William Grimshaw of Haworth

William Grimshaw
of Haworth

❖

Faith Cook

THE BANNER OF TRUTH TRUST

THE BANNER OF TRUTH TRUST
3 Murrayfield Road, Edinburgh EH12 6EL
P.O. Box 621, Carlisle, Pennsylvania 17013, USA

*

© Banner of Truth Trust 1997
First Published 1997
ISBN 0 85151 732 3

*

Typeset in 12/13pt Bulmer MT
at The Banner of Truth Trust, Edinburgh
Printed and bound
at the Bath Press, Bath

TO

MY HUSBAND,

PAUL

CONTENTS

List of Illustrations		ix
Preface		xi
Introduction: Haworth – Now and Then		xiii
1.	'Sober and Diligent'	1
2.	An Ungodly Cleric	9
3.	The Pardoning Love of God	18
4.	Harbingers of Blessing in Yorkshire 1734–1742	32
5.	Haworth – A Barren Wilderness	45
6.	Showers on Dry Ground	57
7.	Full Assurance	68
8.	Haworth – A Garden of the Lord	78
9.	'Strains of Tremendous Eloquence'	88
10.	The Care of Souls	99
11.	A Bona Fide Methodist	110
12.	Not Counting the Cost	123
13.	Anecdotes from Haworth Days	138
14.	Days of the Son of Man	149
15.	'The Great Haworth Round'	161
16.	Every Moment to God's Glory	177
17.	Years of Consolidation	188

18. Grimshaw's Unpublished Writings   200
19. The Unresolved Tension: Church or Dissent   215
20. When Good Men Differ   229
21. Friends and Fellow Workers   245
22. 'What Has God Wrought!'   263
23. 'For to Me to Live is Christ'   274
24. '. . . and to Die is Gain'   284

APPENDICES:

1. Grimshaw's Letters   299
2. Grimshaw's Covenant   309
3. Grimshaw's Creed   314

Bibliography   323
Index   331

ILLUSTRATIONS

Distant view of Haworth   Endpaper

William Grimshaw   Frontispiece

Haworth Old Church after 1755   Title Page

Between pages 112 and 113

Haworth today

Haworth Church after rebuilding of 1879

Sowdens now

Haworth Moor

Between pages 240 and 241

Interior of Grimshaw's Church

Map: Great Haworth Round

ACKNOWLEDGEMENTS

We are indebted to the following for use of the pictures which they have kindly provided for this volume:

Dr Penny Dickson for colour plates, Haworth today, Haworth Church and Sowdens now.

Simon Warner for colour plate of Haworth Moor.

Mrs Judy Coope for the map, Great Haworth Round.

Interior of Haworth Old Church is reproduced by courtesy of the Brontë Society.

Abbreviations and Conventions

Baker, *Grimshaw*   Dr Frank Baker, *William Grimshaw 1708-63* (London: Epworth Press, 1963).

Batty, 'History'   'Church History, Collected from the Memoirs and Journals of the Revd Mr Ingham and the labourers in connection with him. July 14th 1779'. William Batty. Transcribed by Rev. M. Rattenbury, Hull. MS in JRULM.

'Experiences'   William Grimshaw, unpublished manuscript, 'Experiences Gather'd by Conversation with my own & the Souls of others' (JRULM).

Hardy, *Incumbent*   R. Spence Hardy, *William Grimshaw, Incumbent of Haworth* (London: Mason, 1861).

JEN   James Everett's Notes.

JRULM   John Rylands University Library of Manchester.

Laycock, *Heroes*   J. W. Laycock, *Methodist Heroes in the Great Haworth Round* (Keighley: Wadsworth and Co., 1909).

Myles, *Life and Writings*   William Myles, *The Life and Writings of the late Reverend William Grimshaw, A.B.* (London: 1813).

Newton, *Letters*   John Newton, *Memoirs of the Life of the Late Rev. William Grimshaw, A. B. in Six Letters to the Rev. Mr Henry Foster* (Edinburgh: Hamilton, 1814).

Venn, *Sketch*   Henry Venn, *A Sketch of the Life and Ministry of the Late Rev. Mr. Wm. Grimshaw* (Leeds: 1763).

PREFACE

Of all the leaders of the eighteenth-century Evangelical Revival, William Grimshaw has remained one of the least known and least appreciated. It is my hope that this new biography may in some measure redress this imbalance. Myths and misrepresentations have distorted the popular view of Grimshaw's life and labours, while the label of eccentricity has caused even those who value their Christian heritage to dismiss him with a smile. This was my own view of him until the Rev. Iain Murray suggested that, as I 'breathe Yorkshire air', a fresh look at Grimshaw's life would be an appropriate and worthwhile project.

I would first of all thank Mr Murray for making this suggestion. The reading and research involved have immeasurably enriched my own life and set before me an eminent example of Christian character and zeal. But I am indebted to Mr Murray for much more than the seed-thought. He has guided the work throughout, suggested avenues for investigation and important issues to be addressed. More than this, he has lent me valuable books from his own library which I had not been able to obtain elsewhere. For all this help I am most grateful.

The John Rylands University Library of Manchester has given me invaluable assistance in tracing manuscript material and in photocopying Grimshaw's unpublished work for my personal use. Quotations from these manuscripts in this book are reproduced by courtesy of the Director and University Librarian of the

John Rylands University Library. The Evangelical Library in London has facilitated the work in the prompt loan of books I have needed and, like the Dr Williams's Library, has helped me on a number of lines of inquiry. I am also indebted to the Wesleyan Historical Society Library at Westminster College, Oxford, for photocopied material, and not least to my own local reference library in Hull whose staff have searched out rare books for my use.

In any work of this nature there are many who give suggestions and ideas which prove useful. I am most grateful for this, but I would especially mention the help I have received from Michael Baumber, local historian of Haworth and Keighley, who checked through my material on Haworth itself; from the Brontë Parsonage Museum for assistance with early pictures of Haworth; and from the Rev. Michael Rattenbury of Hull for the use of his transcription of William Batty's 'Church History'. Mrs Judy Coope has used her artistic talent to produce a map of Grimshaw's extensive journeys and Dr Penny Dickson of Ripon has spent much time and care in taking photographs of places connected with Grimshaw.

And lastly, I am indebted to my husband, Paul, for many helpful suggestions and for the hours of time he has given to checking and rechecking my work. I could not have accomplished it without his help. His own enthusiasm for William Grimshaw has often rekindled my determination to produce a worthy account of one of the Church's noblest but least remembered sons.

William Grimshaw once wrote, 'Lord, grant that I may never faint till weakness, old age or death invalidate me. By the grace of God, I'm resolved never to flag while I can ride, walk, creep or crawl.' Such was the spirit of devotion to Jesus Christ which motivated this apostolic pioneer of the gospel in the north of England. May a similar passion for God's glory and pity for the souls of men stimulate us to a like zeal.

FAITH COOK
Hull, Yorkshire
April 1997

INTRODUCTION

HAWORTH – NOW AND THEN

HAWORTH IN YORKSHIRE: the words invariably evoke a smile of recognition followed by the comment, 'Oh yes, home of the Brontës.' Haworth has indeed attained eminence because of its link with the Brontë sisters. The poignant story of Patrick Brontë, who arrived in Haworth as the new curate in 1820, together with his wife, Maria, and six little children, has gripped the popular imagination. Maria's death the following year, and four years later the loss of their two school-aged daughters, Maria and Elizabeth, in distressing circumstances; the wasted gifts and pathetic end of Branwell, the only son; the secret writings, publications and astonishing success of Charlotte, Emily and Anne Brontë before their own premature deaths, make the Haworth parsonage a literary shrine, second only to Stratford-upon-Avon, home of William Shakespeare.

Over one hundred articles, pamphlets and books have poured from the publishing houses, dealing with every aspect of the lives and background of the Brontë sisters. Haworth itself has undergone a metamorphosis, from a rugged little Pennine town to a tourist centre, drawing an unending stream of sightseers to its narrow streets.

A climb up the steep old Main Street on a sunny afternoon quickly confirms the commercialisation which has transformed Haworth into a Mecca of the literary world. The uneven flagstones, or setts as they are more correctly called, placed to give the horses' hooves a better grip as they laboured up the hill, and the grey, dismal housing rising sheer above the street, give the place an air of antiquity. But this is quickly dispelled as the visitor passes shops displaying trinkets and souvenirs of 'Brontëland', spilling out their wares onto the pavement. Here Brontë biscuits, Brontë confectionery and even Brontë water may be purchased. Several cafés and restaurants take their names from characters in the novels written by the three sisters. So we discover Villette Coffee House, Heathcliff Café and Rochester House. A wayside busker entertains the passer-by with the lilting tones of Bach's 'Chaconne'. Beyond the church of St Michael and All Angels lies the Brontë parsonage, now converted into a museum. Here, annually, an estimated two hundred thousand visitors, many from far-flung places of the world, wander slowly around trying to recapture the scenes surrounding the brief careers of the Brontës.

Clearly, Haworth and the Brontës are now indissolubly linked. But Haworth has a claim to higher renown than those literary accolades achieved by the attainments of the Brontë sisters. Even a local historian, in a description of Haworth, written in 1879 to meet the insatiable interest of the public in the Brontë sisters, readily admitted that Haworth had known greater days.[1]

Let us then travel back in time, seventy or more years before Patrick Brontë took up his new Yorkshire curacy, to the year 1756. Now we may witness scenes more astonishing than any Haworth has known since. Here, surrounding the old parish church, crammed into every corner of its expansive graveyard, is a vast throng of men and women, numbering possibly upwards of six thousand. Patiently they stand waiting, often in the biting winds that sweep down from the bleak moorland above the church. For what purpose have such crowds been drawn together? They are anticipating the appearance of a preacher – not from the door of the church – but through a window on to scaffolding erected outside to form a makeshift pulpit.

---

[1] J. Horsfall Turner, *Haworth – Past and Present* (Brighouse, 1879), p. 52.

A glance around at the expectant sea of faces tells its own tale. Here are men and women poorly dressed, some prematurely aged by suffering and privation, for the average life-expectancy in Haworth at this time is little more than twenty-six years. But many a face is alight with an inner beauty – transformed by the gospel of the grace of God, for these are the days when the great eighteenth-century Evangelical Revival is sweeping across Britain, altering the whole course of history, as many secular historians were later to acknowledge.

Suddenly there is a hush across the crowded graveyard. A figure emerges from the window. Perhaps it is George Whitefield, John or Charles Wesley, or even William Grimshaw himself – curate of Haworth and instrument in God's hand for the evangelisation of vast areas of northern England. With passion and energy the preacher holds forth to the people the message of forgiveness of sins, of reconciliation with God and the hope of a better world beyond the despair, sorrows and hardship of their earthly circumstances.

The link between Haworth and the Brontës must surely shrink to more balanced proportions as we trace in these pages the extraordinary life and influence of William Grimshaw, Haworth's most illustrious former resident. We will then willingly concur with the estimate of the historian of Haworth to whom reference has been made, who wrote, 'Allow me to say that personally I look upon Mr Grimshaw's ministry as the grandest period in the history of Haworth church. The good accomplished is incalculable.'

1

'Sober and Diligent'

'If greatness is to be measured by usefulness to souls,'[1] wrote
J. C. Ryle in 1866 as he looked back on the eighteenth-century
Evangelical Revival, then, in his estimation, William Grimshaw
would rank among the three greatest men in England during
that period. The lives of the other two, George Whitefield and
John Wesley, are well known, but many who rightly appreciate
their importance know little of this man, whose zeal in the
service of Christ led John Wesley to write, 'A few such as him
would make a nation tremble. He carries fire wherever he goes.'[2]
Not surprisingly, it was William Grimshaw whom Wesley
designated as his successor in the nation-wide organisation of
Methodism, should he and his brother Charles have died first.

But William Grimshaw, evangelist of Yorkshire in the eighteenth century, has largely been forgotten today. This widespread
ignorance of his life and labours may well be explained by the lack
of early biographical material. No significant attempt was made to
evaluate his life until John Newton's account in his *Memoirs of the
Life of the Late Rev. William Grimshaw, A. B. in Six Letters to the*

---

[1] J. C. Ryle, *Christian Leaders of the Eighteenth Century* (Edinburgh:
Banner of Truth Trust, 1978), p. 106f. Ryle's work was first published
between 1866 and 1867 as biographical sketches in *The Family Treasury*, a
monthly periodical, and in 1868 published as one volume.
[2] *The Letters of the Rev. John Wesley, A.M.,* ed. John Telford, Standard
Edition, vol. IV (London: Epworth Press, 1931), p. 160.

Rev. Mr. Henry Foster was published in 1799, nearly forty years after Grimshaw's death.

Grimshaw confined his labours largely to the north of England. This, suggested Ryle in his *Christian Leaders of the Eighteenth Century*, was another possible reason for the neglect: 'The minister who never preaches in London and writes nothing, must not be surprised if the world knows nothing of him. The main reason why the church has done so little to honour Grimshaw's name may be that it had so little opportunity of knowing him.' Since Ryle wrote those words, the recovery of five manuscripts and more than fifty personal letters, all written in Grimshaw's meticulous hand, has much facilitated the task of the biographer. These manuscripts had been held in the family of John Crosse, who was vicar of Bradford from 1784 until 1816. A warm-hearted evangelical, Crosse had made Grimshaw his role model, and understandably so, for he had married Grace Grimshaw, widow of Grimshaw's only son, John.

When Crosse learned that James Everett, well-known Methodist historian and preacher, was planning a full biography of Grimshaw during the 1820s, he made these manuscripts available to him for his research. Everett's work, which he planned to call 'The Curate of Haworth', eventually extended to thirty-eight chapters, with the addition of an appendix. With only the final chapter left to complete, Everett set the work aside, and it was never published.[1] Together with the manuscripts themselves, from which he quoted extensively, it was passed on to Luke Tyerman in the 1860s and subsequently lost from view, stored among unclassified material in the Methodist archives. Not until another Methodist historian, Dr Frank Baker, located all this material and made a thorough study of it for his doctoral thesis

---

[1] One reason for this could be that Everett discovered that Methodists in the early nineteenth century were not readers. Of an earlier work of his, *Methodism in Sheffield,* which he published himself in Sheffield in 1823, four hundred were printed but of those he could only sell one hundred and eighty, leaving himself £40 in debt on the project. Lack of finance and his own poor health at this time could also have been contributory factors.

on Grimshaw, published in 1963 to coincide with the two hundredth anniversary of Grimshaw's death,[1] did these important
documents receive further attention.

Piecing together the scraps of information that may be gleaned
of William Grimshaw's early years, we discover that this tireless
evangelist of Yorkshire was in fact a Lancastrian by birth. Brindle,
his childhood home, is a sleepy village north of Chorley,
hidden away from either of the main roads leading to Preston or
Blackburn. Dominated by its old parish church which dates from
1190, it seems to have changed little as the centuries have come
and gone. Only the occupation of the residents has altered, for
now the attractive new housing suggests that the owners are
harassed professionals working in the surrounding towns who
seek out the peace of village life. But in the eighteenth century,
with a population of little over a thousand, Brindle was an
agricultural community.

Here in the Ribble valley generations of men and women had
lived and died largely unaware of any of the momentous affairs of
state transacted in far-off cities and centres of population. There
was one notable exception, however, for it was in the north-west
of the country that the first Jacobite Rebellion of 1715 gained its
greatest English support. Unimpressed by their new Hanoverian
king, George I, who could scarcely speak their language, the
people rose up in support of the son of James II. Poorly organised
and led, the rebellion eventually petered out not far from Brindle,
after the Battle of Preston when the Jacobites were defeated by
General Wills.

William Grimshaw, born on 14 September 1708,[2] was seven at

[1] Dr Frank Baker, *William Grimshaw 1708-63* (London: Epworth Press,
1963). Hereafter called *Grimshaw*.
[2] Most biographers suggest 3 September, some 8 September, as Grimshaw's
date of birth, but he himself records in his diary that it was 14 September.
'William Grimshaw's Diary', transcribed by Methodist historian, James
Everett, and printed in *Proceedings of Wesley Historical Society*, 1932/3, p. 47.
Original manuscript in John Rylands University Library of Manchester,
hereafter called JRULM.

the time and with all the enthusiasm of little boys for a fight, he would probably have retained clear memories of those days. His parents, Henry and Ann Grimshaw, were at least nominally religious, and William, their first child, was baptised in Brindle parish church. Henry Grimshaw must have had some education, for his spidery signature may still be seen in the Brindle parish register where he became a churchwarden in 1728.

Married to Ann Firth in 1706, Henry Grimshaw was a farm labourer, and had moved around finding employment wherever he could. But after his marriage he settled in Brindle and the family home, long since demolished, is said to have been about half a mile north-west of the church. Little is known of William's childhood days; the old village school had fallen on hard times and had closed, so at the age of five he was sent to Blackburn Grammar School six miles away. Whether he boarded locally or walked the six miles to school each day, we do not know. Certainly he had to be in his classroom by six each morning, as stipulated by the rules governing a charter granted to the school by Queen Elizabeth I. In later years Grimshaw attributed to his teacher, George Smith, the credit for his early academic progress.

Probably St James, the parish church of Brindle, was as sleepy as the village itself, and children growing up there would have had little religious instruction to enlighten their minds and lead them to a knowledge of the truth. Brindle had an absentee rector, Henry Piggott, who found his richer living in Rochdale more congenial, and so arranged for Brindle to be served by a succession of curates throughout his long life, for he lived until ninety-three years of age. When he died in 1722 the Brindle parish register unceremoniously records: 'Exit Mr. Piggott, Rector'.

Throughout William Grimshaw's formative years there appears to have been little spiritual influence to shape his thinking. Our knowledge of his home-life is slight. The only two references to his parents in any of his extant writings suggest a genuine affection for them. One occurs at the death of his father in 1754 when he writes to a friend concerning the loss of her brother: 'I can never be better disposed than at present to sympathise with you ... for since the Lord called home your dear brother, he has called home my dear father.' Such words indicate that in Grimshaw's view his father was indeed a believing man. In contrast, two years later he makes a sorrowful entry in his diary concerning his mother whom he visited on one of his preaching tours: 'Visited at Marsh Lane; but had a sore contention with my dear mother. Lord, renew her heart and save her soul for thy mercy's sake! Amen!'[1]

Whether or not William Grimshaw received any enlightened religious instruction, God was evidently influencing his mind and conscience from a young age. Writing in later years he refers to this in a passage which is clearly autobiographical: 'This I can bear witness to and am persuaded that if any man will but carefully recollect himself, he can date as far back as his infancy, the remembrance of many sharp rebukes, and upbraidings, checks and terrors of conscience for having done amiss. He can very well remember several awful and heart-affecting thoughts about a God and judgment, death and eternity in those tender years.' These 'checks and terrors of conscience' he describes as 'nothing else but the suggestions, drawings and convictions of the Holy Spirit'.[2]

Probably William suffered a severe attack of smallpox during his childhood for he bore the characteristic pockmarks on his face throughout life. But as he grew he developed a powerful physique. Broad-shouldered and well-built, he was tall for those days and was described by one who remembered him as having 'an iron constitution and mighty physical powers'.[3]

During the final years of his schooling Grimshaw was taken from Blackburn Grammar School and sent to Heskin Free

[1]Grimshaw's 'Diary', p. 2.

[2]Grimshaw, *Answer to White*, included by William Myles in *The Life and Writings of the late Reverend William Grimshaw, A.B.* (London: 1813), p. 108. Hereafter called *Life and Writings*.

[3]James Everett's Notes, (hereafter called JEN), compiled for his prospective biography of William Grimshaw, which was largely completed by 1825. Manuscript now held in JRULM.

School, which was ten miles south of Brindle. Perhaps he had shown clear academic promise and his parents wished him to have the advantage of the improved facilities. Better equipped than other schools in the area, Heskin possessed a library of eighty volumes, purchased from a legacy bequeathed by a former headmaster early in the previous century. This compared favourably with other Lancashire schools, including Blackburn Grammar School, which according to a survey conducted in 1674, had at most 'six books too inconsequential to be named'.[1]

Situated in idyllic countryside of 'pleasant rivers and stately woods', Heskin Free School stood in its own grounds with a bubbling spring providing drinking water for the pupils. It is probable that friends helped Henry and Ann Grimshaw finance William's education, for they now had two more children, John and Elizabeth, for whom to care.

From Heskin Free School William Grimshaw proceeded to Christ's College, Cambridge, where he was admitted in April 1726, at the age of seventeen. With a population of six and a half thousand, Cambridge had two widely differing communities. The one, dwelling in humble homes and farms clustered along the banks of the Cam, stood in marked contrast to the other, which was accommodated in the elegant colleges of this ancient seat of learning.

Christ's College itself, backing onto open fields, had been recently renovated and presented an imposing exterior to the young student as he left the secluded precincts of Heskin to be enrolled as an undergraduate. But, though outwardly impressive and renowned for distinguished former graduates such as John Milton, Christ's now, in common with some of the other colleges, attracted no more than a trickle of new students, only nine freshmen entering with Grimshaw in 1726. Christ's had lost its reputation for academic excellence and had slipped from its position as one of the four largest colleges. It now held only

[1] J. P. Earwaker, *Local Gleanings Relating to Lancashire and Cheshire*, cited by Baker, *Grimshaw*, p. 21.

seventh place, even that being contested by other colleges of similar size.

As at Oxford, standards at Cambridge had been in sad decline from early in the century. Manuscripts had been allowed to deteriorate and gather so much dust that students found it almost impossible to read them. A German scholar, von Uffenbach, visiting the English universities in 1710, complained that manuscripts at Caius College were quite illegible, so thick were the layers of dust lying upon them. He had to climb up library steps at Peterhouse which were white with pigeon droppings, while the books at Magdalene were 'with hardly a single exception entirely overgrown with mould'.[1] Clearly the long-established reputation of England's universities had been eroded by indolence and neglect.

University professorships had become mere sinecures held largely by academics wishing to pursue some research. Even the majority of the fellows spent their days in idleness and drunken revelries, leaving most of the lecturing to the tutors. Some of the wealthier students resorted to the expedient of bringing their own tutors with them. When William Grimshaw arrived at Cambridge he would quickly discover that students were largely left to their own devices and that the standards necessary to obtain a degree were scarcely demanding. Proficiency in Latin and logic were essential qualifications for a BA degree at that time, with the inclusion of some theology. But Grimshaw would also be expected to apply himself to rhetoric in his first year, and philosophy in the final year, with a little mathematics as well.

William Towers, Master of Christ's during Grimshaw's student years, largely ignored his students, giving himself to historical research. So, with scant supervision, the temptation to become indolent was strong, and as John Wesley himself reported: 'The moment a young man sets foot in either Oxford or Cambridge, he is surrounded by company of all kinds, except that which should

[1]Rosamond Bayne-Powell, *Travellers in Eighteenth Century England* (London: John Murray, 1951), p. 96.

do him good; with loungers and triflers of every sort; with men who no more concern themselves with learning than religion.'[1] A compensating factor for William Grimshaw was that he had a conscientious and capable tutor, Thomas Cartwright, to supervise his studies, and under his watchful eye the young man settled well to his academic work.

William Grimshaw was admitted to Cambridge as a sizar, or poor student. This description, used only in Cambridge and at Trinity College in Dublin, was equivalent to that of 'servitor' at Oxford. It meant that the student would be granted assistance with board and reduced fees in return for menial tasks performed for the wealthier students. A sizar, distinguished from the rest of the students by special clothing, was excluded from many of the privileges enjoyed by other undergraduates and was often the butt of jests and even physical abuse from better-placed young men. William Grimshaw's hefty physique probably protected him from some of the torments suffered by other sizars.

Despite the lax academic standards, some aspects of university discipline were harsh in the early eighteenth century, even unnecessarily rigorous in some respects. If Grimshaw had felt like a quick dip in the River Cam, he would discover the misdemeanour punishable by a public flogging for a first offence, and for a second offence he could face expulsion. Sabbath rules were so strict that even shaving on a Sunday carried a heavy fine. William Grimshaw's training at Heskin Free School had, however, inculcated good habits of learning and discipline and he describes himself as 'sober and diligent' for the first two years of his university course. Probably he had an ulterior motive for his diligence, for if he could gain one of the coveted scholarships awarded at the end of the first year, he would be released from the thankless position of a sizar and enjoy the full privileges of student life. This he achieved in May 1727, and, under the surveillance of his tutor, Thomas Cartwright, Grimshaw continued to study well for a further year.

[1] J. H. Whiteley, *Wesley's England* (London: Epworth Press, 1945), p. 269.

2

An Ungodly Cleric

WILLIAM GRIMSHAW BEGAN HIS STUDIES at Christ's College as a basically serious young man. His early religious impressions, coupled with clear academic promise, led him to determine to devote himself to a career in the Church. For two years he held fast to his purpose and studied well, but as he entered his third year he succumbed to the pressures all around him and joined 'the triflers and loungers' of whom Wesley had complained. Describing the pressures an undergraduate faced at Oxford, Wesley was to write, 'Is he not surrounded with those who are often more pernicious than open libertines, men who retain something of outward decency and nothing else . . . who seriously idle away the whole day and revel until midnight and if not drunken themselves, yet encourage and applaud those that are so?'[1]

Though conditions were as bad in Cambridge, there was no equivalent to the Oxford Holy Club, begun in 1729 to gather together young men of a more serious disposition. And on Grimshaw's own confession, he 'learnt to drink and swear and became as vile as the worst'.[2] As a friend was later to write, 'Bad example deplorably prevailed to seduce him . . . and having no

---

[1] John Wesley, quoted by Luke Tyerman, *The Oxford Methodists* (London: Hodder and Stoughton, 1873), p. 18.

[2] Letter from Joseph Williams to Malachi Blake, cited by J. W. Laycock, *Methodist Heroes in the Great Haworth Round* (Keighley: Wadsworth and Co., 1909), p. 32. Hereafter called *Heroes*.

root in himself, the torrent of impiety in the college carried him away so far that . . . he seemed utterly to have lost all sense of seriousness.'[1]

Not surprisingly Grimshaw's academic work suffered in consequence. He drifted through the remainder of his course, managing only to scrape through his degree. Published lists of Cambridge graduates in 1730 contain 112 names, arranged in order of merit and achievement. We find Grimshaw's name near the bottom of the list: a commentary not so much on his ability as on his way of life.

Despite all this, he still intended to enter the ministry of the Church of England, apparently seeing no incongruity between such a desire and his behaviour. Finding himself a few months too young for ordination, Grimshaw returned to Brindle where he intended to spend the time seeking an appointment as a curate – a prerequisite for ordination. Perhaps he had not been home since he left four years earlier as a youth of seventeen – the journey across the country from Cambridge to Lancashire would have been an arduous one in those days.

Back in Brindle he must have found himself something of a celebrity, but here Grimshaw was immediately faced with a problem. How could he hide his indisciplined way of life from his parents and from the generous friends who had helped to finance his education? Describing this situation in later years, he confessed that he sought cleverly to conceal his worldliness rather than to reform his ways. He 'refrained as much as possible from gross swearing, unless in suitable company, and when he got drunk would take care to sleep it out before he came home'.[2]

Not many months elapsed before the vicar of Rochdale, Samuel Dunster, himself a graduate of Trinity College, Cambridge, noticed the young man in nearby Brindle and offered him

[1] Henry Venn, *A Sketch of the Life and Ministry of the Late Rev. Mr. Wm. Grimshaw* (Leeds: 1763), p. 30. Hereafter called *Sketch*. This consisted of an eight-page appreciation attached to the published form of his sermon at Grimshaw's funeral.

[2] Joseph Williams in Laycock, *Heroes*, p. 33.

a curacy in Littleborough. This was then a small community on
the outskirts of his own lucrative Rochdale living to which he
had been appointed on the death of the aged Henry Piggott, nine
years earlier. Perhaps Dunster took a fatherly interest in Grimshaw;
certainly he donated several books to him out of his personal
library. These Grimshaw duly inscribed with his own name and
the name of the one from whom he had received them.

Nothing more remained then for William Grimshaw except to
seek out his bishop and request ordination. For this he had to
travel to London, for Bishop Peploe, the Bishop of Chester, in
whose diocese Brindle was located, could seldom be found at
home. This was not unusual for bishoprics tended to be awarded
for political services and a bishop was expected to take his place
in the House of Lords for a considerable part of each year. As
remuneration from different bishoprics varied widely, prestige
and eloquence in debate, coupled with frequent appearances in
the House, were the surest ladders to preferment and the offer
of one of the more lucrative bishoprics. Few bishops, therefore,
were able or willing to give adequate time and attention to the
spiritual concerns of the churches in their charge. Problems of
distance and communication made any sort of oversight of can-
didates for ordination difficult, and it is unlikely that Grimshaw's
bishop knew anything of his background, beliefs or credentials
for the ministry.

On 4 April 1732, at the age of twenty-three, William Grimshaw
was ordained by Bishop Peploe in a private chapel in Queen's
Square, Westminster. It appears he was the only candidate at
that time and for a few fleeting moments the young man was
impressed by the solemnity of the occasion and the awesome
nature of the task to which he was committing himself. He was
'much affected with a sense of the importance of the ministerial
office and the diligence which ought to be used in the discharge
of it'. But these convictions, soon wore off and 'were but as the
chaff scattered by the wind of temptation'.[1]

[1]Venn, *Sketch*, p. 30.

So William Grimshaw took up his duties in Littleborough, ill-fitted as he was to care for the souls of others. But he was not alone in his worldliness and spiritual darkness, as a glance at the condition of the Established Church in England at this period, and the political and ecclesiastical circumstances which had brought it about, soon confirms. Since 24 August 1662, just seventy years before young Grimshaw presented himself for ordination, the Church of England had been in a parlous condition. On that day – Black Bartholomew's Day – it could be said to have lost its soul, as over two thousand Puritan preachers and school teachers were ejected from their livings and employment. This was for their refusal to comply with the terms of the Act of Uniformity, which required 'unfeigned assent and consent' to everything contained in the 1662 Prayer Book. Charles II's promise of 'liberty to tender consciences' had proved to be worthless.

Bereft of so many of their spiritual guides, the people became as sheep without a shepherd, for the men who filled the empty pulpits were, commonly, poorly-taught men-pleasers and time-servers. The historian J. R. Green has asserted: 'No such sweeping alteration in the religious aspect of the Church had ever been seen before.'[1] Weakened and often worldly, the Church of the Restoration was ill-prepared to check the tide of immorality and godlessness that now swept through a society suddenly released from the high expectations of its Puritan pastors – a society which noted and copied the abandoned behaviour of Charles and his dissolute court.

Given this vacuum of conviction, it would not be difficult for heresy and corruption to gain widespread acceptance among the people. So it is not surprising that in the last decade of the seventeenth century a philosophy, later to be known as Deism, began to command a considerable following. Like many heresies, its central ideas were merely another expression of the aversion of

[1] J. R. Green, *A Short History of the English People,* vol. III (MacMillan & Co., 1874), p. 375.

the natural man for biblical revelation. Popularised by the writings of the philosopher, John Locke, whose work *The Reasonableness of Christianity* was published in 1695, it objected to the profundities of Puritan writers. Locke purported to restore Christianity to its 'original simplicity' and made reason the touchstone of truth.

Although Locke himself did not deny revelation or the supernatural, his followers used his thinking as a springboard for their philosophies, until revelation itself was discredited. Man's reason was elevated as the supreme arbiter in all matters. Christianity was set forth as a natural religion in which God as Creator, or even the First Cause, had set the world in motion and then left it to its own devices. By the time Thomas Woolston was writing in 1729, the supernatural in Christianity had largely been denied and he could say in his *Discourses on the Miracles of Christ* that such supernatural acts were 'foolish, trivial, contradictory and absurd'.

Young William Grimshaw himself had imbibed some of these Deistic notions during his Cambridge days, and such teachings fitted the mood of a society where morals had all but collapsed and people were tired of religious controversy. Denial of God's revelation in the Scriptures removed any basis for an absolute authority; and consequently men lost any sense of accountability for their actions. Little wonder then that standards plummeted and religion for most people became an empty formality.

England was still largely a rural community at this time. Five out of every six people lived in the villages and here the spiritual impoverishment of the churches took its heaviest toll. Parishes were regarded chiefly as sources of revenue and many an absentee rector drew his income from a string of village parishes, and like Henry Piggott, the non-resident rector of Brindle, seldom visited the churches except to collect his dues. Hundreds of parish churches had only one service a week, conducted mainly by visiting curates.

The Bishop of Carlisle, who set out to investigate the state of his diocese, described the situation he found. Of one church he wrote: 'The roof is miserably shattered and broken. Not one pane of glass in any of the windows. No flooring. No seats. No reading desk. They happened to bring in a corpse to be buried, according to the custom of the place without any service, whilst we were there. I desired my chaplain to officiate, but he could only find some few scraps of a Prayer Book and an insufferably torn Bible . . .'[1]

The church in Littleborough to which William Grimshaw was commissioned by Bishop Peploe, with the customary official licence, signed and sealed, was in a far superior condition to those the Bishop of Carlisle discovered on his itinerary. The simple rectangular building, with its hexagonal tower and seating for about two hundred worshippers, stood adjacent to the track that ran through the hamlet. Perhaps still under some sense of the serious nature of his calling, Grimshaw soon discovered and joined with a small group of men and women in Rochdale who met together each week for prayer, singing, reading the Scriptures and mutual spiritual encouragement.

Dr Samuel Dunster, the rector of Rochdale, concerned to encourage his young curate, continued to pass on books which he thought might benefit him. One such book, a work by the Puritan divine, Thomas Brooks, may well have intrigued Grimshaw by its quaint title, *Precious Remedies against Satan's Devices*. Putting it on his shelf, he possibly intended to peruse it further when he had time to spare. Little did he realise the significance that book was to have in years to come.

Unfortunately Grimshaw's connection with the group of believers in Rochdale came to an early end, for within a few months he moved from Littleborough to Todmorden six miles away, although still within the same parish. In all likelihood this was an exchange with a friend, who wished to combine his clerical duties with that of teaching at Rochdale Grammar

---

[1]Bishop Nicolson, *Miscellany Accounts of Diocese of Carlisle*, cited by G. R. Balleine, *A History of the Evangelical Party* (London: Longmans, Green and Co., 1909), pp. 19–20.

School. But this move distanced Grimshaw from the beneficial influence of the Rochdale society and their weekly gatherings. Cut off from this spiritual encouragement and challenge, it is not surprising that he soon relapsed into his former ways, becoming a jovial and not untypical curate of his day.

Todmorden lies about eight miles from Halifax and is set in the midst of steep hilly countryside. Even Daniel Defoe, as he conducted his epic tour of Britain in 1725, only six years before Grimshaw took up his curacy in Todmorden, found his journey across the Pennines almost intolerable when he reached this area. 'We had not gone fifty yards . . . but we found our way began to ascend again, and soon after to go up very steep, till in about half a mile we found we had another mountain to ascend, in our apprehension as bad as the first . . . Thus it is up hill and down, so that I suppose we mounted to the clouds and descended to the water level eight times in that little part of the journey.'[1] Not only was the terrain rough and inhospitable, the people too were of similar character. Another contemporary historian described them in these words: 'The inhabitants of the district between Todmorden and Halifax are as wild, uncouth and rugged as their native hills; and indeed, it is positively dangerous for a person to pass that way.'[2]

Criminal proceedings in nearby Halifax were brutal. Defoe describes in detail the arrangements for executions – carried out for even the most trivial offences. He colours his report with an account of a local custom by which the accused – if he were adroit enough – might remove his head from the block between the signal for the axe to fall and the moment it landed. If he could then race down the hill (with the executioner in pursuit) and leap into the river he would be exonerated from his felony. This seems to have been a feat seldom accomplished. Such local barbarity gave rise, in Defoe's opinion, to the proverbial saying, still repeated even today:

[1]Daniel Defoe, *A Tour through the Whole Island of Great Britain* (repr. Exeter: Webb and Bower, 1989), p. 174.
[2]Cited by Baker, *Grimshaw,* p. 28.

From Hell, Hull and Halifax,
Good Lord, deliver us.

Why Hull should be included in the couplet, Defoe could not determine!

The fear of witchcraft with its accompanying incredulity was still widespread in the area, and though the burning of witches had largely died out,[1] the phobia and superstition lingered on among the people. An illustration of this, derived from William Grimshaw's early days in Todmorden, is provided in the following anecdote, which also illustrates his aptitude for a practical joke – a characteristic which was always to be a feature of his life.

Evidently a young man in the parish had made one of the local girls pregnant. Instead of marrying the girl, the young man added to his offence by ridiculing her, putting her to public shame. Grimshaw was indignant at such behaviour and determined to teach the fellow a lesson. So he dressed up as the devil, donning a large and ugly mask, complete with horns. Knowing that the young man always came home over a certain stile, Grimshaw lurked in the shadows waiting for him. As the unsuspecting youth mounted the stile, this horrifying spectre slowly rose up and laid hold on him with an iron grip. Believing that the devil himself had come to take him away for his misdemeanours, the youth cried out in alarm and begged for mercy. No, mercy would not be shown him; the apparition indicated that he must and would have him away to his infernal abode. At last, knowing full well the cause of the encounter, the youth promised to marry the girl forthwith and so the 'devil' was prevailed upon to release him.[2]

Failing as he did to preach the gospel, Grimshaw had few other means than such bizarre methods as this to improve standards in his parish. And so he continued for a further three years, but a day of change was approaching – a day when God himself was to intervene in the life of this carefree and godless young curate. For

---

[1] The last known case was in Sunderland in 1722.
[2] JEN.

him, as he later confessed, the Church was simply a means of earning his bread, and the duties involved were therefore to be discharged with as little inconvenience to himself as possible. John Newton, who established a friendship with Grimshaw in later years, adds the following description of this period of Grimshaw's life:

He did duty, as the phrase is, in the church once on the Lord's day; that is, he read prayers and a sermon. With this his conscience was satisfied. Whether his flock were satisfied or not, he neither knew nor cared. Nor did he attend more to useful studies. He was a gentle casuist, a compliant companion, a man of the world.[1]

With his easy-going nature and his instinctive love of fun, Grimshaw sought popularity at the expense of his parishioners' true welfare. His days were spent in hunting and fishing – and the woods and rivers of West Yorkshire would have provided ample scope for such pursuits – while his evenings were passed in socialising with the more influential members of his parish, playing cards, drinking and swearing. He sought to curb these last two activities to the extent that he avoided entering the pulpit under the influence of drink, and reserved his swearing for like-minded company. Still only twenty-three years of age, William Grimshaw had become a typical early eighteenth-century cleric. 'O what a scandal to religion are swearing, drunken, horse-racing, gambling and ungodly priests; and what a jest or stumbling block to the world!'[2] exclaimed Erasmus Middleton, as he surveyed this sorry period of Grimshaw's life.

---

[1]John Newton, *Memoirs of the Life of the Late Rev. William Grimshaw, A. B. in Six Letters to the Rev. Mr Henry Foster* (Edinburgh: Hamilton, 1814), p. 8. First printed 1799. Hereafter called *Letters*.

[2]Erasmus Middleton, *Biographia Evangelica*, vol. IV (London: 1786), p. 398. Hereafter called *Biographia*.

3

THE PARDONING LOVE OF GOD

CERTAIN TIMES AND EVEN PARTICULAR YEARS become turning points in the purposes of God and such a time was now dawning. After many decades of spiritual decadence, God's power was beginning to be manifested simultaneously on both sides of the Atlantic and in parts of Europe. In 1734 while William Grimshaw, nearly twenty-six years of age, was leading his easy-going life among the hills of West Yorkshire, cut off from any external influence, God was preparing men whom he would use in his work. George Whitefield, only twenty years of age, was then striving by physical austerities and painful searching to find peace of conscience. 'God only knows', he wrote in his journal, 'how many nights I have lain upon my bed, groaning under the weight I felt, bidding Satan depart from me in the name of Jesus.'[1] He was converted the following year.

John Wesley, eleven years Whitefield's senior, was about to leave his homeland for Georgia, in the New World. Devoted, ascetic and zealous though he was, he too was to learn through frustration and failure the impotence of his own righteous deeds to save his soul. Declaring, as he arrived home once more in February 1738, that 'the faith I want is a sure trust and confidence in God that through the merits of Christ my sins are forgiven and

---

[1] *George Whitefield's Journals* (London: Banner of Truth Trust, 1960), p. 52.

I am reconciled to the favour of God',[1] John Wesley too found the forgiveness he had earnestly sought for so long, and in May of that year was granted, in addition, an inner assurance of his acceptance with God. Howell Harris, far off in Wales, and like Grimshaw largely isolated from the main streams of life, was also awakened and converted to God early in 1735.

How William Grimshaw began to be aware that all was not well with him, we do not know. Possibly his inability to deal with the sorrows of two of his parishioners may have awakened him to his own state. When James and Susan Scholfield's infant daughter Mary died at only five weeks old, the mother was distraught. She could not accept her baby's death, and tried to tend the little body as if the child had been still alive. Grimshaw attempted to console the grieving parents, but no advice could he give them save barren worldly counsel: 'Put away all gloomy thoughts, and go into merry company and divert yourselves, and all will soon be right.'

But all was not soon right. Had their pastor any other guidance for them, the Scholfields wondered? This time Grimshaw confessed himself unable to advise them, admitting his own spiritual plight. Yet one ray of light pierced the gloom, for, he added, 'To despair of the mercy of God would be the worst thing of all.'[2]

From this time a new note of seriousness characterised Grimshaw. Gone were the merry evenings drinking with his friends, gone was the passion for entertainment, and in its place came an austerity, even a rigour, as he strove to please God. A

[1] *Journal of John Wesley*, Standard edition, ed. Nehemiah Curnock, vol. I (London: Kelly), p. 424.

[2] These details were first provided by R. Spence Hardy, in his *William Grimshaw, Incumbent of Haworth* (London: Mason, 1861), p. 20. He was given them by John Scholfield, a grandson of James Scholfield. There is also a sequel to this incident. Susan and James Scholfield were both later converted, and James became a Methodist lay preacher. Remembering his own inadequacy to help them, Grimshaw said, 'O Susan, what a blind leader of the blind I was when I came to take off your burden, by exhorting you to live in pleasure and follow the vain amusements of this world! But God has in his mercy pardoned and blessed us all three. Blessed be his great name!'

marked change came over his ministry: now he was diligent in warning his parishioners of their spiritual danger, urging upon them a strict and upright life. No longer did he neglect his duties, but visited the parishioners in their homes and catechised their children. Grimshaw quickly found, however, that neither he nor they had the power to attain to the standards he felt were necessary to obtain the favour of God. 'My friends,' he would cry out in despair in the middle of a service, 'we are in a damnable state, and I scarcely know how we are to get out of it'.[1] Sometimes he would ask the whole congregation to remain kneeling as if he felt that this posture 'might atone for his own delinquencies'.[2]

At this point Grimshaw supposed that if he were to keep a ledger of all his conduct, he could monitor his life more strictly in order to improve his ways. So he began to keep a careful record, entering all his sins on one side of the page and on the other side matching his misdeeds with his acts of righteousness. At the end of each day he hoped the accounts would balance, so bringing peace to his troubled conscience. This he did for seven years: but it was a hopeless task, which led him further into the mire.

As he sank into depression and hopelessness, an event occurred which definitely acted as a distraction to Grimshaw's disturbed state of mind. One day a young widow, two years his junior, came cantering along the road leading to the parsonage. Catching sight of Grimshaw, she called out merrily, 'I am come to bid a penny at you.' In the local parlance of the day such words were tantamount to a proposal of marriage. The young curate was captivated. Lonely and dejected, he felt deeply the need of human love and Sarah Sutcliffe, well-known heiress of Ewood Court, made an easy conquest.

Sarah was a Lockwood by birth, a long-established family owning extensive property in Midgeley, a village to the west of Halifax, not far from Todmorden. Ewood Hall, part of Ewood Court, the Lockwood estate, was Sarah's family home and was later to figure in John Wesley's *Journal* as a centre for Methodist

---

[1] James Everett, 'The Curate of Haworth' (JRULM).
[2] Ibid.

activity in the area. Part of the complex still stands in its commanding position, surrounded by trees, and overlooking the Calder Valley. The family worshipped at St Mary's, Luddenden, and in the recently modernised church plaques commemorating generations of Lockwoods can be seen on the walls.

In 1735 they were married. Grimshaw loved his high-spirited bride tenderly, but there were clearly problems in the home from the beginning. A tradition has survived, recorded among local reminiscences, which suggested that Sarah was addicted to drink – a not uncommon failure in the light of the fact that the period known as the 'gin age' in English history was now approaching its height. When the government banned imported alcohol in 1689, people began to brew cheap liquor in their own homes. This rapidly became a craze until it was said that in London every sixth house had become a gin shop.

Nor did Sarah encourage her husband in his quest after spiritual light. From a reference in a record of his personal experiences compiled in later years, it would appear that Grimshaw was referring to his own circumstances when he wrote: 'Where husband and wife observe prayer in their family, to frustrate that exercise and the blessings attending it, Satan will prejudice the wife against her husband for praying, so the husband will be prevailed upon to leave off. This is a grievous and dangerous device of the adversary.'[1]

So, with new-found domestic joys and cares, William Grimshaw clearly pushed his spiritual concerns to the back of his mind, at least temporarily. Heiress though she might be, Sarah brought no great wealth into her marriage and as they set up home in the Todmorden parsonage, they did not find it easy to manage on the slender income derived from Grimshaw's curacy. The pressures must have increased when Sarah presented her husband with a son in April 1736. John was probably born at Ewood Court where Sarah's stepmother and younger sister

[1] William Grimshaw, unpublished manuscript, 'Experiences Gather'd by Conversation with my own & the Souls of others' (JRULM). Hereafter called 'Experiences'.

would be on hand to care for mother and child: certainly his baptism was recorded in the church register of nearby St Mary's, Luddenden. Just eleven months later, another child, Jane, was added to the family.

But God did not allow his work in Grimshaw's soul to be retarded for long. By the time John was two and Jane nearly a year old, there is clear evidence that all the aspirations and heart-searchings had reasserted themselves. There was nothing he did not try in order to gain peace of conscience. 'He reformed in every branch and every relation, abstained from every immorality, said many prayers, spent much time in reading and meditation.'[1] Now also he began to pray four times daily – a habit which he maintained to the end of his life. He also spent seasons in fasting and self-searching; and yet to Grimshaw's burdened conscience it all seemed of little avail: those spiritual consolations he longed for seemed as elusive as ever. His reformation of character, however, was clear to all. Even Sarah could not fail to recognise the change in her husband's demeanour and outlook: 'In a little time he was cried up for a saint and the wife of his bosom could bear witness that never was man so altered for the better.'[2]

But it was at this point that William Grimshaw suffered a bereavement, painful enough in any circumstances, but to one in so troubled a state of mind, a crushing blow. His young wife Sarah died at the age of twenty-nine. No details are known of the circumstances of her death – just the bare statement of the fact in Luddenden parish church records: 'Sarah, daughter of John Lockwood of Ewood, Gent., the wife of the Revd. William Grimshaw, Minister of Todmorden, who died November 1, 1739.'

Left a widower at the age of thirty-one, Grimshaw's immediate and pressing concern was the care of his two children, John who was now three years old and Jane who was two. This he settled by sending them to Ewood Court where Sarah's younger sister, Mary, and her stepmother undertook to care for them. Less easy

---

[1] Joseph Williams, cited by Laycock, *Heroes*, p. 33.
[2] Ibid.

to resolve was his own broken spirit and the despair that threatened to engulf him.

The many rooms of the Todmorden parsonage now seemed empty and desolate. Instead of the bustle of family life there was only silence. Grimshaw began to brood in a melancholy fashion on his own death and felt it necessary to make careful and detailed arrangements for his funeral. So, only three weeks after his loss, he drew up a document entitled: 'The Form of My Burial'.

Longing for Sarah's nearness and company, he first specified that he should be buried 'as near to her as convenience will permit'. Funerals in that area were always followed by an 'arvill' or feast at a designated alehouse. On these occasions alcohol flowed so freely that it often degenerated into a drunken riot. So Grimshaw specified with clinical exactness the quantities of alcohol and other refreshments which were to be allowed at his own funeral:

To attend my funeral I desire that 20 persons be invited (of my next relations and intimatest acquaintances) and entertained in the following manner: Let 5 quarts of claret (which will be everyone a gill) be put in a punch bowl, and drunk in wine glasses round until done. Let everyone have a penny roll of bread to eat therewith; let everyone be come and let all sit down together to the same as an emblem of Christian love ... In this form I hope my executors will bury me, as I hope to rise again to a blessed resurrection, through the merits of my dear Redeemer, Jesus Christ.   Nov. 26, 1739[1]

[1] Grimshaw continues: And I have by will ordered five pounds to bury me: it will be disbursed in the following manner:

	£	s	d
To a funeral sermon, 10s.6d, To church dues 5s	0	15	6
To a horse litter, £1 1s. To a coffin, £1	2	1	0
To 2 gallons of claret, 6s.8d. per gal.			
5qts. at home, 3qts. at drinking house,	0	13	4
To 20 2 penny cakes, 3s.4d. To 20 penny rolls 1s.8d.	0	5	0
To 25 prs gloves £1. To expense of inviting to funeral 3s	1	3	0
To parson and clerk each a penny cake [and other oddments?]	0	2	2
	5	0	0

R. Spence Hardy, *William Grimshaw, Incumbent of Haworth* (London: Mason, 1861), p. 12. Hereafter called *Incumbent*.

Apart from being a fascinating document in terms of the social customs and costs of the times, the fact that Grimshaw should draw up such detailed requests gives a clear indication of the burdened state of his mind.

Broken by his bereavement and despairing of the grace of God, Grimshaw was an easy target for the venomous onslaught of Satan. He was tempted to blaspheme his God, believing him to be both cruel and implacable and was 'often ready to accuse God as dealing harshly with one who was now no more profane or careless, but seeking in earnest to obey him',[1] as he confessed long afterwards. Immoral suggestions tormented his imagination and Deistic notions, which he had accepted in his Cambridge days, came flooding back to add to his spiritual confusion. Now he was tempted 'to believe that Christ was a mere man; to undervalue and despise the work of creation as being no more than for a man to make a top or any little machine'.[2]

One day, during this season of intense soul-distress – a period Grimshaw was to describe as 'the melancholy months of my soul's sorrow for sin',[3] – his eyes alighted on a book on his shelf, probably untouched for many years. It was the Christian classic by Thomas Brooks, *Precious Remedies against Satan's Devices*. Surely, if ever he needed such a book, it was at that moment. In God's purposes, however, this work produced in Grimshaw a yet deeper sense of his own sins. As Brooks described over two hundred devices Satan may use to capture the unwary soul, Grimshaw read his own condition into them all, and 'finding the cases there described to tally with his own exactly, he was convinced that he was Satan's easy prey and led about captive by him as he pleased, which brought him to the brink of despair'.[4] So a book that has brought timely aid to many Christians since it was first published in 1652 intensified his struggle, at least

[1] Venn, *Sketch*, p. 31.
[2] Joseph Williams, cited by Laycock, *Heroes*, p. 34.
[3] Letter to Mrs Gallatin, 30 November 1758, cited by Baker, *Grimshaw*, p. 41.
[4] Laycock, *Heroes*, p. 33.

temporarily. But in God's purposes it was designed to deepen the work in Grimshaw's soul.

Throughout these days Grimshaw attempted to carry on his ministry, but on one Sunday his depression led to such a measure of debility, that he could hardly mount the steps into his pulpit. His robust health was failing beneath the mental and spiritual strain. Symptoms, real and imaginary, began to manifest themselves. It scarcely comes as a surprise to learn that after Grimshaw had been called out on two occasions to aid parishioners who had attempted suicide, the final strategy in Satan's armoury was to lure him on to end his own sorrows in a similar fashion.

In all this protracted spiritual conflict Grimshaw was isolated from any who might help him. Fearing that none would understand and many might conclude he was merely depressed, or even question his sanity, he did not speak of his inward trials. He imagined that no-one else had ever experienced such mental anguish. John Newton, describing Grimshaw during this period, writes:

His troubles were aggravated by having no kind friend to whom he could disclose them . . . but in the midst of all his discouragements he persevered in prayer, and in the study of the Scriptures; and in due time, when he had learnt by painful experience the depravity of his nature, his utter unworthiness and insufficiency, his prayers were answered.[1]

Cut off as Grimshaw's location was from the main thoroughfares of English life, he probably knew little of the momentous events taking place at that very time. He did not know that first in Bristol, then in London and further afield, George Whitefield was preaching to the people, in vast open-air gatherings, the message of forgiveness of sins through faith in Christ. John and Charles Wesley, too, had broken through the strictures of their Anglican background and were preaching wherever they could gather the people.

[1] Newton, *Letters*, pp. 12–13.

But two incidents occurred at this time, both designed to lead the curate of Todmorden out of his spiritual darkness. The first, though it might appear negative, showed Grimshaw where his thinking was leading him astray. An itinerant minister (whom he did not choose to name but who could well have been Benjamin Ingham) often passed that way and frequently rebuked Grimshaw for his legalistic views of salvation. 'Mr Grimshaw,' he would say, 'you are a Jew. You are no believer in the Lord Jesus Christ. You are building on the sand.' In vain Grimshaw tried to avoid the itinerant with his unwelcome message; but even if he succeeded, the words rang again and again in his mind: 'You are building on the sand, Mr Grimshaw . . . you are building on the sand.' Grimshaw became increasingly apprehensive of meeting this faithful man. 'I have heard him say,' continues the writer who has preserved this anecdote, 'when he was out walking in the evening, if a brier had caught hold of his coat, he was afraid it was this minister; for when Mr Grimshaw attempted to shun his company he would in affectionate manner lay hold of him and drop some word of Scripture for his conviction.'[1]

The second incident occurred early in 1741 as Grimshaw was visiting a friend. Lying on a table in his friend's room was a book which attracted his attention and finding it was a theological work, he picked it up with quickened interest and crossed the room with it. He stood facing a small shelf of pewter dishes and there examined the book, which he discovered to be written by the Puritan divine, John Owen. 'Instantly', a friend recalled in after years, 'an uncommon heat flushed in his face.' Puzzled, he turned towards the fire, wondering if the sudden wave of heat had come from a reflection of the flames radiated from the pewter dishes.

Turning again to the volume he now held, he opened it at the title page and read, *The Doctrine of Justification by Faith*. As he pondered on the title another flash of heat suddenly passed over him. Astonished by a second occurrence of this phenomenon, he

[1]*Christian's Magazine*, 1792, p. 433.

reasoned that this must be a divine indication that the volume would be of crucial relevance to his need and so requested a loan of the book. We can well imagine that he lost little time in finding opportunity to read a book so strangely brought to his attention.

Owen's preface quickly showed Grimshaw that the book was directed to those who were in the very distress in which he found himself. Even the contents pages confirmed this conviction as Owen set forth the purpose of his treatise, pointing out the need of 'a due sense of our apostasy from God, the depravation of our nature thereby, with the power and guilt of sin, and the holiness of the law necessary to a right understanding of the doctrine of justification'.[1] Grimshaw readily assented to all this, having learned these lessons from his own experience. As he read on, he discovered his experiences were not unique. Many had trodden the same tortuous path as he – Justin Martyr, Ambrose and Chrysostom among them.

Light began to filter into his mind. He turned from section to section until he came to a crucial matter, possibly the crux of his problem. It was Owen's teaching on the doctrine of the imputed righteousness of Jesus Christ – a doctrine which was to form the bedrock of Grimshaw's thinking for the rest of his life. With scriptural illustration from the Mosaic law concerning the 'scape-goat' which, bearing a man's unrighteous deeds, was turned into the wilderness, backed up and elucidated by New Testament teaching, Owen showed that the justified man no longer seeks by his own efforts to please God but is counted by God as possessing the obedience and righteousness of Christ apart from any merit of his own.

Then Owen confronted his reader with a crucial question: 'whether he will trust unto his own personal inherent righteousness or, in a full renunciation of it, betake himself unto the grace of God and the righteousness of Christ alone'.[2] The choice for Grimshaw was now obvious. 'He saw his need of a Saviour and

[1]*The Works of John Owen*, ed. W. H. Goold (Edinburgh, 1852; repr. Banner of Truth Trust, 1967), vol. 5, *Faith and Its Evidences*.
[2]Ibid., p. 230.

the freeness, fulness and suitableness of his grace and merits, and embraced him in both his arms.'[1] Describing the spiritual transaction that took place at this time, Grimshaw told his friend Henry Venn nearly twenty years later:

I was now willing to renounce myself, every degree of fancied merit and ability, and to embrace Christ only for my all in all. O what light and comfort did I now enjoy in my own soul, and what a taste of the pardoning love of God![2]

Joy and relief swept over him like a flood – 'heaven in the soul' was his later description of those days. The Bible became full of fresh meaning and, if God had 'drawn up his Bible to heaven and sent him down another, it could not have been newer to him'.[3]

Aspects of his ministry now changed significantly as he mingled extempore prayers with the set prayers of his Church's liturgy. A new evangelical dimension was added to his preaching. During the years of his search after forgiveness and peace, his preaching had not been without effect. Although sin and judgment had been his constant themes, and he could then only thunder denunciations and exhort his hearers to live a moral life, increasing numbers had travelled in from outlying areas to hear him preach. Some who had previously been awakened to their own need now found peace through the grace and forgiveness of Christ. 'As he was taught of God from his own experience,' wrote Henry Venn, 'so his preaching in the year 1742 began to be clear and profitable. He dwelt much in representing the nature and excellence of Christian faith and salvation by Christ alone.'[4] But others were not so pleased. To silence 'the objections of many hot churchmen'[5] Grimshaw began to preach on portions of the Thirty-Nine Articles, pointing out that in his ordination oaths

---

[1] Williams, cited by Laycock, *Heroes*, p. 32.

[2] Venn, *Sketch*, p. 32.

[3] Extracts from the *Diary, Meditations and Letters of Mr. Joseph Williams of Kidderminster*, ed. B. Hanbury (1826), p. 201.

[4] Venn, *Sketch*, p. 32.

[5] *Christian's Magazine*, November 1792, p. 434.

he had sworn to preach those very doctrines he now held forth to them.

It cannot be supposed, however, that Satan, who had rejoiced to hold Grimshaw captive for so long, would not endeavour to bring him once again into spiritual bondage. Soon he was buffeted once more by doubts and fears. 'Great joy, or our first love is short-lived,' he later wrote in a manuscript account of his experiences, 'with some it lasts but a month or two, and seldom longer; with others not more than a week or two . . .'[1] for so he had found it. Perhaps his new-found joys were but an illusion, he wondered; perhaps God did require a certain standard of holiness before he was willing to accept a sinner after all. Dejected by such misgivings, Grimshaw described the experience as being in 'a spiritual wilderness'. But help was at hand, and once more, cut off as he was from external aid, God used the printed page to help him. This time it was through a booklet loaned him by a young man in a neighbouring parish.

Paul Greenwood, who was about seventeen years of age, lived six miles north of Todmorden, not far from Haworth, where his father kept a smallholding. As the incumbent of Haworth church, Isaac Smith, had been suspended by the vicar of Bradford, it is probable that Paul travelled down to Todmorden to hear Grimshaw preach. Certainly he came under much spiritual concern in 1740. But Grimshaw could not help him to find a peace with God which, as yet, he did not know himself. A small pamphlet, however, came into the youth's possession, which filled him with hope. Written by Robert Seagrave, a friend of George Whitefield, it was published in 1738 and intended for distribution as a tract. Carrying a long title, *A Draught of the Justification of Man, different from the Present Language of the Pulpit,* it was an exposition of Galatians 3:24, 'The law was our schoolmaster to bring us unto Christ', and set forth the same teaching as Grimshaw had found in John Owen's work, only in a more popular style. Robert Seagrave is best remembered today

[1]'Experiences'.

for his hymns,[1] but in his own day this pamphlet, and another entitled *Letter to the People of England,* were widely used by God and were among the earliest publications of the revival.

Greenwood's first reading of Seagrave's pages moved him so deeply that he had to slip out of the house in search of a place where he could pray. The barn seemed ideal for here he would not be disturbed. He fell on his knees and began crying out to God for mercy and forgiveness. The hours passed and still he wrestled for the blessings he so earnestly desired. His father became concerned about him and while searching for him heard sounds coming from the barn. Opening the door, he stood motionless for some moments. There was his son praying. Overpowered by a sense of his own sins, Paul's father knelt down beside him, and there he also pleaded with God for mercy. When Greenwood's mother discovered her husband and son praying in the barn, she too was deeply affected and knelt beside them, earnestly seeking the forgiveness of God. Before long they were joined by another brother and sister who also felt compelled to cry out for mercy. Together the whole family, mingling their tears of repentance, found the favour and forgiveness of God.

Naturally Paul Greenwood, who already knew Grimshaw personally, was eager to share the account of God's dealings with his family and to lend him the pamphlet which had been so helpful. When Grimshaw read *The Draught,* he rejoiced once more in the truth of justification by faith through the imputed righteousness of Jesus Christ. 'Really virtuous persons are glad to renounce their own righteousness for that of Christ.' This he could readily affirm, and it was not long before he knew once again an inner peace through confidence in the finished work of Christ.

As he gained peace of heart, William Grimshaw's thoughts began to turn towards a second marriage. His children needed a mother, and he longed to have them back with him again and to

---

[1]Best known is 'Rise, my soul, and stretch thy wings', *Christian Hymns* (Bryntirion: Evangelical Movement of Wales, 1977), No. 638.

know once more the comforts and joy of family life. His brother, John, who was three years younger than he, had also been ordained and had settled in a curacy at Cross Stone, within walking distance of Todmorden. Probably Grimshaw often called on his brother in the period of his bereavement and loneliness. So when John married a local girl, Mary Cockcroft, his brother was sure to have become acquainted with her family and during the summer of 1741 Grimshaw chose Mary's cousin, Elizabeth, to be his bride. They were married on 10 August, and soon John and Jane, now five and four years of age respectively, joined them in the Todmorden parsonage.

4

HARBINGERS OF BLESSING IN YORKSHIRE
1734-1742

FOR SEVEN YEARS, FROM 1734–1741, Grimshaw had been searching after a knowledge of the forgiveness of his sins and peace with God. All through those years he had experienced an isolation and loneliness of spirit for, apart from Paul Greenwood and possibly one or two others, few would have understood his inner conflict. But, apparently unknown to him, there was a parallel work of God progressing in Yorkshire throughout that period, and often not far distant from his own Todmorden parsonage. His experiences were but part of a significant and widespread movement of the Spirit of God.

Yorkshire had known little gospel light in the past. Here and there godly men had laboured and seen fruit for their toil, but most of the people had lived and died without any spiritual enlightenment. One exception to this prevalent condition was to be found in the village of Rowley, in East Yorkshire. Here Ezekiel Rogers, cousin of the better-known John Rogers of Dedham, had ministered to the small community for twenty-two years. Like his cousin, whose powerful preaching had been formative in the life of Thomas Goodwin and many others, Ezekiel Rogers was also silenced because of his non-conformity. Being a younger man, however, he decided to emigrate to the New World – but he did not go alone, rather his whole congregation accompanied him in search of religious liberty. They sailed from Hull in 1638 and established a settlement north of Boston, Massachusetts, calling it

Rowley in memory of their home village. There Rogers ministered to his flock for a further twenty-two years.

Another Puritan, often called the Northern Puritan, was Oliver Heywood. Born in Lancashire like William Grimshaw, he too spent his life ministering to the people of Yorkshire. In 1650 he took charge of the parish church in Coley, a rural area on the moors north of Halifax. Although initially well-disposed towards Charles II, Heywood was one of the first to feel the restrictive rigour of the new regime. Continually harassed for his nonconformity, he was cited to appear at York, and ejected from his charge several months before Black Bartholomew's Day in August 1662. For the next twenty-five years he had no settled pulpit, but always sought opportunities to preach wherever he could, travelling from his home in Northowram, between Halifax and Bradford. He itinerated in West Yorkshire and parts of Lancashire, preaching to small groups of God-fearing people – Christians prepared to face the hazard of prohibitive fines and the loss of position and property in order to worship God in accordance with principles of Scripture and their conscience. Even though Heywood himself was harried, tracked down and sometimes imprisoned, nothing could deter him from preaching. Finally, when religious liberty was granted after 1688, his people erected a chapel for him near Coley, and when he was too infirm to mount his pulpit, they would carry him up, so that he could still preach to them.

Perhaps the small group of praying men and women, which Grimshaw discovered in Rochdale when he first went to Littleborough in 1731, was the fruit of Heywood's ministry; certainly Heywood's diary records frequent visits to Rochdale. But, apart from a few pockets of spiritual life, darkness and ignorance of biblical truth rested over the county as a whole until the year 1734, the same year that William Grimshaw began to be concerned over his way of life in the sight of God.

The first glimmer of a new day of grace in Yorkshire came with the return of Benjamin Ingham from Oxford to his native Ossett, south of Leeds, in 1734. Born in 1712, young Ingham had been serious from an early age, reading the Scriptures each night and often finding secret places where he could pray alone. He had entered Queen's College in 1730 and soon after sought out John and Charles Wesley, becoming a member of the Holy Club. A private diary compiled by Ingham during the summer of 1734 has recently been discovered and decoded: its contents reveal that same degree of devotion to God which characterised other members of the Holy Club, but also the same restrictive legalistic spirit that hindered them.[1]

Back in Ossett in July 1734 after completing his studies, Ingham continued to maintain a similar level of spiritual endeavour, coupled with the philanthropic work that had been his preoccupation during his Oxford days. We read in a contemporary account of his life, written by William Batty: 'He began to keep religious meetings in his mother's house every night: he read and expounded the scriptures and other good books, sang hymns, psalms and prayed.'[2] Soon the neighbours were affected, first an old man, then two widows and later many others asked to join the little gathering. Before many months had passed, the first religious society in that area had been formed.

Benjamin Ingham then extended his influence, beginning classes for children, for the poor and the illiterate. Finding this

[1]'April 6 [1734] Resolutions for observing the Passion Week:

1. Monday, Tuesday, and Thursday, to eat no bread; one flesh meal at dinner; and to have supper on bread and milk.

2. Wednesday, Friday, and Saturday to make one meal on dry diet.

3. To spend at least seven hours a day in public and private prayer, religious meditation and reading and works of mercy . . .

Monday, April 8. 5[o'clock] Dressed. 5.15 Private prayer. 5.30 Wrote diary. 5.45 Read chapter. 6[o'clock] E[jaculatory prayers]; showed Smith and Evans the Chapel. 6.30. Read *Country Parson*. 7.15 Public Prayers. 8.15 Went to visit the sick woman; she had sent for the person to administer the sacrament . . .' *Diary of an Oxford Methodist,* ed. R. P. Heitzenrater (Durham: Duke University Press, 1985), pp. 155–6.

[2]'Church History, Collected from the Memoirs and Journals of the Revd Mr Ingham and the labourers in connection with him. July 14th 1779'. William Batty. Transcribed by Rev. M. Rattenbury, Hull. MS in JRULM, p. 1. Hereafter called 'History'.

ministry also owned by God and numbers awakened to their lost condition, Ingham began preaching in the surrounding villages and towns and by 1735 a number of religious societies had been formed, dotted around his native Ossett.

In June 1735 Ingham was ordained and in September of that year decided to sail with John and Charles Wesley for Georgia in the New World. Like them he felt the urgent need of the un-evangelised Indians and fully intended to devote his life to this work. But God had other purposes behind this mission to Georgia, for on the ship he and the Wesleys met some Moravians whose conversation and testimony to the need of justifying faith was to affect all three profoundly. For, despite all the good accomplished in Yorkshire, Benjamin Ingham was still looking to his own righteousness to earn his acceptance with God. We read of him:

The Spirit of the Lord began to convince him of his sin in the ship as they were going over to Georgia but he laboured hard to establish his own righteousness . . . at length [after several months in Georgia] having used all means and finding them ineffectual and in deep distress he looked unto Jesus, called on him for mercy and instantly obtained it.[1]

Although Ingham had made significant progress in acquiring an Indian language, God's eventual purpose for each of these three men was far other than they thought or intended. By differing circumstances they all returned to England: Charles Wesley in December 1736, broken by illness and disillusioned; Ingham in July 1737, ostensibly to recruit new workers for their endeavours; and John Wesley early in 1738.

Losing little time after disembarking, Benjamin Ingham returned home, but as he approached Ossett he reined in his horse and stopped for a while. William Batty describes the scene:

On Wooley Moor, a hill about six miles from Ossett, he sat down, having a prospect of the country where the Lord soon after made him an instrument of calling many souls, and there the Spirit of the Lord

[1] Ibid., p. 2.

was poured upon him in a particular manner and then and there he was ordained of God to be a preacher of the gospel and was anointed by the Holy Ghost for the work.[1]

The consequences of these things were immediate: everywhere he preached the power of God accompanied him. His biographer continues:

Every Sunday he preached in a different church or chapel till he had preached in all the churches or chapels in the neighbourhood. The word was attended with power, numbers were astonished and affected, and crowds flocked to hear. At the same time G. Whitefield preached in many churches in London: from their meeting together in London this year [1737] may be dated the spreading of the work of the Lord and the beginning of the general awakening in England.[2]

May 24, 1738 has rightly been regarded as a date of major importance in the annals of the Christian Church, for on this day, as we have noted, John Wesley received an inward assurance of salvation. Then, as he later confessed, 'I did trust in Christ, Christ alone for salvation; and an assurance was given me that he had taken away my sins, even mine, and saved me from the law of sin and death.'[3] Charles had found the same assurance a few days earlier. But another significant date, though less spoken of, must also be mentioned because of its far-reaching effects on the work of God in Yorkshire. On 1 January 1739 the Wesley brothers, George Whitefield and Benjamin Ingham, together with about sixty others, were in the old Moravian Chapel in Fetter Lane at a love feast.[4] On this memorable day these men received a further effusion of divine power, equipping them for the travail and the

---

[1] Ibid., p. 3. [2] Ibid.
[3] John Wesley, *Journal*, vol. I, p. 95.
[4] John Wesley describes the scene: 'About three in the morning as we were continuing instant in prayer, the power of God came mightily upon us, insomuch that many cried out for exceeding joy, and many fell to the ground. As soon as we recovered a little from the awe and amazement at the presence of the divine majesty, we broke out with one voice, "We praise thee, O God, we acknowledge thee to be the Lord!"' *Journal,* vol. II, p. 121f.

glory of the work of evangelising vast tracts of the country which were 'for the most part in a state of heathen or worse than heathen ignorance'.[1]

Ingham's preaching was now attended by even more evidences of the power of God, and by the end of 1739 he had gathered together little groups of new believers in many different places around Leeds and Halifax, forming them into 'societies' for mutual encouragement, fellowship and prayer. Forty societies were established in the West Riding in that year alone. But such a work of God could not be expected to go unchallenged, and in June 1739, Benjamin Ingham, still only twenty-seven years of age, was arraigned before the church courts in Wakefield and forbidden to preach in the churches of Yorkshire.

Fifteen years after these events, William Grimshaw himself was to write a letter to Dr John Gillies, a minister in Glasgow who was compiling an account of the great works of God in revival in past generations. In this letter Grimshaw was to give him a careful account of the events that were then taking place in Yorkshire, though he himself had scarcely been aware of all that was happening at the time:

In the year 1738, our gracious Redeemer was pleased to revive his work in the West Riding, as we call it, of the county of York. Now were poor souls among us brought to know Jesus alone, for their wisdom, righteousness, sanctification and redemption. The first instrument sent hither by our dear Immanuel, was one Mr Benjamin Ingham, a clergyman and one of the Oxford Methodists. He was born in Ossett in this Riding. The clergy at first received him in their pulpits, the churches were soon crowded, and a great stirring up of the people to seek salvation by faith alone, in the merits of the crucified Saviour quickly appeared. But Satan, perceiving his kingdom to be in danger, began to roar, and the clergy (as I have been informed) were forbid to receive Mr Ingham any more. Wakefield, Ossett, Leeds, Halifax and many other churches and chapels he preached in, until he was prohibited. And greatly were the people blessed. He then betook himself (as did Messrs

---

[1] Robert Southey, *Life of John Wesley*, vol.1 (London: Longmans, 1846), p. 206.

Wesley and Whitefield, and others at the same time,) to our Saviour's manner, field preaching. And eminently did our Lord soon testify that this was his good pleasure. Multitudes assembled everywhere, and it soon appeared that conscience rather than curiosity was the main motive thereto. Man's fall and degeneracy, his redemption through Christ Jesus alone, the nature and necessity of the new birth, justification by faith alone, sanctification by the indwelling Spirit of our Redeemer etc. These were (and still are) the main doctrines and subjects of all discourse. Many people not only heard but were convinced, converted and brought to a saving and experimental knowledge of these truths. The kingdom of God soon appeared to be a kingdom within by righteousness, peace and joy in the Holy Ghost.[1]

As Grimshaw pointed out, the attempt on the part of the clergy to check this work of God, by prohibiting Ingham to preach in the churches, had a counter-productive effect: the people gathered in yet greater numbers to hear him preach. This increased measure of blessing could also be accounted for in another way. William Batty in his biographical sketch of Ingham tells us:

At Ossett, Aug. 24th, [1740] the Lord Jesus manifested himself to B. Ingham in a particular way. The great Mystery of Godliness was made clear to him. He then experimentally knew what the white stone meant & the new name [and] the Passover of the blood of sprinkling. From the beginning of the year 1737 he had had a lively hope of his interest in Christ which had grown up in him stronger and stronger; so that he was freed from doubts and fears about his salvation: but now he was fully assured of his eternal salvation.[2]

We are not surprised, therefore, to read in Batty's next paragraph: 'In this year 1740 the word of the Lord went on gloriously in Yorkshire.' He continues by giving an impressive list of sixty places in West Yorkshire where Ingham established societies – places such as: Horbury, Dewsbury, Brighouse, Gomersal, Mirfield, Bingley, Baildon, Cleckheaton, Bradford, Heaton and

---

[1]Grimshaw in a letter to Dr John Gillies, 19 July 1754, appendix to *Historical Collections of Accounts of Revival* (first published 1754, republished, Edinburgh: Banner of Truth Trust, 1981), pp. 506–7.

[2]Batty, 'History', p. 4.

many others. Ingham would travel tirelessly amongst them, encouraging believers to hold fast in spite of opposition. Each month he would announce a united meeting for all these small groups and two thousand would regularly gather. Batty adds, 'He was acquainted with 800 whom he believed were united to Christ, & with several hundred more who were concerned and seeking salvation.'

Not far from Ossett, to the east of Leeds, lay Ledstone Hall, the stately home of Theophilus, Lord Hastings and Earl of Huntingdon. His four daughters by his second wife: Lady Anne, Lady Frances, Lady Catherine and Lady Margaret Hastings, often came to the family home in Yorkshire where their half-sister, Lady Betty Hastings was living. The ladies soon heard of the young itinerant preacher from Ossett and curiosity turned to concern after they had listened to Benjamin Ingham for themselves; he then found himself frequently invited to preach at Ledsham Church, the Earl's private chapel. Back in London, the sisters availed themselves of every opportunity to hear Methodist preaching and before long all four turned from their own righteousness to Jesus Christ. Benjamin Ingham naturally became a frequent visitor at Ledstone Hall whenever they were in Yorkshire and, in 1741, he and Lady Margaret Hastings were married and made their home in the village of Aberford, five miles north of Ledstone Hall.

Hindrances to such a work of grace in a part of the country hitherto little touched by the gospel came not only from the opposition of the clergy, but, more subtly, through division and mistrust between those who should have been united in spiritual endeavour. Problems first arose in London where the Wesleys and the Moravians had hitherto been working in close union in the Fetter Lane Society. Misguided teaching had been introduced among the Moravians by a newcomer, Philip Molther, who had only recently joined the Moravians, having arrived from Germany in October 1739. Because of this, Wesley eventually had to withdraw from the society and he and his diminished band of followers were obliged to find new premises where they could meet. In July 1740 an old foundry became the centre where they worshipped and from where John Wesley organised Methodism's rapidly expanding activities. So began the first Methodist Society. But Molther's influence spread and this erroneous Moravian teaching extended from the Fetter Lane Society and soon began to damage the work taking place in Yorkshire. It has been summed up by A. C. H. Seymour in his *Life and Times of the Countess of Huntingdon:*

Many of the Moravians had joined the society in Fetter-lane, and now began to introduce some fatal errors among them. All was confusion. By some it was contended that believers had nothing to do with ordinances – were not subject to them and ought to be *still:* that they ought to leave off the means of grace; not go to church; not to communicate; not to search the scriptures; not to use private prayer, till they had living faith; and to be *still* until they had it. And it was further explicitly affirmed, that there were no *degrees* in faith – that none had any faith who had ever any doubt or fear, and that none were justified until they had clean hearts, with the perpetual indwelling of Christ, and of the Holy Ghost – and that everyone who had not this ought, until he had it, to be *still* . . . not to use ordinances or *means of grace.*[1]

Initially Ingham resisted such teaching, travelling down to London to try to bring about some better understanding between Wesley and their former friends. Ingham's views on the assurance of faith certainly contrasted markedly with the Moravian teaching.[2] But Benjamin Ingham owed a considerable debt to the Moravians, having been led to right views of justifying faith through them. A visit to Herrnhut, the Moravian headquarters in Germany, with John Wesley in July 1738 had cemented these bonds, making him predisposed to a sympathetic interpretation of their ideas. Because of this, and also his increasing dislike of Wesley's teaching on Christian perfection, his relationship with

[1] A. C. H. Seymour, *The Life and Times of Selina, Countess of Huntingdon,* vol. I (London: W. E. Painter, 1840), p. 36. Hereafter called *Countess of Huntingdon.*

[2] 'We may be heirs of heaven before we know it.' See Ingham to John Wesley, 20 February 1740, quoted by L. Tyerman, *Oxford Methodists,* p. 92.

John and Charles Wesley cooled considerably from this period onwards. Faced with the immense task of evangelising Yorkshire, Ingham had invited a prominent Moravian leader John Toeltschig to come and help him in 1739. Toeltschig had been well received by Ingham's societies and so now, in 1741, by popular request, the Moravians were invited to begin a 'Yorkshire Congregation'.[1] For a time, Ingham himself was carried away by their new emphases, though he did not himself become a member of the Moravian Church.

The men whom God chooses to accomplish his designs often differ widely from each other in personality and gifts and Benjamin Ingham was not the only man whom God raised up at this time to bring the light of the gospel into Yorkshire. Few could have been more dissimilar than the scholarly Ingham and the stonemason from Birstall, south of Leeds, John Nelson. Born in 1707, a year before William Grimshaw, Nelson also had experienced terrifying dreams and convictions of sin as a child, yet grew to 'love pleasure more than God'. Restless in spirit, he at last determined to travel to London to seek work. Here he joined the crowds who flocked to Moorfields to hear George Whitefield preach in the open air. On at least twenty occasions he listened to the preacher's passionate and searching appeals but remained unconverted still.

On 19 June 1739, however, a man rose to preach to the throng of eager hearers whom John Nelson had never seen before. It was John Wesley, and this was the first occasion he had addressed the people in Moorfields. God's hour had come for John Nelson. Writing long afterwards, he exclaimed: 'O that was a blessed morning to my soul! As soon as Mr Wesley got upon the stand, he stroked back his hair and turned his face toward where I stood, and I thought fixed his eyes upon me. When he spoke I thought his whole discourse was aimed at me ...' Alone in his rooms after that sermon, he 'prayed until he could pray no more'. At last he was able to declare: 'Jesus Christ was as evidently set forth before

---

[1]James Hutton, *History of the Moravian Church* (London: Moravian Publications Office, 1909), p. 306.

the eyes of my mind as crucified for my sins as if I had seen him with my bodily eyes; and in that instant my heart was set at liberty from guilt and tormenting fear, and filled with a calm and serene peace.'[1]

Returning to Yorkshire shortly after these things, Nelson could not refrain from speaking everywhere of his experience of the forgiveness of sins – something almost unknown among the people. His wife, sceptical at first, was soon converted and from that moment she supported her husband wholeheartedly though suffering, abuse and pain were often her only earthly recompense. Within three weeks of Nelson's return to Yorkshire seventeen of his neighbours, family and friends had been converted to God.

News of these things spread from town to town, and many were the requests for John Nelson to come and explain the way of peace to small gatherings of concerned men and women. Labouring all day at his stonemasonry, Nelson would go straight from his toil to a meeting, still clad in his leather apron, with his hammer and trowel slung round his waist. Without design he had become one of the earliest Methodist lay preachers.

Before long Benjamin Ingham heard of the Birstall stonemason who had turned preacher. This could well have proved an offence to Ingham for Nelson was unordained, uneducated and untrained. In addition, Nelson's preaching was clearly after the pattern heard from Wesley and impressed on his heart by the Holy Spirit and, as we have seen, there was a degree of rift between Ingham and Wesley. Sending for John Nelson, Ingham questioned him carefully, and then, revealing the true greatness and generosity of his spirit, declared to all who gathered on the occasion: 'Before you all I give John leave to exhort in all my societies,' adding, 'John, God hath given you great honour, in that he hath made use of you to call sinners to the blood of our Saviour, and I desire you to exhort in all my societies as often as you can.'

[1]*The Journal of Mr John Nelson, The Lives of Early Methodist Preachers*, vol. I (London: Wesleyan Conference Centre, 1875), p. 14.

This was in 1740, but sadly, as Ingham became more deeply involved with the Moravians, he found Nelson's preaching an embarrassment and retracted his permission, and, as Nelson recalled it, said instead, 'You ought not to tell the people that they may know their sins forgiven; for the world cannot bear it.' Not intimidated by Ingham's social and educational advantages, Nelson had replied stoutly, 'I love every man and fear no man; and I will tell all I can . . . I believe it is a sin not to declare to the children of men what God has done for my soul that they may seek for the same mercy.'[1] So from 1742 onwards the two men worked largely independently of each other, Ingham throwing in his lot increasingly with the Moravians, who established an extensive base for their work near Halifax.

William Grimshaw, in his letter to Dr John Gillies from which we have already quoted – a letter he wrote in 1754 at the request of George Whitefield – sums up these events:

In the year 1740 or 1741, one, John Nelson of Birstall in this Riding, a mason, converted among the Methodists in London, was raised up to preach the gospel, came down to preach it to his countrymen, and joined Mr Ingham in the work. The parson and the mason laboured together with great success for some time, and formed societies, whose exercise consisted in praying, singing, reading, conferring together about the work of God in their souls. These men are still living and still labouring, I trust with great success, but not together.

In 1742, I am informed they separated, and shortly afterwards the Lord sent down first I think the Rev. Charles Wesley, and then the Rev. John, his brother, to Birstall. John Nelson joined them. Towns, villages, and country received the word with gladness, and great was the ingathering of souls. Leeds, Birstall, Halifax, Ossett, Gumersell [Gomersal], Horton and many other places have cause to praise God for those seasons.

Wherever Nelson travelled, the people congregated. He was the first Methodist preacher to introduce the gospel into many of the towns, villages and rural areas of Yorkshire. A moving

[1]Nelson, *Early Methodists*, p. 44.

description has survived of Nelson's preaching in Halifax among rough and often hardened people: 'A washing tub, mouth downwards, served for a pulpit, and here among the huge rocks with which the house was surrounded, far from the din and tumult, Nelson preached and the people were much affected; a grey-headed man near eighty years of age, the owner of the house, listened with deep concern while the big tears trickled down.'[1]

William Grimshaw, though nearby, was probably unaware of these circumstances. Poor roads and slow communications isolated him from surrounding areas, but, even had he heard rumours of such things, he might well have been suspicious. Clearly, however, these things were a harbinger of the blessing of God soon to be poured out in full measure on the people of Yorkshire and the north of England; and in those blessings the curate of Todmorden, humbled and converted, was to be another notable instrument in his hand.

[1]Laycock, *Heroes,* p. 18.

5

HAWORTH – A BARREN WILDERNESS

TODMORDEN, SCENE OF WILLIAM GRIMSHAW'S FOLLIES, his bereavement, his travail of soul and his new birth was now responding to the message he proclaimed from its pulpit. But after nearly eleven years there, and with new spiritual confidence, he felt there would be advantage in a change and a fresh beginning where, together with his new bride Elizabeth and the children, he could set up home. Hearing that the curacy in nearby Haworth had become vacant, Grimshaw applied for this appointment in the spring of 1742. Nine miles north-east of Todmorden and four miles south of Keighley, this small Pennine town was to become God's chosen arena for some of the most striking displays of his power during the eighteenth-century Evangelical Revival.

John Newton paints a dismal pen picture of conditions in Haworth as Grimshaw would have found them when he arrived in May 1742: 'The bleak and barren face of the adjacent country was no improper emblem of the state of the inhabitants; who in general had little more sense of religion than their cattle, and were wild and uncultivated like the mountains and rocks which surrounded them.' But all this was soon to change, as Newton hastened to add: 'But by the blessing of God upon Mr Grimshaw's ministry, this desert soon became a fruitful field, a garden of the Lord . . . and the barren wilderness rejoiced and blossomed like the rose.'[1]

[1] Newton, *Letters,* p. 43.

Probably Newton's description was a little too severe. Conditions in Haworth were not markedly worse than in surrounding areas. But the spiritual darkness which rested over the whole land prior to the revival was certainly deeper in areas like Yorkshire which had known little of the light that had illuminated many parts of the country during the previous century. The grip that gin and other alcoholic liquor held over the people of Haworth was reflected in the number of drinking houses that flourished in the township relative to the population, which consisted of little over two thousand at the time that Grimshaw began his ministry. Described as 'this liquid fire by which men drink their hell beforehand', gin brought dissipation with its resulting privation and sorrow to many homes in Yorkshire.

Oliver Heywood, the ejected minister of Coley in the previous century, had often passed through Haworth on his travels into Lancashire during the years when he was prohibited from preaching in his own pulpit. His first visit was in June 1672 when he wrote in his diary: 'Upon a solemn invitation I went to Jonas Foster's house in Haworth parish, where I was never before in all my life.' Unimpressed with the spiritual conditions he found in this remote Pennine village, he reported that it was 'a very ignorant place where there was never good preaching'. But on this occasion he continues, 'multitudes of people flocked to hear me, some were affected, God helped my heart graciously in praying and preaching about four hours together. It was strange preaching amongst them, who knows what work God may have on some hearts? Oh that some soul might be awakened!'[1] There followed a number of visits after this, the last recorded twenty years later in 1692, when Heywood wrote,

I rode . . . to preach at Haworth town. God greatly helped my heart in weeping and wrestling with God for the conversion of sinners, and in preaching on Isaiah 55:7. There was a great crowd of people and they were attentive. Who knows what good may be done? The same day

[1] *Oliver Heywood's Diary*, vol. III, ed. J. Horsfall Turner (Brighouse: 1882), p. 108.

being Easter Monday, the Vicar of Bradford sat all day in an ale-house gathering his dues, in Haworth parish . . . I had nothing for my pains except that four or five thrust sixpence apiece into my hand. I rode fourteen miles there and back, and was greatly comforted in my day's work and thought it was far better than his.[1]

Perched high up on the edge of the moors, the parish church of St Michael and All Angels to which William Grimshaw was now appointed, probably dated back to Tudor times. There had been a place of worship on that site for at least four hundred years before Grimshaw's day. Robert Towne, who had become its curate in 1655, was ejected in 1662, like Oliver Heywood, for being unable to comply with the terms of the Act of Uniformity. Described as 'a notoriously rabid Independent' by his detractors, Towne died in 1664, and we have little other information about him. Another curate, Edmund Robinson, was executed in York Castle in 1692 after two or three earlier warnings, for commissioning counterfeit coinage.[2] And yet another, William Clifford, incumbent in 1703, confessed he 'would rather dye in the pope's bosom than in the Presbyterian faith'.

William Grimshaw's immediate predecessor was Isaac Smith who had been appointed as curate of Haworth in 1726. Contradictory opinions, some highly commendatory but others quite the reverse, have been recorded about Smith, whose stormy years as curate ended with his suspension by the vicar of Bradford in 1739, and finally his dismissal by the Consistory Court in 1740. Probably neither judgment is entirely true. The son of a dissenting minister who had also been ejected from his charge in 1662, young Isaac Smith would have known suffering and deprivation in his earlier days. Subsequently he had argued his way back into the Established Church; but going even further, had veered towards a High Church position. Some of his Haworth parishioners were unhappy about this; one disgruntled woman complained that her minister was 'deeply tinctured with popery';

---

[1]Ibid., vol. III, p. 349.
[2]Turner, *Haworth – Past and Present,* pp. 40–46.

that when he came to church on a Sunday morning 'he always
went to the baptismal font, dipped his finger in the water, crossed
himself and walked twice or three times round the aisles muttering something which nobody could understand'.[1]

Tardy in paying money owed to Benjamin Kennet, the vicar of
Bradford, Isaac Smith soon fell into disfavour with him. And the
Haworth people also complained that their curate extorted his
financial dues in an insensitive and rigorous manner. But this is
not the whole story. An examination of old documents reveals
that Smith was only paid a pitiful twenty guineas for his annual
stipend[2] and was probably reduced to deep poverty – which
explains to some extent his apparent perversity over money
matters. To supplement his meagre income he resorted to the
expedient of conducting clandestine marriages ('clog and shoe'
weddings, as the church register describes them) and pocketed
the fees which would otherwise have gone to Benjamin Kennet.
Smith defended himself robustly over this issue, maintaining that
the practice was commonplace; it had been customary 'from time
immemorial to publish and marry people from Bradford parish at
Haworth church, without contradiction or opposition'. But it
annoyed the vicar, and provided him with the opportunity he had
been seeking to discipline the unpopular curate of Haworth. And
so in 1739 he arranged for Smith to be suspended temporarily
from his clerical duties.

Spence Hardy, in his biography of Grimshaw, quotes at length
from an open letter which Isaac Smith published in an early
Yorkshire newspaper, the *Leeds Mercury*, on the occasion of his
suspension, entitled 'A Letter to the People of Haworth'. It gives
a different picture of Smith's character:

And if I first look at myself, I must confess with weeping eyes, I have not
been so careful and diligent in doctrine and life as I ought to have been:
therefore, the Lord is holy in all his ways and righteous in all his works,

[1] JEN.
[2] From archives of Borthwick Institute for Historical Research, York, R III
xxxii E3, August 1727.

and I am punished infinitely less than what my sins deserve: not to mention that fault . . . or rather misfortune, for which I now lie under the censure of suspension from the ministry.

Such a confession could indicate Christian humility or, alternatively, it might simply suggest that Smith knew that there had been defects in his preaching and ministry. Nevertheless he continued by protesting his earnest endeavour in Haworth, and then concluded,

I hope I can truly say, to my great comfort and joy that some of you, and I heartily wish the number was far greater, have through the blessing of God upon my poor endeavours, been delivered from the power of Satan and translated into the kingdom of our Lord Jesus Christ . . . but this boasting is almost over when I consider what numbers in Haworth parish are yet in the gall of bitterness . . . strangers to God and Christ and strangers to their duty.[1]

Although Isaac Smith had sought, according to his light, to arouse the people of Haworth to their spiritual duty, the majority had remained unresponsive. But his own understanding of the gospel was defective, for in this same letter to his people he contends that 'alms deliver from death and make atonement for sins' – a comment which adds credence to the parishioner's complaint who said the curate was 'deeply tinctured with popery'.

Among Isaac Smith's other activities during his fourteen years in Haworth was the erection of the church clock and barn, both largely at his own expense, in spite of his low income. Perhaps the best thing he accomplished, however, was the purchase of a parsonage: a farmhouse known as Sowdens, with its accompanying outbuildings. This he dedicated on 15 May 1739, with 'prayers, aspersions, acclamations and crossings'.

Nestling into the hillside on the moors above Haworth, about half a mile south-west of the church, Sowdens was an excellent choice for a parsonage. Sturdily constructed and spacious for the

---

[1]*Leeds Mercury,* 4 December 1739, cited by Hardy, *Incumbent,* p. 32f.

day, the whole complex may have been built in Stuart times; certainly one of the outbuildings carries the date 1659. An article in *The Methodist Recorder* for January 1899 describes Sowdens as follows:

Today it stands very much as it stood a hundred and fifty years ago on the edge of the great Yorkshire wilderness, where winter storms howl across the bare hills and heather clothes the moors up to the edge of the quarries . . . The old parsonage is built of stone dug out of the everlasting hills. It presents as little surface as possible to the fierce blasts, and is sheltered by trees and outbuildings and a long stone wall.[1]

But Sowdens had an important advantage – one which must have influenced Isaac Smith in his choice of a parsonage. This was a nearby running spring which could provide six gallons of pure drinking water every minute for the household at Sowdens. This resource would have proved a great benefit to William Grimshaw and his family. Over a century later an enterprising resident found a way of piping the water from Sowdens spring to augment the town's supply.

In spite of his efforts to placate the annoyance of his vicar, Isaac Smith was finally discharged from his duties in 1740, after being arraigned before the Consistory Court for 'not being grave and decent in his apparel on Sundays and Holy days . . . and for not wearing such as is the usual habit of clergymen'. Given Smith's ritualistic leanings, this may refer to the wearing of unlawful vestments rather than appearing in slovenly clothing. He died a year after his unceremonious dismissal; meantime the people had been served by a temporary curate, whom Smith had nominated. But he too had fallen into disfavour – this time for propagating Arian views.

After the death of Isaac Smith, we may well imagine that both the trustees of Haworth parish church and the parishioners were anticipating the appointment of a new curate who would serve

---

[1] *The Methodist Recorder*, 'The Yorkshire Storm-Centre of the Evangelical Revival', by H. K. and H. D. W. January 1899.

them more satisfactorily. The number of communicants had dropped to a mere handful, with nearly four hundred young people eligible, at least nominally, for confirmation.[1] So when the curate of nearby Todmorden expressed interest in the appointment, it seems that the trustees decided that this was to be the man of their choice.

But when William Grimshaw initially applied to the vicar of Bradford for the vacant charge at Haworth, Benjamin Kennet refused. In all probability he had heard of the style of preaching recently introduced at Todmorden and preferred to appoint a curate in Haworth who he could be sure would create no further problems. In Haworth, however, the stipend of the curate was paid from a special trust raised from the rents of four farms in the adjacent village of Stanbury, especially bought for the purpose.[2] By 1742 the annual yield was £42-16s-6d, with an additional £8-15s-6d[3] raised from the mortgage of another property. This would give Grimshaw a considerably better income than his predecessor, though it was still modest for the times.

This circumstance gave the trustees the power to overturn any appointment the vicar of Bradford might make, because the trust instrument endowed them with the authority either to pay or withhold the stipend due to the appointee. And these men, with true Yorkshire recalcitrance, insisted on having William Grimshaw. Even though Kennet resorted to the Ecclesiastical Court in York, he was out-manoeuvred when the trustees entered a caveat against him, preventing, 'Mr Kennet, Vicar of Bradford chusing a Minister to serve in our Church'.[4] The vicar had no

[1]From Archbishop Herring's Visitation Returns, 1743 (Yorkshire Archaeological Society, Record Series, vol. LXXII, eds. Ollard and Walker, vol. II (Wakefield: 1929), p. 40.

[2]For further details of this trust see *The Brontës*, Juliet Barker (London: Weidenfeld and Nicolson, 1994), p. 80.

[3]Archives of Borthwick Institute for Historical Research, York, RIII xxxii E4, September 1743.

[4]Michael Baumber, unpublished MS, 'Revival to Regency, Keighley and Haworth', 1740–1820, p. 162.

option but to give way, for until he acquiesced to their demand he too would be deprived of his dues. And so, despite the machinations of the vicar, William Grimshaw arrived in Haworth during May 1742. In the church register he entered the following biographical note:

May 16th. 1742

The Revd. William Grimshaw A.B. of CHRIST's College, Cambridge, succeeded the Revd. Mr: Isaac Smith, A.M. deceas'd, in the Parish Church of Haworth, May 16th: having been Minister of the Parochial Curacy of Todmorden, Lancashire, 10 years 9 Months: He was born in Brindle near Preston: sometime educated at ye: Free School of Blackburn by Mr: Geo: Smith H: Master: Afterwards at Heskin Free School by Mr: Thomas Johnson H: Master thereof in the County aforesaid, & from thence sent to & admitted Member of the University and College above said. Witness my hand

W. Grimshaw   Minr: of Haworth

Now thirty-four years of age Grimshaw, with his burly frame and resilient personality, was well-suited to handle his indisciplined and tough parishioners, and was to remain in Haworth for the rest of his eventful life. The people of Todmorden still retained a high place in his affections, however, and he frequently visited them. The town later became one of the earliest centres of Methodism in the area.

The village of Haworth was part of a 'chapelry', made up of Haworth itself, together with three adjacent areas: Stanbury, Near Oxenhope and Far Oxenhope; the whole being described as a township with a total population of about 2,200. Although several unsuccessful applications had been made to Parliament for Haworth to become a separate parish, it remained in the chapelry throughout Grimshaw's life and for nearly a century afterwards. This meant that the incumbent of Haworth could only occupy the position of curate, and never that of vicar in his own right. However, two kinds of curacy existed: the temporary, where the incumbent was employed, as Grimshaw had been at Todmorden, as assistant to the vicar, and under his authority; and the perpetual curacy. This latter position meant that though Grimshaw was ostensibly under Kennet's jurisdiction, in fact only a bishop had the final power to remove him from office – a circumstance which was to prove important in the future.

The centre of the old village of Haworth to which William and Elizabeth Grimshaw came over two hundred and fifty years ago has not changed significantly. It still consists of one long main street, straggling up the steep hillside for three quarters of a mile. Houses and shops, constructed in a continuous block in the local grey stone, seem to cling precariously to the windswept slope. At last the road levels out and then divides, forming a triangle of housing near the church. Here the majority of the villagers lived. No map exists of Haworth in Grimshaw's day, but from later maps it is possible to form a fairly accurate picture of the village. At the foot of the hill, then and now, stands the Old Hall, built in the Elizabethan era and one-time home of the Emmott family. Opposite was the ducking pond, where the village scold would be tied to a chair at the end of a long plank and dipped unceremoniously into the stagnant water, to cure her of a sharp tongue. Three ale houses ringed the church: Black Bull Inn, White Lion Inn and King's Arms; while the church itself was surrounded by a treeless graveyard, almost an acre in extent, overcrowded with flat gravestones.

'What a map cannot show you', writes a local historian, 'is the topography of the place. The triangle is on a small plateau from which there are sharp descents in practically every direction, except on the left of Main Street towards Sowdens, which is on the moor edge. The gradient between the Old Hall and Bridge-house is pretty steep and the road up the other side is like the north face of Everest!'[1]

William Grimshaw was soon to discover, if he did not know already, that Haworth was not a healthy place in which to live. Its primitive sanitary arrangements formed a constant source of

[1]For this, and other details in the chapter, I am indebted to local historian, Michael Baumber of Keighley.

infection, leading to epidemics and a high death toll in the community. Over a century later, the people of Haworth at last drew up a petition to the General Board of Health requesting an inspector to be sent to the township to report on the situation. So, in April 1850, Benjamin Herschel Babbage arrived and carried out a detailed investigation. The resulting report, which he compiled and published under the Public Health Act, makes disturbing reading. And if conditions were so rudimentary in 1850, it is not hard to conjecture what they must have been like in Grimshaw's day.

Babbage discovered that 41.6% of the children of Haworth died before the age of six – many from unrecorded conditions. Burials took place without adequate depth of earth and coffins were often merely topped by a heavy flat stone. These things would have been much the same in the previous century. Refuse from houses and shops flowed down the open gutters and Babbage was to note with dismay that 'There are no water-closets in the town, and only 69 privies, being little more than one privy to every four and a half houses ... I found 24 houses lower down in the main street with only *one* privy between them.'[1] The crude methods for disposing of sewage which Babbage exposed make us surprised that the effects were not worse. Little wonder that life expectancy was not much more than twenty-five years in Grimshaw's Haworth, with many dying of dysentery, typhus fever, consumption and epidemics of influenza, while smallpox accounted for numerous childhood deaths.

The West Riding of Yorkshire was a centre for the worsted industry, as Daniel Defoe had discovered in his mammoth journey across the British Isles in 1726. Here he found 'an infinite number of cottages or small dwellings in which dwell the workmen which are employed ... [and] the women and the children ... so that all can gain their bread, even from the youngest to the most ancient'.[2]

[1] Benjamin Herschel Babbage, *Report to the General Board of Health ... of the Hamlet of Haworth* (London: 1850), p. 12.
[2] Defoe, *A Tour ... of Great Britain*, p. 175.

Worsted, a fabric made of long-fibred threads which were combed rather than carded, had been known in England since the fourteenth century, but it had not flourished in the West Riding until the beginning of the eighteenth. Haworth was second only to Halifax as a centre for the combing industry, making the village a complex of mini home-factories. There was scarcely a woman or child who was not employed in the business of washing, dyeing, combing or spinning the wools to make the worsted materials. The men folk would farm the small-holdings around the cottages, fetch raw materials and utensils for the industry and take the finished products to market in Bradford.

Although the Industrial Revolution, which gathered pace during the second half of the eighteenth century, had inevitably brought changes into the lives of the people of Haworth with the building of three mills in the neighbourhood, in 1850 Babbage found only about two hundred employed in these mills, with the majority of the community still working from their own cottages. We may assume, therefore, that the working conditions Babbage described would have been equally true in Grimshaw's day:

This business [the worsted industry] is carried on in their houses. In order to obtain the proper temperature for this operation, iron stoves are fixed in the rooms where it is carried on, which are kept alight day and night, and the windows are seldom, if ever, opened excepting in the height of summer. In some cases I found that this business is carried on in bedrooms, which consequently became very close and unhealthy, from the high temperature maintained by the stoves, and the want of ventilation.[1]

Clearly Haworth could offer little either spiritually or environmentally to the young family from Todmorden as they settled down at Sowdens. But its needs and challenge would have been evident to William Grimshaw. 'It is one of those obscure places which, like the fishing towns of Galilee favoured with our Lord's presence, owe all their celebrity to the gospel. The name of Haworth would scarcely be known at a distance were it not

[1] Babbage, *Report,* p. 6.

connected with the name of Grimshaw,"[1] wrote John Newton in 1799, little knowing the eminence that the small town would gain among literary circles in the following century. Commenting on those words of Newton's, G. E. Harrison was to write:

We shake our wise heads and are anxious to correct Cowper's mentor by telling him that when he wrote the Brontës had not been born . . . that wide grave for the mother and her children had not been opened in Haworth church. And yet . . . John Newton wrote better than he knew. The whole epic [of the Brontë family] cannot be separated from the gospel . . . Had there been no Wesley, the fire had not kindled. Had there been no Grimshaw, there would have been no fierce tale of *Wuthering Heights* .[2]

---

[1]Newton, *Letters,* p. 43.
[2]G. E. Harrison, *Haworth Parsonage, A Study of Wesley and the Brontës* (London: Epworth Press, 1937).

6

SHOWERS ON DRY GROUND

'IN THIS YEAR [1742] OUR DEAR LORD was pleased to visit my parish', wrote William Grimshaw to Dr John Gillies as he continued his description of the work of God that had been taking place in the north of England. Writing in 1754, twelve eventful years after he had first come to Haworth, Grimshaw could only give Gillies a brief summary of the unfolding acts of God's grace as he had witnessed them.

It would be easy to assume from Grimshaw's words quoted above that the remarkable events which he describes began as soon as he arrived in Haworth. But this would be inaccurate. Clearly the work started slowly, for Grimshaw continues in his next sentence, 'A few souls were affected under the word, brought to see their lost estate by nature and to experience peace through the blood of Jesus.' Such an understanding of the beginnings of the great revival in Haworth is also in keeping with other comments which we may glean either from Grimshaw himself or from those who wrote about these events.

Grimshaw was to tell the Archbishop of York, Matthew Hutton, in 1747 that he had only had twelve communicants when he first arrived; and, recalling his early days in his new parish, he had once said to John Newton as they stood together on the moors overlooking Haworth, 'When I first came into this country, if I had gone half a day's journey on horseback towards the east, west, north or south, I could not meet or hear of one truly serious person.'[1] Perhaps these words were a little gloomy, for there had been some conversions in Todmorden during his final months there, and certainly Paul Greenwood and his family at Ponden Hall, only two miles from Haworth, were 'truly serious'. But such an observation reflects the isolation of spirit Grimshaw must have experienced as he began his new ministry in Haworth.

One of the first improvements he effected in the church building itself was the replacement of the old pulpit. An imposing new structure, part of which may still be seen today in Stanbury parish church, was soon installed, marking the priority which Grimshaw placed upon the preaching ministry. Around the sounding board above the pulpit he had two verses of Scripture carved: first, 'I am determined to know nothing among you save Jesus Christ and him crucified', and secondly, a verse which he was to take not only as the keynote of his own spiritual life but as a watchword for his preaching ministry, 'For to me to live is Christ and to die is gain.'

Several comments have survived concerning Grimshaw's preaching at the outset of his ministry in Haworth. 'He presently began to preach Christ and the necessity of conversion and brought forth early fruits of his ministry amongst people as ignorant and brutish as the country is wild and savage,'[2] wrote Joseph Williams, a merchant from Kidderminster, to whom we are indebted for much of our first-hand information about Grimshaw. Henry Venn confirms that Grimshaw's early preaching disturbed the spiritual indifference of his hearers, and brought many under a deep conviction of sin: 'Very soon the good effects of his preaching became visible. Many of his careless flock were brought into deep concern for the salvation of their souls.'[3]

As we have seen, the emphasis of Grimshaw's ministry in Todmorden had changed markedly after his conversion, but it would seem that during his first two years in Haworth it was not

[1]Newton, *Letters*, p. 86.
[2]Williams to Blake, cited by Laycock, *Heroes*, p. 34.
[3]Venn, *Sketch*, p. 32.

yet that full-orbed presentation of the gospel which it later became. Instead, like John Bunyan whose spiritual pilgrimage was similar to his own in many respects, Grimshaw would have been able to say, 'I preached what I felt, what I smartingly did feel, even that under which my poor soul did groan and tremble to astonishment.'[1]

The law of God and divine punishment for sin were still his predominant themes at this time. John Newton saw this emphasis in Grimshaw's ministry as an important precursor to a fuller preaching of the gospel, particularly when addressing a congregation which had received little previous instruction:

When he removed from Todmorden to settle at Haworth, he had a deep sense of the evil of sin, a warm compassion for sinners, who, ignorant of their state and danger, he saw were going careless and unconcerned in the path that leadeth to destruction. He likewise knew for himself and was able to point out to others the way, the way of salvation by faith in the Son of God. But his knowledge and judgment were not yet fully ripened. He was more acquainted with the conflicts than the comforts of the believer. He was harassed by distressing doubts and fears and fiercely assaulted by the temptations and fiery darts of the enemy. Perhaps a minister at this stage of experience, which some undervalue as legal, is peculiarly adapted to preach to ignorant and wicked people, whose habits of sin have been strengthened by long disregard for the holy law of God, and who have had no opportunity for hearing the gospel.[2]

Newton maintains that Grimshaw was 'not wholly free from a legal spirit himself', but for that very reason 'was well qualified to speak to those who are sleeping securely in their sins'. 'Thus', he continues, 'many of our most eminent evangelical modern preachers were led. They set out as it were in the twilight, but the dawn is a sure presage of advancing day. They have lived to see many mistakes and defects in their first efforts . . . but perhaps

[1] John Bunyan, *Grace Abounding to the Chief of Sinners,* para. 276, in *Works,* vol. 1 (Edinburgh: Banner of Truth Trust, 1991), p. 42.
[2] Newton, *Letters,* p. 44.

their greatest success in awakening sinners was when their views of the scheme of salvation were much less clear and distinct.'[1]

Most probably Newton's authority for such a view came from Grimshaw himself, for the two men met on several occasions towards the end of Grimshaw's life. And Grimshaw's own writings bear out the fact that in his early days as a believer he was often tempest-tossed, sometimes knowing 'great joy arising from an exquisite sense of pardon and peace'; and then, perhaps only hours later, experiencing a desolation of heart which he was to describe as 'a spiritual wilderness'. At such times, he confesses, 'We think we are not God's children, that we are not justified, nor pardoned, that we are mistaken with ourselves, and it was only a delusion to think so.'[2]

The effect of Grimshaw's passionate appeals to the conscience of his hearers, and his powerful denunciations of sin, soon became apparent. The empty pews gradually began to fill. Not Haworth people only but men and women from all the surrounding areas began to pour into Haworth to hear the new curate whose preaching was affecting his congregation so deeply. Venn describes the scene: 'This lively powerful manner of representing the truths of God, could not fail of being much talked about, and bringing out of curiosity many hundreds to Haworth church.' Awakened to a realisation of the offensiveness of sin to a holy God, the people wept openly. 'The whole congregation have been often seen in tears on account of their provocations against God, and under a sense of his goodness in yet sparing them and waiting to be gracious to them.'[3] A graphic tribute to the power of the curate of Haworth to sway the hearts of the people through the preached word comes from one who heard him in those days, and who could never forget it, even though the preacher's voice had long since been silenced in death. 'He frequently rolled with thunder,' he recollected, 'but mingled tears like the Redeemer's over Jerusalem, with his severity.'[4]

[1] Ibid., p. 46.
[2] 'Experiences'.
[3] Venn, *Sketch*, p. 33.
[4] JEN.

'My church began to be crowded, insomuch that many were obliged to stand out of doors,' wrote Grimshaw to Gillies as he recalled these days. And still the stream of visitors from other parishes continued to pour into Haworth each Sunday. Men awakened to their spiritual needs would be anxious that their wives and families should also hear the preaching. Some came willingly – others did not. One anecdote, told by an anonymous writer who had heard the story first-hand, illustrates this second category of hearers. He reports that after hearing so much of the new preaching in Haworth, a local farmer attended the services one Sunday out of curiosity:

It pleased God that day to make him a monument of his mercy, to the great surprise of all his neighbours. This good man found himself much distressed on account of his wife, whom he knew to be in a lost condition; he could not bear the thought of her being lost; he frequently reasoned with her, but she hated the ways of God, and particularly the late change made in her husband. When he endeavoured to persuade her to go with him to hear Mr Grimshaw, she would reply, "I'll not go to hear that Black Devil." One Sabbath morning, being distressed, he told her he could not leave her behind him, and that if she would not consent to go with him, he must be obliged to use violence; she absolutely refusing, he put on her better clothes, took a rod, and in a violent passion declared that every time she refused to walk along, or turn aside, he would not spare her; for he was determined she should hear Mr Grimshaw that very day.

They lived about six miles from the church; (she told me the story when her husband was sitting by). She said, "He drove me as men drive a beast to market; I went calling and abusing Mr Grimshaw all the way." Yet that was the very day which God had fixed upon to shew mercy to her precious soul. She returned in great distress, and the next Sabbath went without any invitation. Mr Grimshaw, observing her particularly affected, went after sermon and asked her where she lived. When she had informed him, he said, On such a day I will come and see you, and preach in your house.[1]

---

[1] *Christian's Magazine*, 1792, p. 433.

This woman became 'one of the most affectionate hearers he had', and her home a preaching outpost which Grimshaw was to use frequently in years to come.

Before the year 1742 was over, it became obvious that the present church building would have to be enlarged. No longer could it suffice to meet the needs of the people now awakened to their spiritual concerns and flocking into Haworth. So Grimshaw began to draft an official request for permission to start the work of enlargement and also for the necessary funding from the ecclesiastical authorities in York. Two copies of this request are extant: one written on a fly-leaf of the parish register. Evidently this must have been Grimshaw's original draft, and in it he gave as the reason for the request that 'we are greatly interrupted and disturbed by out-comers from divers parishes'. Realising, doubtless, that such a reason was scarcely politic, given the strict observance of parish boundaries that prevailed in that day, he started again. The second version, clearly the final one, was copied out on parchment inside the register itself and merely complained of 'too crowding a congregation of people':

We, the Minister, Church Wardens, Freeholders and other inhabitants of Haworth Parish aforesaid do for the more open and orderly Attendance of the publick Worship of Almighty GOD wherein We are in the said Church greatly interrupted and disturbed by too crowding a Congregation of people, agree & determine, yt: ye: said Church be enlarged . . . and we do permit William Grimshaw ye: Minister to undertake ye: accomplishing of ye: said Enlargement by such Contributions or otherwise as He shall obtain for that purpose . . .

Signed on 11 January 1743 by Grimshaw and nine others, the request was granted and some of the expense met out of an existing fund, but it was specifically stated that the rest of the money for the project must be raised by the Haworth parish itself. This proved a real obstacle for the people were poor, and not for another ten years could Grimshaw start on the enlargements. Completion of the work was not until 1755.

Much of the initial response to Grimshaw's preaching was

coming from outside his immediate parish. Here and there in the records of these days we have hints that, like Isaac Smith before him, Grimshaw discovered that the indigenous community were more resistant to his preaching. Some made the excuse that their clothes were too poor for them to attend a place of worship, but the new curate had an answer to that problem. He invited all who felt too ashamed of their clothing to come to Sowdens on a Sunday evening where he would hold a special service for them. Henry Venn tells us that at these Sunday evening gatherings Grimshaw would expound a chapter of Scripture or a psalm, and adds, 'God was pleased to give great success to these attempts which animated him still more to spend and be spent in Christ's cause.'[1]

In February 1743 William Grimshaw had his first meeting with Benjamin Ingham of which we have a definite record. Ingham, who had been feeling the increasing burden of the sixty or more societies which he had formed in Yorkshire and Lancashire, had decided in the previous July to transfer them all to the care of the Moravian preachers whom he had invited into Yorkshire. This left him free to do the work he loved best: itinerate from place to place breaking new ground with the message of God's grace to sinners. A pressing invitation from residents in Colne, Lancashire, brought Ingham to within ten miles of Haworth. Doubtless, as he travelled around, Ingham had heard reports of the awakening ministry that had recently begun in Haworth and, if they had not met earlier, would have been curious to meet the new incumbent. So on 23 February, William Batty records in his 'Christian History', 'He came the first night to Haworth and lodged at the clerk's house, whereby he became acquainted with Mr Grimshaw, the minister of the church who invited him to preach in his parish.'[2]

Clearly an immediate rapport was established between the two men, with Grimshaw giving Ingham freedom to preach in his parish. How interesting it would have been if some record of their

---

[1]Venn, *Sketch*, p. 33.   [2]Batty, 'History'.

conversation had been preserved as they sat together either in the parlour of the Black Bull Inn or in the kitchen at Sowdens. Ingham had shared unforgettable days with John and Charles Wesley and knew the Methodist movement from the beginning. He would have told Grimshaw of the societies he had been forming, and of the Moravian movement which had established its headquarters at nearby Halifax. Perhaps he invited the curate of Haworth across to Ledstone Hall to meet the Countess of Huntingdon, Lady Margaret's sister-in-law, when she came on one of her regular visits to Yorkshire with her husband.

Although William Grimshaw had received Ingham into his parish gladly, he was not prepared to afford a similar welcome to any Methodist itinerant who wished to preach in Haworth. A far different reception awaited John Nelson when he came later in 1743. Possibly Ingham had given Grimshaw a jaundiced report of the faithful stonemason-preacher whose views had differed from his own since he had linked his work with the Moravians. Certainly, Ingham's relationship with John and Charles Wesley was less cordial than it had been formerly. Not surprisingly, when John Wesley first visited Yorkshire in May 1742, it was at Nelson's home in Birstall that he called, even though Ingham had been one of his closest friends.

Tradition tells us that when Nelson came into Haworth in the summer of 1743, he preached in Emmott Hall. But instead of trying to discover the nature of his message, Grimshaw charged his people not to attend the meetings. He warned them that 'wherever the Methodists went, they turned everything upside down'. Some of his parishioners dared to risk the curate's wrath and resolved to hear Nelson preach. When the stonemason announced his text, they were forcibly reminded of their pastor's warning for his text was: 'These that have turned the world upside down are come hither also.' And one woman, who had previously resisted Grimshaw's own message, was converted.[1]

---

[1]This anecdote was passed on to Rev. Thornley Smith during his period in Haworth and inserted into *Christian Miscellany*, February 1858. Cited by Hardy, *Incumbent*, p. 38.

All who record the story of Grimshaw's life insist that he had no contact with any Methodist leader until 1746. The above anecdote is sometimes used to illustrate how little he knew of Methodist work. But the importance of his early link with Benjamin Ingham cannot be overlooked. Grimshaw must have known much more about the Methodists than is usually suggested. It cannot be a coincidence that only a few months after Ingham's visit, in the summer of 1743, he took the step of dividing his parish with its ever increasing congregation into small units or 'societies'. Each unit was to consist of six to ten families. Twelve such groups he designated, which were to meet weekly in the four hamlets of which his parish was composed: Haworth, Stanbury, Near Oxenhope and Far Oxenhope.

Initially, these groups were intended to supplement his Sunday preaching: 'By [this] means,' wrote Henry Venn, 'the old and infirm who could not attend the church, had the truth of God brought to their houses; and many who were so profane as to make the distance from the house of God a reason for scarce ever coming to it, were allured to hear and receive with joy the word of life.'[1] Grimshaw would then visit every group once a month, so establishing personal contact with his numerous congregation.

Describing this practice in a letter to John Wesley over four years later, in November 1747, Grimshaw was to acknowledge how beneficial it had been:

I visit my parish in twelve several places monthly, convening six, eight or ten families in each place, allowing any people of neighbouring parishes that please to attend that exhortation. This I call my monthly visitation. I am now entering into the fifth year of it and wonderfully, dear sir, has the Lord blessed it.[2]

Another source of information about William Grimshaw's early work in Haworth is to be found in the records compiled by the Archbishop of York, Thomas Herring, when he visited his

[1] Venn, *Sketch*, p. 34.
[2] Grimshaw to John Wesley, November 1747. For whole letter see Appendix III.

[65]

entire diocese in 1743 to investigate conditions in each parish. Known as Herring's Visitation Returns, the information was gathered by means of questions put to each incumbent (although out of 836 parishes, Herring discovered that 393 had no resident incumbent). On 21 June 1743 the archbishop arrived in Haworth. He learnt that there were 326 families in the chapelry, only three of which were Dissenters and there was one small school catering for 40 children, financed by an annual endowment of £18. At the time of the archbishop's visit Grimshaw used to conduct two services each Lord's Day, and catechise those awaiting confirmation between Easter and Whitsun. He celebrated communion five times a year and normally had between fifty and sixty communicants on these occasions. This last fact shows that in the thirteen months of Grimshaw's ministry the numbers of communicants had risen markedly from the twelve he found when he first came to Haworth, but were not as yet the astonishing figure of twelve hundred during the summer months which he could report four years later.

Grimshaw added a further interesting piece of information in answer to the archbishop's questions which suggests that his own parishioners were not as responsive as those from other places:

I give notice [of a communion service] the two Sundays immediately foregoing the celebration. The parishioners do not send in their names [as they were required to do]. I never, praised be to God for it, have seen cause to refuse the sacrament to anyone. I have sometimes administered to such as come out of other parishes, but they were my common hearers, and their lives and conversations well known to me ... I will also insist carefully upon my own parish communicants sending in their names as required.[1]

So it would appear that though there were early fruits from Grimshaw's ministry during his first two years in Haworth, much of his labour was directed at breaking up the fallow ground by calling the people to forsake their sins. Such preaching was

[1]Herring's Returns, 21 June 1743, pp. 40–1.

leading to a widespread spiritual concern both among his own parishioners and in the surrounding areas, an anxiety which in God's mercy would shortly turn to a powerful converting work, and yield an abundant harvest of blessing not only among the people of Haworth but also in many other parts of Yorkshire and further afield.

7

FULL ASSURANCE

NOT LONG AFTER JOHN NELSON'S VISIT to Haworth, another itinerant preacher, of whom William Grimshaw was equally suspicious, came to the area. William Darney, a Scotsman, reputed to be a giant of a man, was travelling around from village to village preaching. Known as 'Scotch Will', Darney was a shoemaker by trade, but he was also described as a pedlar, so doubtless he sold the footwear he had made and other small items at the same time. Wherever he went he seized the opportunity to gather a small crowd and would preach to them, composing 'hymns' for the people to sing – hymns as unpolished as the pedlar himself, and yet popular with his hearers. Doggerel they might have been, and certainly Charles Wesley was most disparaging about Darney's lack of poetic gift, but they were an effective means of communicating truth.

Interesting details about Darney's movements came to light earlier this century with the discovery of a manuscript diary written by a Leeds man, Richard Viney, for the year 1744. Overlooked for almost two centuries, this diary contains fascinating insights into the development of the work of God in Yorkshire from the perspective of a man whose livelihood – the making of ladies' corsets – brought him into acquaintance with most of the better-known personalities involved in the revival. Vacillating between the Methodists and the Moravians, Viney knew both Benjamin and Lady Margaret Ingham as well as John and Charles

Wesley. On 5 January 1744 Viney has a quaint entry in his diary under the heading 'Occurrences':

A man, commonly called Scotch Will, who carries a Pack, sells Handkerchers, Stockings &c, and who often Preaches about here, having some connexion with John Nelson: Call'd here . . . with his goods, and I bought two handkerchers of him, Intending to have some talk with him.[1]

Viney met the rugged pedlar-preacher from Scotland on a number of occasions, providing clear evidence that Darney was in West Yorkshire from late 1743 onwards. A colourful personality, he was possibly converted in 1740 under the preaching of James Robe in Kilsyth, ten miles north-east of Glasgow. In that year Robe had begun placing an increased emphasis on the doctrine of regeneration, but saw little spiritual fruit until 1742 when Kilsyth and Cambuslang (near Glasgow), fifteen miles further south, experienced a powerful work of God. Although we have no precise information about the date of Darney's conversion, we know from the preface to one of his hymns that he felt a call from God to preach in October 1741, becoming the first herald of the gospel in the Rossendale district of Lancashire.

Darney was a man of fervent zeal and indomitable courage. His huge frame and broad Scottish accent, combined with his fearless denunciation of sin and his declaration of the wrath of God upon the impenitent, made his messages unforgettable. Little wonder then that the news of his preaching spread quickly throughout the area. Wherever there was a converting work, Darney banded the converts together into small societies, in the same way that Benjamin Ingham had done, that they might meet on a regular basis for mutual encouragement.[2] When he returned to that area,

---

[1] 'Richard Viney's Diary', *Proceedings of the Wesley Historical Society*, vol. XIII, p. 109.

[2] Viney records how Darney formed a society in Pudsey in January 1744: 'Scotch Will Preached again today as on this day 14 night twice, here in Pudsey, and appointed next Wensday evening to preach again and take down ye names of as many as think well to form a Society.' 'Diary', p. 190.

he would visit these groups of believers, teaching and strengthening them in the faith.

If William Darney was in the Pudsey area of Leeds where Viney lived in January 1744, it comes as no surprise to discover that he was on the outskirts of Haworth, little more than fifteen miles away, later that year.

William Grimshaw was not pleased. Perhaps he was unhappy that an unordained man should be preaching or he could have been concerned lest Darney should spread error among his people. Whatever the reason, Grimshaw determined to attend one of the meetings himself, possibly planning to refute Darney publicly.

An anecdote relating to this occasion has been preserved by William Myles in his biographical sketch of Grimshaw, first published in 1808 – an anecdote which he received from one who had known both Grimshaw and Darney personally. But though Myles was convinced that the incident he related was broadly true, he suspected some details, most particularly the subject matter of the conversations said to have taken place between Darney and Grimshaw which seemed to him to have become garbled in transmission.[1] These we have omitted.

Myles records that as Grimshaw entered the room where Darney was already preaching, he discovered that the pedlar was addressing the people on the subject of justification by faith. As he listened, however, his suspicions were gradually allayed, for with skill and spiritual energy Darney demonstrated the truth of this doctrine, backing up his arguments by references both to the Scriptures and to the Articles and Liturgy of the Church of England. This was the very truth that had brought light and comfort to Grimshaw's own soul and soon all his antagonism melted away. He bowed before teaching which he knew to be the Word of

[1]Myles, *Life and Writings*, p. 18. Myles' informant, James Ashworth, suggested that the subject under discussion between Grimshaw and Darney was Grimshaw's own lack of understanding over justification and he was not a converted man at this time. Clearly this is inaccurate.

God. Now he was convinced that Darney proclaimed the same gospel as he did.

After this initial meeting, Grimshaw lost no opportunity to seek out Darney's company and to converse with him, for many matters still perplexed the curate of Haworth. Although he had met Benjamin Ingham, Grimshaw had enjoyed little opportunity to discuss spiritual concerns at length with other like-minded men. At first the two met secretly. Perhaps Grimshaw feared the comments of his parishioners or maybe he was troubled about what his wife Elizabeth might think, for she had shown little sympathy with the spiritual work which had been going on in Haworth.

On the moors above his home at Sowdens there were some old quarries and here in one of these isolated spots Darney and Grimshaw would meet. If even a dog were to bark, so the story goes, Grimshaw would exclaim nervously, 'Hush! there is someone coming!' But at last his fears were dispelled and before long he took a public part in one of Darney's meetings, giving out a hymn and even leading in prayer.

A genuine bond sprang up between the two men, a fact amply borne out by other contemporary records. From this time onwards, Grimshaw, whose humility and readiness to learn from others was a marked characteristic throughout his life, freely acknowledged the debt he owed to Darney. Unlike Grimshaw, William Darney had clearly had the privilege of solid scriptural teaching as a foundation to his faith. This is demonstrated by his ability to set out his beliefs as he did in a three-hundred page book entitled *Fundamental Doctrines which are Contained in the Scriptures.*[1] One of the themes which he and William Grimshaw were likely to have discussed was the question of the full assurance of faith. On this subject Darney was to write confidently, 'He hath given me to know in whom I have believed . . . without doubting for many years past, and I am assured that he

[1]William Darney, *Fundamental Doctrines which are Contained in the Scriptures* (Glasgow: Archibald McLean, 1755).

hath sealed unworthy me to the day of eternal redemption'.[1] Even Richard Viney noted in his diary that Scotch Will seemed to enjoy a strong sense of spiritual security, though Viney confused this with perfectionism – a teaching which was no part of Darney's belief.

It may seem an anomaly that after having preached to ever-increasing congregations since his arrival in Haworth in May 1742, two years later Grimshaw himself should still be lacking that same deep inward assurance of which Darney had spoken. But, as we have noted, Grimshaw's early years as a believer were far from smooth. This is borne out in the manuscript to which we have already referred which carries the title, 'Experiences gather'd by Conversation with my own & the Souls of others'. Written later in his life, probably with little revision and bound together between rough brown boards, this manuscript records the unusual work of God's grace that he had known personally and had also observed in the lives of others whom he counselled. In the opening paragraphs he describes the spiritual struggles believers often face and the fierce temptations with which they may be assailed during the early stages of the Christian life:

Young Christians . . . are by and by, like their Master, led into the wilderness, and that too not merely by permission, but by the Holy Spirit of God . . . Upon their entrance into this spiritual wilderness, their joys leave them . . . At this time we think (I mean at our first coming into this wilderness) that we are not God's child, that we are not justified nor pardoned, that we are mistaken with ourselves, that it was only a delusion or chimera to think so; now we are grieved that we affirmed our being forgiven to anyone and are ready to recant it. But this is only Satan's suggestion – and it is generally the first thing he tempts us with. So it was the first thing he tempted our blessed Saviour with – to question whether he was the Son of God. If the devil can but make us doubt of this, so long as it prevails, the progress of grace may seem to be totally stopped.

After the devil has tried us thus for a season, he then assaults us with evil imaginations and blasphemous thoughts; doubts about the authority

[1]Darney, *Fundamental Doctrines*, cited by Frank Baker, *Grimshaw*, p. 57.

of the holy Scriptures, scruples about the divinity of our Saviour. This he probably does to prevent our reading or hearing the Word of God; or to make us, as his second devise, to question the truth of our new state. At these times we are apt to reason with ourselves, saying, Surely we are not born again; surely we are not sons of God, for if we were, why are we thus?

Clearly these words were drawn from his (Grimshaw's) own trials of faith as a young believer. Subsequently he deleted much of the material, often scoring out entire pages, not intending any eye save his own to read some of these disclosures.

Experiencing so many alterations in his moods and feelings as a believer, Grimshaw must have found in William Darney's calm assurance of 'being sealed unto the day of redemption' a little-known dimension of the Christian life. Perhaps he realised that he had been placing too much importance on his own variable feelings and not enough on the unchanging Word of God. We know for certain, however, that on 8 August 1744, Grimshaw entered upon a second covenant with God, the first having been made in 1738 in the midst of his intense spiritual turmoil as he sought peace with God. So now he felt the need to make another such covenant.

This covenant and the circumstances which followed make 8 August 1744 a significant date in Grimshaw's entire life and in his ministry. Writing eight years later, Grimshaw himself associated it directly with another experience which took place less than a month afterwards:

Thou knowest, O Lord, I solemnly covenanted with thee in the year 1738; and before that wonderful manifestation of thyself unto me at church and in the clerk's house between the hours of ten and two o'clock on Sunday, September 2nd, 1744, I had again solemnly devoted myself to thee on Aug. 8 1744.[1]

Some spiritual experiences, like that of the Apostle Paul when he was 'caught up into the third heaven', are of such a nature that a believer rarely feels able to talk about them. Such was the case

---

[1]Grimshaw's 1752 covenant, see Appendix 2.

with William Grimshaw. John Newton, who had first met Grimshaw in 1758 when he had spent some days with him, and who had also spoken with him at length on several other occasions, had never heard him mention it. Had it not been for the description which Grimshaw gave to Joseph Williams, the Kidderminster merchant, when he had visited Haworth in 1746, Newton would never have known of it.

When Newton was writing his biographical sketch of Grimshaw's life, he was anxious to verify the account which Williams (who had died in 1755) had left on record, fearing that Williams 'might [have] incautiously inserted some particulars in his narrative which he received from less authentic information'. During a later visit to Haworth Newton discovered a woman who had been in service in Grimshaw's household in 1744. She recollected the incident reported by Williams, having been actually present on the occasion. While perhaps understanding little of its spiritual significance, she was able to supply Newton with several extra details not mentioned by Williams. But her version of the events that occurred that Sunday in September 1744 harmonised perfectly with the account Williams had given. This confirmation gave Newton the added assurance he was seeking.

Grimshaw's maid recalled that when she began her duties on that Sunday morning, she found her master was already up, even though it was only five o'clock in the morning. He was praying alone in a small upstairs room – a room now musty and dark and used as storage space in the present Sowdens farm. A little later Grimshaw left the house and went to the home of one of his parishioners where he conducted an early service with some of his people. Returning home, he went upstairs once more to pray and prepare for the worship of the day. As far as the maid could recall, Grimshaw had eaten nothing that morning and before long he set off for the morning service at the church.

As the service was in progress, Grimshaw began to feel faint and as he was reading the second lesson was overcome with dizziness. He beckoned to someone who was standing near to help him out of the church, saying that he felt very ill. According to the maid's account, he then collapsed, falling at the reading desk. As soon as he recovered a little, he was helped from the church to the parlour of the nearby Black Bull Inn.[1] Joseph Williams continues at this point: 'Under some apprehension that this seizure might issue in death, he all the way through the church and churchyard to the clerk's house very earnestly exhorted the people to prepare to die; to be always ready to fly to Christ and to abide in him; to trust in him only for salvation etc.' His maid added the information that before leaving the church he asked his people not to disperse, for he hoped to return as he had something extraordinary to tell them.[2]

'As soon as he was sat down in the parlour,' continues Williams, 'he found that his arms for a hand-breadth above the elbows and his legs for a hand-breadth below the knees were cold as death.'[3] His maid and others spent the next hour trying to stimulate his circulation. In the manner of the day, they rubbed him continually with heated cloths, but all to no avail; he seemed to remain as chilled as ever. All this time Grimshaw appeared to have remained conscious, though sitting with his eyes fixed on the ceiling.

But unknown to those who were trying to help him, thoughts far other than of his physical condition were preoccupying William Grimshaw's mind. To Joseph Williams he confided that he had fallen into a trance, and saw and heard unforgettable things. In this state he had found himself standing at the entrance of 'a dark foul passage', and understood that he had to pass along it. As he went, he discovered that on each side of the passage ran a wall of great height. Beyond the wall on the right side lay the heavenly country, but on the left lay hell. Groping his way along this passage, he could hear a discussion in progress. It was God

---

[1] Joseph Williams says he was taken to 'the clerk's house', but this was in fact the Black Bull Inn because the proprietor, Jonathan Whitehead, was also the parish clerk. It was much nearer than Sowdens.

[2] Newton, *Letters*, p. 31.

[3] Joseph Williams, *Diary*, ed. B. Hanbury (1826), p. 201.

the Father conferring with God the Son about the eternal destiny of Grimshaw's soul. For a long time it seemed that things were going very badly for him. God the Father would not save him, nor admit him to the heavenly country, because he had not yet wholly relinquished his own righteousness, neither had he cast himself solely and entirely on the merits of the Lord Jesus Christ for his salvation. But just as the case seemed to be swinging irrevocably against him, he heard the Lord Jesus Christ pleading his cause. For a long time he remained in suspense, torn between hope and fear, and still the outlook for his soul appeared bleak. About to despair, he suddenly saw a sight which caused hope and joy to course through his whole being. He saw the Lord Jesus Christ showing to him his wounded hands and his wounded feet. And as he gazed at the sight, he realised that those hands and those feet were freshly pierced. 'Instantly', reported Williams, 'he was filled with a joyful sense of his interest in Christ.'[1]

Simultaneously, the circulation in Grimshaw's arms and legs returned to normal and his limbs became comfortably warm once more. Standing up, he appeared perfectly well, and his maid added that 'he seemed to be in a great rapture', declaring, 'I have had a glorious vision from the third heaven.' But to those present in the parlour, he gave no further details of all that had taken place. Shortly afterwards he returned to the church to conduct the afternoon service, which began at two o'clock. So elated was

---

[1] Philip Doddridge referred to this incident in Grimshaw's life when he published the life of Colonel James Gardiner in 1749. Colonel Gardiner had had a similar experience in 1719 which had led to his conversion. Commenting on the extraordinary nature of such an event, Doddridge writes, though without naming Grimshaw, 'I hope the world will be particularly informed that there is at least a second that does very nearly approach it, whenever the established church of England shall lose one of its brightest living ornaments, and one of its most useful members, which that, and perhaps any other Christian communion can boast. In the mean time, may his exemplary life be long continued and his zealous ministry abundantly prospered.' P. Doddridge, D.D., *Some Remarkable Passages in the Life of the Hon. Colonel Jas. Gardiner* (London: Hamilton, 1808), p. 44.

he with all that he had seen and heard, that he preached and spoke to the people until seven o'clock in the evening, before finally dismissing them and returning home.

Although at no time since his conversion had Grimshaw's acceptance with God been in any doubt, his own lack of assurance of his state often left him anxious and depressed. But in God's overruling purposes this experience gave Grimshaw an unshakeable confidence in the steadfast love of God the Father on the grounds of the sacrifice of Christ. Now he was certain that he would persevere to the last – a conviction which sustained him in hope even though he would often grieve over his shortcomings. From that day onwards, and for the rest of his life, he was delivered from that debilitating insecurity which had so clouded the early years of his Christian life.

As Joseph Williams records, 'He never again lost sight of his evidence, and he has a flaming love to the Lord Jesus Christ. His heart is warm with the blood and love of Christ.' Now love for God and for his 'dear Redeemer', a term Grimshaw never tired of using, became the mainspring of all his service. Never, as he later declared, could he do enough for Christ, who had done so much for him.

Nor did William Grimshaw ever confuse this manifestation of the love of Christ with that experience which the Methodists were later to call 'entire sanctification'; and which they were to claim brought a Christian into a state of perfection or 'perfect love'. Far too conscious of the daily struggle against the sin still remaining within and of the insidious assaults of the evil one on his soul, Grimshaw remained always a vigorous opponent of any such ideas. Instead, as had been the case with both John Wesley and Benjamin Ingham, this full assurance became the spring-board for his further abundant labours, labours which were soon to extend far beyond the boundaries of his own parish, and even of his county.

8

HAWORTH – A GARDEN OF THE LORD

SET FREE FROM DOUBTS and the tyranny of an accusing conscience,
William Grimshaw began to preach with an accession of power
and freedom he had not known previously. Indefatigable in toil
for the kingdom of God before, he now redoubled his efforts.
'Too happy himself in the knowledge of Christ,' wrote Henry
Venn, he could not 'rest satisfied, without taking every method he
thought likely to spread the knowledge of his God and Saviour.'[1]

Certainly, by any standard, there had already been a remarkable work of God in Haworth, but now the showers that had
been refreshing the thirsty ground began to fall as torrents. The
arid waste was soon transformed into 'a garden of the Lord,
producing many trees of righteousness, planted by the Lord himself', as Newton aptly commented. The minds and consciences
of Grimshaw's hearers were yet more readily subdued under the
truth. Some of his astonished parishioners, who knew little of the
spiritual transaction that had taken place in the parlour of the
Black Bull Inn, could only suppose that the added passion and
power in their curate's preaching sprang from his new-found
friendship with William Darney. So they said with a mixture of
surprise and perhaps a degree of derision, 'Mad Grimshaw is
turned Scotch Will's clerk,' or alternatively, 'Scotch Will leads
and guides Mad Grimshaw.'[2]

[1] Venn, *Sketch*, p. 33.   [2] Myles, *Life and Writings*, p. 18.

In the eighteen months following September 1744, Grimshaw had reason to believe that at least one hundred and twenty people were converted – people whose subsequent life gave every indication that their profession was genuine. Describing the revival that broke out in its fullness at this time, Joseph Williams wrote:

Since that trance . . . he reckons six score souls savingly renewed, whom as fast as he can discover evidences [of] a thorough work in their hearts he forms into classes . . . He observes there is such a diversity in the Spirit's operations, that scarce any two of them have been wrought upon in the same way. Some have sunk down in the church under a terrifying sense of divine wrath, while others have been drawn with the cords of love. Some have received a sealed pardon in a few weeks or days, while others have been held many months under a spirit of bondage.[1]

Grimshaw's own comment on this wide variety of spiritual experience is expressed with his unique turn of phrase:

There is but one way in nature into this world, and a 100 ways out of it into another; but there are a 100 ways into the spiritual world, or into CHRIST, and but one way, which is CHRIST, into the world to come. Nay, there are not two in 500 of God's children that are born again or brought into CHRIST, every way alike.[2]

Nor was the work confined to any single grouping of people – though mainly affecting the young, the old were not excluded – and from among landed farmers, cottage workers and labourers alike, many were brought under conviction of sin and converted. Writing of these things to Dr John Gillies, Grimshaw was later to record:

In this present glorious work of God, which he, glory, glory, glory be to him for ever ascribed for it, is now carrying on in these and various other nations, the young people are mostly stirred up to seek and find the Lord. They are of all ages, from children to 30 years old; many are

[1]Williams to Blake in Laycock, *Heroes*, p. 35.
[2]'Experiences'.

converted between then and 40 years old; but fewer between [that] and 50, fewer again between [50] and 60, and but very few from that age upwards.[1]

The group meetings which Grimshaw had established in 1743 to cater for those living at some distance from the church now became yet more significant. New converts were placed in these classes and Joseph Williams adds, 'He takes care to set over every class one man who hath the gift of prayer, who also watches over his class, marks the increase or decay of the work . . . and gives an account to the pastor at meetings he now and then holds with them.'[2]

One of the most notable characteristics of these days – a feature which had been present from the beginning of his ministry in Haworth – was the depth of emotion with which the people listened to Grimshaw's preaching, and also the physical phenomena which accompanied it. 'It was amazing', wrote Grimshaw to Gillies, 'to hear and see what weeping, roaring and agonies many people were seized with at the apprehension of their sinful state and the wrath of God.' Such phenomena, so often an accompaniment of a revival in its early stages, appears to have been unexpected and spontaneous. But Grimshaw could soon see that these extremes of response were often unhelpful to the work. Like John and Charles Wesley, he came to realise that Satan was only too ready to take advantage of heightened expressions of emotion and spiritual turmoil, in order to counterfeit the true, and so bring the work of God into disrepute.

Commenting further on this to Gillies, Grimshaw wrote:

Soon after the devil observed such cryings and distress of soul, and agitation of body to affect people under the word, he also began to seize people under the word with strange unnatural distortions, convulsions, hideous roarings; to bring, as we plainly saw, contempt and disgrace upon the true work of God.

[1]Ibid.
[2]Williams to Blake, Laycock, *Heroes*, p. 35.

Grimshaw added that most of the physical phenomena, attributable to Satan's counterfeit, were also associated with spurious professions of conversion. Almost all such heightened manifestations of emotion died out after 1747, as he explains to Gillies. 'For seven years past, the cryings and agitations in sincere penitents are in a manner ceased and are rarely seen or heard of.'[1]

This letter which William Grimshaw wrote to John Gillies in 1754 is a fascinating record of the progress of the gospel in the north of England up until that date. We are conducted on a rapid tour across the area and given intriguing flashes of information about the revival as it spread outwards from Leeds, Birstall and Haworth in ever-widening circles. 1744 was a remarkable year in West Yorkshire. After sketching John Nelson's activities from the time he separated from Ingham, Grimshaw continues:

About the year 1744 God was pleased to visit Keighley, (a market town three miles from Haworth), Siliden [Silsden], Sutton, Addingham, Meastone [Menston], Bingley, Baleden [Baildon] and many other places. The Lord has done wonderful things in all these places. One Thomas Colbeck has been one main instrument with some others, Jonathan Maskew, Paul Greenwood, &c., in his gracious hands here.

Keighley, like Haworth, was to be a significant centre in the revival in Yorkshire, and for some years God had been preparing the men whom he would use in that work. A young and poorly-educated shoemaker, John Wilkinson, had visited Birstall, near Leeds, at the invitation of his brother-in-law to hear the strange preaching of a local stonemason, newly returned from London. This stonemason was declaring that men might know forgiveness of sins and be justified in God's sight through faith in Christ. Listening to John Nelson's preaching, Wilkinson was deeply affected, and returned to Keighley to gather a small group of seriously-minded men and women around him in order to search the Scriptures. With none to guide them, and Wilkinson himself only partially understanding Nelson's message, the group made

---

[1]Letter to Gillies, *Historical Collections,* p. 507.

little headway until a letter from a friend in Birstall brought Wilkinson into a full understanding of gospel truth. Now with clear convictions and even a measure of eloquence, he began to preach.

Thomas Colbeck, a neighbour of Wilkinson's, was unable to comprehend the change in Wilkinson and found it even more strange that his friend should wish to preach. So Colbeck decided to hide in an adjacent room while Wilkinson was preaching so that he could hear without being detected. But God's Word found him out, convicted him of his sin, and he too was converted. Soon he joined his friend in his labours for the spread of the gospel. Scarcely more than a teenager, Colbeck had considerable business acumen, and was already running his own grocery shop. Heir to a substantial fortune, he now fixed his affections on a more enduring inheritance, and set out with heart aflame to bring to the people in neighbouring villages the same life-transforming message. And as Grimshaw reported to Gillies, 'The Lord has done wonderful things in all these places.'

Soon Colbeck ventured into Haworth itself, seeking to gather together the converts from John Nelson's preaching there in 1743, which as we have seen, had not pleased Grimshaw at the time. So began the first Haworth Methodist Society, precursor of many such societies in the great 'Haworth Round', as it was later called, a name which was to become synonymous with the massive labours of William Grimshaw himself.

Finding the spiritual demands which the revival engendered in Haworth greater than he could meet on his own, William Grimshaw made an important innovation in the life of his parish during 1745. It was an innovation to which his prejudices as a churchman would have made him naturally disinclined – he began to use the gifts and services of lay preachers. This practice had become the hallmark of Wesley's Methodism since first John Cennick and then Thomas Maxfield had begun to preach in 1739. But in 1745 Grimshaw was yet to meet either of the Wesley brothers or George Whitefield. Most probably, therefore, the seed-thought for such a change came from his conversations with

Benjamin Ingham; but it was also a natural by-product of his new-found friendship with William Darney who became the first layman to help him.

During 1744, as we have seen, Darney had been preaching in the outlying areas of Grimshaw's parish. By 1745 he was preaching in Haworth itself as Grimshaw records in his letter to Gillies:

In the year 1745, William Darney, a Scotchman, who had been stirred up to preach the gospel with much blessing about Bradford, Manningham, and divers other places a few miles east of my parish, came and preached in it.

Tradition points to the very spot at the top of Main Street near the Black Bull Inn where Darney stood to deliver that first message, and Grimshaw commented graciously to Gillies, 'The Lord was with him indeed. I have cause to bless God for it.' In addition to this assistance, which could only be spasmodic, for Darney's other societies of young believers also needed him, Grimshaw selected two other young men to help him in the work.

Paul Greenwood was an obvious choice as one of Grimshaw's early assistants. After his dramatic conversion, he was full of zeal for the conversion of others and had already developed an affection for his curate which was to last throughout his life. Together with Paul Greenwood, Jonathan Maskew also became widely known as one of 'Mr Grimshaw's men'. Born in 1713, Maskew was also the subject of a work of grace, before he had heard any gospel preaching. Living in Otley, about fifteen miles from Haworth, he came from a poor family background, and had received little educational advantage. But from early childhood upwards he had experienced convictions of sin, which increased in intensity until he reached manhood when God enlightened him, apparently without any human agency. When he was converted, his parents disowned him, casting him out of the home. Hearing of his plight, Grimshaw befriended the young man and offered him accommodation under his own roof, in return for labouring services on the farm land attached to Sowdens. Here Maskew was to remain until his preaching and travels took him further afield to various parts of Yorkshire and Lancashire and then, after 1752, to Newcastle-upon-Tyne.

Describing Grimshaw's early use of laymen to help him in Haworth, Joseph Williams adds further details of their work:

In all this work he [Grimshaw] acknowledges he has had a great deal of assistance from two laymen in his parish, who, with his approbation, expounded the scriptures and gave exhortations to great numbers, who almost every day attend on them in private houses; and more than once he told me with an air of pleasure, that he verily believed that God had converted as many by their services, as by his own.[1]

But the task which these two young men undertook was fraught with perils. Lacking the respect and consequently the protection normally afforded to the incumbent of the parish, they both met with vicious and mindless persecution as they travelled around the vicinity exhorting the people. Words written of Maskew could equally apply to Greenwood: 'The unction of his word, and the warmth of his address are well remembered, when in the vigour of life, fearless of danger, the inclemency of seasons, and in the midst of violent and barbarous persecutors, he preached the gospel of Christ.'[2]

Another expedient William Grimshaw employed to further the work of God in Haworth during 1744–45 was the use of tracts, both to encourage young converts and to awaken those who as yet showed little spiritual concern. Remembering how Robert Seagrave's booklet had been used in his own conversion, Grimshaw wrote to John Syms, George Whitefield's agent in London, requesting a parcel of tracts to be sent to him. This fact indicated that though Grimshaw had not yet met any Methodist leaders, he was now well aware of the awakening taking place in other parts of the country. In the event Syms sent Grimshaw one or two large parcels of tracts which he 'sold and caused to be sold and circulated round that country for the good of souls'.[3]

[1]Laycock, *Heroes*, p. 34.
[2]Jackson, *Early Methodist Preachers*, vol. IV, p. 208.
[3]Letter to Mrs Gallatin, 13 July 1756.

In May 1745 Benjamin Ingham again visited Haworth. By this time a firm friendship had been established between the two men, cemented by Grimshaw's visits to Ingham's home in Aberford, not far from Leeds. This was in order to meet the Countess of Huntingdon on her regular visits to Yorkshire each summer. The Countess herself, whose role in the great eighteenth-century revival runs like a shining thread throughout the whole narrative, had been converted by means of a simple remark of Ingham's wife, Lady Margaret. With heart overflowing with spiritual joy, Lady Margaret had said artlessly, 'Since I have known and believed in the Lord Jesus Christ for salvation, I have been as happy as an angel.' An upright and God-fearing woman, the Countess was still stranger to such heart religion until during a time of serious illness she recalled Lady Margaret's remark and this caused her also to cast herself upon Christ.

From the time of Lady Margaret's marriage to Ingham in 1741, or soon after, the Earl of Huntingdon and Lady Selina used to make annual visits to Yorkshire. The Earl died in 1746 but the Countess' biographer A.C. H. Seymour states that 'For a few years during Lord Huntingdon's life, Ledstone Hall was visited every summer, and on these occasions there was always frequent preaching at the church.' He continues by asserting, 'Mr Grimshaw invariably attended these meetings, never troubling himself to ask the consent of the minister of the parish, or caring whether he liked it or not.'[1] The Countess quickly appreciated the warm-hearted but determined curate of Haworth, and he became a firm favourite with the people at her northern preaching festivals.

Clearly by 1744–45 Grimshaw had become what John Wesley called 'irregular'. By this Wesley meant that in forming societies, in beginning to preach outside his own parish boundaries, and in welcoming the help of laymen to preach and exhort, Grimshaw was acting outside the terms of his brief, as an ordained minister of the Church of England. Neither the Wesleys nor Grimshaw found such a pathway easy, but the needs of the people, destitute

[1]Seymour, *Countess of Huntingdon,* vol. 1, p. 259.

of spiritual light, and the zeal of these men to please God above all else was their all-compelling motive. A letter from John Wesley, written in 1756 to another clergyman who was struggling with the same issues, suggests strongly that in his view the abundant harvest of blessing which came to Grimshaw's parish in 1744 was partly due to the fact that he was prepared to make personal considerations secondary and become 'irregular'.[1]

News of the preaching in Haworth, which God was using to turn men, women and young people from their sins, spread far and wide. 'Haworth soon became the common subject of conversation all around the country,' comments one who knew Grimshaw personally, 'and there were such undeniable proofs of God being there as his most inveterate adversaries could not possibly deny.' These 'undeniable proofs' were most eloquently expressed in the changed homes of the people of Haworth. Newton had complained that Grimshaw went to 'a people wild and uncultivated like the mountains and rocks which surrounded them'. But through the power of the gospel the lives of the people were lifted to a new level. They enjoyed their religion. Worship and spiritual conversation were a delight. Homes devastated by alcohol and cruelty were restored. 'Families in which sin had made the most miserable havoc, and in which all the comforts of life were destroyed, now were made happy in the fear of God.'[2]

This transformation affected every part of their lives bringing significant social and moral change to the town. Grimshaw himself, answering the accusation that the Methodists attended so many meetings that they had become idle, causing trade and industry to suffer, could say of his parishioners that they were

[1]John Wesley to Thomas Adams, *The Letters of the Rev. John Wesley, A M,* ed. Telford, vol. III (Standard Edition, London: Epworth Press, 1931), p. 151. In this letter Wesley states that not one person was converted in Haworth until Grimshaw became 'irregular'. Clearly this is inaccurate, but it adds weight to the suggestion that the revival in Haworth accelerated greatly after 1744.

[2]*Christian's Magazine,* November 1792.

now 'more industrious in their trade and other occupations' and that they 'maintain their families better than they ever did before'.[1]

And still his congregations grew until Grimshaw was often obliged to address the people in the expansive graveyard which surrounded the church. From far and near they came, some travelling as many as twenty miles each Sunday to be under the life-transforming preaching of the Word of God. One example must suffice. John Madin lived near Bacup and in May 1744 first heard William Darney preach at Heap Barn, a farm about a mile and a half from his home. Opposition had flared up as Darney was preaching. 'A fierce looking and gigantic woman with up-lifted dungfork threatened to knock him down unless he desisted.' But God had chosen a people for himself from that rough gathering, and as John Madin declared his new-found peace, Darney had hugged him, saying, 'You are the first fruits of my labour in this place.'

But Darney could not stay with these young believers, and so John Madin and his friends tramped the twenty miles each Sunday to Haworth 'over lone and desolate hills . . . some of which were 1500 feet above sea level, across deep and rugged valleys; but their new-born zeal surmounted all difficulties.'[2] So it was that the 'barren wilderness' to which William Grimshaw came in 1742 had indeed become 'a fruitful field, a garden of the Lord'. The preaching was providing sustenance for the needy souls of men and women not only in Haworth but far beyond its borders.

[1]Grimshaw, *Answer to George White*, see Myles, *Life and Writings*, p. 140.
[2]Laycock, *Heroes*, pp. 42–43.

9

'STRAINS OF TREMENDOUS ELOQUENCE'

NATHANIEL DRACUP, who lived in Bradford, could often be found amongst the crowds of worshippers drawn from many miles around to Haworth. Attracted by all he had heard of God's work in this moorland village, Dracup was also drawn by Grimshaw's unusual gifts as preacher. He later wrote a tribute in verse which expresses something of the power of the preaching that brought him and many others back again and again to Haworth:

> *'Twas now his heart ran o'er with peace and joy,*
> *His eyes with tears, and all his sweet employ*
> *Was publishing the Saviour's worthy name,*
> *And setting forth the honour of the Lamb.*
>
> *And now his soul felt sweet angelic fire;*
> *His bosom glowed with love and strong desire,*
> *To seek and save the wandering souls of men*
> *And bring them back to peace and rest again.*
> *He knew the Christ he preached; he never dealt*
> *In the base trade of preaching truths unfelt.*

Not only did Dracup recall the tender pleadings with the souls of the people which he had heard from the Haworth pulpit. Equally he remembered the faithful warnings of judgment directed to those who rejected such offers of mercy:

> *See there he stands! the pious crowds among,*
> *Celestial eloquence flows from his tongue:*
> *Lo! on his reverend brow the frowns arise,*
> *And from his tongue the awful threat'ning flies:*
> *He tells the sinner what must be his doom;*
> *He thunders out the awful wrath to come:*
> *He treads self-righteous schemes to dust, and then,*
> *Knocks down the props on which poor mortals lean:*
> *And thus with zeal divine, he tears away*
> *All but a Christ whereon to rest or stay.*

It was not this aspect of Grimshaw's ministry, however, with which Dracup wished to close his elegy:

> *But now his face a milder aspect wears*
> *And conscious pleasure in his eye appears;*
> *He points the sinner to the Lamb of God,*
> *And tells the virtue of atoning blood.*[1]

No doubt, if Grimshaw himself could have read those lines, he would have been highly displeased at such a fulsome portrayal of his ministry. He would have repudiated such commendations in the strongest terms. It was the subject not the manner of his preaching which mattered to him. As he wrote to his friend William Romaine in 1761, 'I live at Haworth when I am at home; and when I am abroad [preaching elsewhere], I am abroad; but at home or abroad my work is the same: *'Tis to preach Jesus and him crucified; and to help, thro' him, poor sinners to God, grace and glory.*'[2]

Another description has survived of Grimshaw's preaching, this time recalled by William Darney, Paul Greenwood and several others. They had asked Grimshaw how he would preach if a congregation seemed 'remarkably inattentive and stupid'. The answer Grimshaw gave them, as these men remembered it, was

---

[1] W. W. Smith, *Wesleyan Methodism in Bradford* (1841), pp. 117–118.
[2] Letter to William Romaine, 29 January 1761.

that his usual plan was 'to preach the law and to prove that all mankind were guilty before God; if that seemed to produce no effect, he enlarged on the sufferings of Christ; his boundless love to perishing sinners; if unaffected by the agonies and dying cries of our blessed Redeemer, he then addressed them on the torments of hell', and, they added, this would be 'in strains of tremendous eloquence'.[1]

It is a sad loss to the Christian Church that we now have none of Grimshaw's actual sermons.[2] However, his own recommendation of the sort of preaching a believer should seek out for the good of his soul provides an accurate summary of the type of ministry he considered important:

Hear the best men. Hear a soul-searching, a soul-winning, a soul-enriching minister; one who declares the whole counsel of God ... who makes hard things easy and dark things plain. Many, to gain the vain admiration of the ignorant and the praises of men, affect in their preaching high-flying words, pompous language, rhetorical strains and philosophical terms. A sanctified heart in a minister is better than a silver tongue.[3]

'To make dark things plain' was clearly uppermost in Grimshaw's mind when he chose to preach in what he termed 'market language'. Though a well-educated man and capable of a more polished style, he deliberately exercised self-denial in refusing to address his congregations in anything but the most basic terms, that he might strip away any excuses they could offer for neglecting the message. Some of his expressions sound unrefined, even crude, to our ears but he purposed the highest spiritual good of his hearers.

[1] Letter from C. Radcliffe, Methodist preacher in Haworth, to Everett, 1827.

[2] In 1861 Spence Hardy recorded the fact that thirty of Grimshaw's sermons, carefully written out, were to be found at Scaitcliffe Hall, near Todmorden (*Incumbent*, p. 230). These, together with Grimshaw's first will and his 1752 covenant with God, were also there but can no longer be traced. See Baker's footnotes, *Grimshaw*, pp. 40, 80.

[3] Grimshaw, unpublished manuscript, 'The Believer's Golden Chain'.

Much of his language was common parlance of the day, coloured with imagery from daily life. 'A tup which had fastened its head in a bunch of briers', was Grimshaw's homely rendering of Abraham's 'ram caught in a thicket'. Urging young people to repent, he would enquire, 'Do not think you can dance with the devil all day and then feast with Christ at night! Will you hang the most sparkling jewels of your young hearts in the devil's ear?'[1] Pressing home the duty of everyone to give God thanks for the blessings of food and drink, he would say pointedly: 'Some of you are worse than the very swine; for the pigs will *grunt* over their victuals, but you say nothing.'

Never did Grimshaw strive after effect for its own sake, but he was clearly a preacher of outstanding abilities. He could hold a congregation spell-bound for two hours or more, with many moved to tears as the Word of God came to them with convicting power. 'He commanded their attention,' wrote John Newton, speaking with 'earnestness and authority as one who was well assured of the truth and importance of his message.'[2] Realising that his sermons were often long, he explained to Newton that he dared not leave off sooner in case he left anything unsaid which might enlighten even one soul in the way of salvation.

If they do not understand me, I cannot hope to do them good; and when I think of the uncertainty of life, that perhaps it may be the last opportunity afforded, and that it is possible I may never see them again, till I meet them in the great day, I know not how to be explicit enough ... I can scarcely tell how to leave off lest I have omitted something for the want of which my preaching and their hearing might prove vain.[3]

And on another occasion he exclaimed in despair, 'I may talk to you till my tongue is as small as a sparble [a small nail used in the repair of boots and shoes], but you will go to hell after all.'[4]

When Grimshaw was preaching in the open air on the Prodigal Son, one who had been listening with rapt attention remembered

[1]Grimshaw, unpublished manuscript, 'The Nature, State and Conduct of a Christian'.
[2]Newton, *Letters,* p. 48.   [3]Newton, *Letters,* p. 55.   [4]JEN.

him suddenly pointing and calling out with energy: 'Yonder he comes! Yonder he comes, all in rags; yonder he comes, rag, tag and bobtail!'[1] Involuntarily the whole congregation turned to gaze across the valley to catch a glimpse of the returning prodigal. John Newton sums up Grimshaw's preaching memorably in these words: 'The solemnity of his manner; the energy with which he spoke; the spirit of love which beamed in his eyes and breathed through his addresses were convincing proof that he did not trifle with his people.'[2]

Another account of one of Grimshaw's early preaching services comes from the autobiography of Richard Burdsall, commonly known as 'Dicky' Burdsall, who later became a well-known Methodist lay preacher. Dicky, aged fifteen, first heard Grimshaw preach while he was spending a few days with his brother and his wife at Eldwick, not far from Bradford. On a raw December day, with bitter winds whipping up the newly-fallen snow, Dicky and his brother had set off for nearby Bingley, where they had heard that Grimshaw was expected to preach. It never occurred to them that the conditions might make it impossible for the preacher to brave the five-mile trek from Haworth along isolated moorland paths, possibly obliterated by snow. If Grimshaw had promised to come, it was safe to assume that he would find a way of being present.

Burdsall describes the occasion:

When we got to the place, I trembled so much with the cold that I thought it would be impossible for me to bear it long. The place of worship was a barn, which had been fitted up for the purpose with deal seats and a pulpit . . . After waiting for a short time, a broadset, sharp-looking little[3] man appeared habited as a layman, and buttoned up from the storm. Having quickly loosed his garments, in a moment he was in the pulpit, and giving out a hymn; the people sang like thunder. His voice in prayer seemed to me as it had been the voice of an angel. After

---

[1]Ibid.   [2]Newton, *Letters,* p. 57.

[3]In fact, Grimshaw was not far off six feet tall, but his broad shoulders and chest gave some the impression that he was short.

prayer he took a little Bible out of his pocket, and read the following words for his text: 'Glory to God in the highest, and on earth peace, goodwill toward men.' The Holy Ghost now shone upon my heart, and discovered to me that both myself and all mankind were in a lost and perishing condition while in a state of nature. I wept and wished that my parents had been there, knowing them to be in the same perishing state.[1]

John Pawson, also later to become prominent in Methodist circles, began his ministry as a lay preacher in Haworth in 1763. In an article for a Methodist magazine written in 1795, Pawson adds his own testimony to Grimshaw's preaching gift: 'Mr Grimshaw enjoyed great liberty and freedom when engaged in preaching the glorious gospel of Christ. He was a natural orator, and spake with the greatest facility. His public discourses were adapted not only to the state but likewise to the capacity of his hearers; the greatest part of whom were of the lower class, and consequently ignorant and wild beyond conception; he therefore addressed them in the most familiar language possible.'

'I shall never forget', wrote Pawson in 1803, 'a sermon and prayer which I heard from him near fifty years ago.' Preaching on Psalm 34:9, Grimshaw had become particularly animated as he explained the meaning of the promise, "There is no want to them that fear him." As Pawson relived the occasion, he could still hear the preacher speaking 'in a most encouraging manner to the poor, despised and persecuted people. And, in the fulness of his heart he said, "Why, before the Lord will suffer his promises to fail, he will lay aside his divinity – he will un-God himself!"' At the close of the service he recalled Grimshaw's unconventional benediction:

Lord, dismiss us with thy blessing: take all these people under thy care and bring them in safety to their homes, and give them their suppers when they get home. But let them not eat a morsel till they have said grace: then let them eat and be satisfied, and return thanks to thee when

[1]Cited by Baker, *Grimshaw*, pp. 106–107.

they have done. Let them then kneel down and say their prayers before they go to bed: let them do this for once at any rate and then thou wilt preserve them until morning.[1]

Perhaps a better tribute to Grimshaw's style of addressing men and women than such fragments that remained impressed on the mind of his hearers, are passages to be found in several of the manuscripts he left, possibly with a view to publication. The most important of these is the treatise already alluded to written in 1755. Entitled 'The Admonition of a Sinner', it is an exhortation to his readers to fulfil their spiritual duty to their friends and neighbours by urging them to turn from their evil ways. But in these exhortations he inadvertently also provides us with a sample of his own passionate preaching:

Most men when spoken to of the evil of their sins, the danger of their souls, their need of Christ and the necessity of regeneration will airily wave and put off all with a sigh and a wish: 'God forgive us, we are all sinners; and so make an end' . . . But heaven and hell are at hand and God is just and jealous, his threatenings real. The judgment day is terrible, death is approaching and life is uncertain . . . God still waits to be gracious to you and takes pleasure in showing mercy. His patience bears, his justice forbears, his mercy entreats. Christ stands offering his blood and merits freely to you. The Holy Spirit is persuading you; ministers are calling and praying for you; your conscience is accusing you; yea, and the devil is waiting for your death that he may have you into hell.

Is not this your accepted time? Is not this *the day of your salvation?* What! Had you rather lose heaven than your pleasures and profits? Would you rather burn in hell than repent on earth? Would you rather have the devil your tormentor there than Christ your governor here? Would you rather renounce Christ and glory than renounce your cursed sins? Is a holy life too much for heaven? And would you rather at last be in hell than deny yourselves the pleasures of sin for a season? Oh friends! What do you think of these things?

Behind the passion and urgency of Grimshaw's preaching, lay the habit of continual personal communion with God in prayer.

[1] John Pawson, *Methodist Magazine,* 1803, p. 453.

Since the early days of his spiritual quickening, he had maintained the practice of praying four times a day. One who stayed under his roof for a period of six months bore testimony to the long periods of time he devoted to this exercise. Not surprisingly then, those who remembered Grimshaw's pulpit prayers were gripped by the immediacy and reality of his access to the throne of grace: 'He was like a man at times with his feet on earth and his soul in heaven. In prayer he would indeed "take hold (as he used to express himself) of the very horns of the altar", which, he added, he could not, he would not let go until God had given the blessing.'[1]

Worship of the God of glory was to Grimshaw so solemn an undertaking that he would tolerate no disturbances in the services. Considering the overcrowded church and the lack of adequate seating, it was no mean feat to attain silence and reverence in the congregation throughout a service, sometimes prolonged over two or three hours. From his elevated position in his pulpit, he could quickly notice any disturbance. If an interruption should occur, he would break off either prayer or preaching and wait until every worshipper was wholly attentive. If he spotted anyone nodding off to sleep or trifling around, the embarrassed culprit might find the attention of the whole congregation directed towards him. Once Grimshaw interrupted his benediction to rebuke worshippers who were reaching for their hats in order to make a hasty exit: 'Let your hats alone,' he exclaimed, ever conscious of any unusual movements among the people, 'they'll stay if you let them.'[2]

Another problem arose from the custom of those times for people to bring their dogs into services of worship with them. So great a nuisance had this become in some churches that official dog-whippers had to be appointed to deal with troublesome animals. Grimshaw knew a better expedient. On one occasion, when a dog-fight broke out in the middle of a service in Haworth,

[1]Middleton, *Biographia*, vol. IV, p. 403.
[2]John Bennet's 'Diary', 26 January 1751 (JRULM).

three or four men struggled ineffectually to separate the animals. Then from the reading desk where Grimshaw was waiting came his booming voice: 'What! Have you no feet?' As he passed from the lectern to the pulpit he demonstrated his meaning on one of the offending animals.[1]

Grimshaw regarded it as his God-given duty to ensure that every soul under his charge should hear the preaching of eternal life. If any were disinclined to attend, he might, with all the authority vested in his position as incumbent of the Established Church, announce that a service would be held at the home of the reluctant parishioner during the coming week. 'I know I am not welcome,' he would announce, 'but I will speak to every one under my care concerning his soul. If you will not come and hear, you shall hear me at home: and if you perish, you will perish [and in broad Yorkshire dialect] wi' t' sound o' t' gospel i' yer lugs!'

Even though his congregations could be numbered at well over a thousand, Grimshaw never lost a personal concern for his hearers. Sometimes he would break off in the middle of a discourse and apply his words directly to some individual present. One term of endearment he frequently used in describing the elderly members of his congregation was 'old moss-crops'. And when he became very animated as he preached, he would often exclaim, "Ye old sinners – ye moss-crops!" On one occasion he was preaching at Colne, not far from Haworth. His heart moved with compassion for the people as he held forth Christ, the Saviour of sinners, and showed that there was mercy reserved even for the vilest, no matter how long they had lived in ungodliness or how deeply they had sinned. Sitting in the front row was an elderly man with a crop of white hair. Forgetting himself, Grimshaw leaned forward in his pulpit, looked directly at the old man and declared in kindly tones, "And for thee also, old moss-crop!"

In general Grimshaw avoided dealing with controversial matters in his preaching, particularly in the light of the doctrinal

[1] JEN.

differences of his day which held such potential for division among those who would otherwise be united in spiritual endeavour. 'Let us take care', he would say, 'to preach up Jesus, and him crucified.' Or, as he put it on another occasion, 'My business is to invite all to come to Christ for salvation, and to assure all that will come of a hearty welcome.'[1]

A succinct summary of the themes reiterated many times over from that imposing Haworth pulpit can be found in Grimshaw's only work to be published in his lifetime. Defending the Methodists from the calumny heaped on them by their opposers, Grimshaw set out the content of Methodist preaching, and we may safely assume that this was also the content of his own preaching. Having demonstrated the doctrines of man's original bliss in the Garden of Eden, his fall and subsequent alienation from God with all its grievous repercussions, Grimshaw continued:

What do these Methodists preach? . . . Why sir, that God foreseeing before the foundation of the world the fall of man, that in consequence thereof his divine justice must needs punish the same, and that his mercy would by no means interpose for his redemption, without a previous and adequate satisfaction made to his justice for man's transgression, graciously sent his only begotten Son, co-equal with himself . . . who suffered also and died for us upon the cross; and shed his divine and most precious blood, each drop of which is worth infinitely more than ten thousand worlds to accomplish this redemption.[2]

In 1762 Grimshaw was to write a more expanded version of his beliefs.[3] Full of warmth and life, this statement of faith reflects the character and spirit of the preacher. Its final words, addressed to William Romaine at whose request it was written, summarise the most prominent features of Grimshaw's ministry:

I think, we are both agreed to pull down man, and when we have the proud chit down, to keep him down. For this is the main. – And never

[1]Williams, *Diary*, p. 203.
[2]Grimshaw, *Answer to White*, reprinted Myles, *Life and Writings*, pp. 91–92.
[3]Full text in Appendix 3.

let him recover so much as his knees, till with a broken heart and a contrite spirit, the dear REDEEMER raise him.

As already indicated, Grimshaw not only preached to large congregations. On the contrary, he was prepared to travel many miles to minister to a handful of hearers. John Fletcher of Madeley, writing to a friend who wished to move in order to preach to greater numbers, cautioned his correspondent with these words: 'You must not be above being employed in a little way. The great Mr Grimshaw of Haworth was not above walking some miles to preach to seven or eight persons; and what are we when compared to him?'[1]

John Newton's assessment of Grimshaw's preaching fully concurs with Fletcher's words:

But though Mr Grimshaw often preached to great numbers, he was a no less attentive servant to a few. When any were willing to hear, he was willing to preach, and often cheerfully walked miles in the winter, in storms of wind, rain or snow, upon lonely unsheltered moors, to preach to a small company of aged, decrepit people in a cottage.

In a word, he was a burning and shining light. His zeal was not an angry unhallowed fire . . . it was the bright flame of that love which the knowledge of Christ had kindled in his heart . . . He had drank deeply into the spirit of his Lord and Master: and perhaps this century has not produced another who could say with more justice and propriety to his hearers (if his great humility would have permitted him), "Be ye followers of me, as I am of Christ."[2]

---

[1] L. Tyerman, *Wesley's Designated Successor* (London: Hodder and Stoughton, 1882), p. 384.
[2] Newton, *Letters,* pp. 61–62.

10

THE CARE OF SOULS

WHEN JOSEPH WILLIAMS first visited William Grimshaw early in 1746 he received a cordial welcome – a welcome which formed a marked contrast to the weather. Crossing the Pennines in February was likely to be hazardous and so Williams had found it to be. In his diary for 23 February he records the journey he had undertaken from his home in Kidderminster in connection with his business as a clothier, travelling first into Lancashire, then Cheshire and lastly into Yorkshire until he reached Haworth. 'On Wednesday the 13th instant I reached Haworth, intending to get the company of the minister of that parish, of whom I had heard an excellent character, and, indeed, the conversation I had with him abundantly compensated for all my sufferings and extreme dangers arising from the severity of the season.'[1]

News of the revival in Haworth, Keighley and many of the surrounding villages and towns was becoming more widely known by this time and clearly Joseph Williams was anxious to meet the incumbent of Haworth about whom he had heard many reports. Visitors such as Williams, described as 'a truly pious man ... a Christian in his closet, in his family, in the world and at the house of God',[2] would be welcome indeed to Grimshaw, who must often have felt a measure of isolation in his remote parish.

[1] Williams, *Diary*, p. 199.
[2] Ibid., p. 444.

Hour after hour the two men talked, doubtless sitting beside the eight feet wide open hearth in Grimshaw's kitchen at Sowdens, the warmth of the fire shutting out the severity of the season. Finally they retired to bed at two in the morning. Grimshaw gave Williams the most detailed account we have of God's dealings with him up until that date, an account to which we have already referred a number of times. Williams in turn set down all he had heard, as he remembered it, first in his diary on 23 February, and then ten days later, on 5 March 1746, in a lengthy letter to a friend, Malachi Blake, vicar of Blandford. On 21 July an unknown correspondent transcribed portions of this letter, adding further details. There are, therefore, at least three versions of this narrative extant and by piecing them together we can obtain as complete a record as possible of the events Grimshaw described to Williams.

As a Nonconformist, Williams might have expected to be regarded with a measure of suspicion by an incumbent of the Established Church. But far from this, he records that 'our hearts were so knit together in love, though I told him I was a Presbyterian, that he almost conjured me to make his house my home, house and all, as oft as I go that way in my business; and at parting once and again, on bended knees gave me his benediction'.[1] Already the breadth of Grimshaw's love for all other believers, regardless of their denominational label or minor differences of opinion, was beginning to express itself.

Joseph Williams was amazed by all he saw and heard in Haworth. Far from the main thoroughfares of population, he discovered evidences of that same breath of new life now moving in the hearts of people in other parts of the land. He confirmed that by this time Grimshaw was regularly preaching to congregations numbering between a thousand and twelve hundred people. The pressures on Grimshaw's time and strength were considerable, for the pastoral needs of such a congregation weighed upon him continually. Even on a Sunday when he had three sermons to

[1] Laycock, *Heroes*, p. 36.

preach, Williams noticed that 'Many wait for him and open their cares to him freely before whomsoever.'

A further testimony, corroborating his own eyewitness, comes from a landlady of Joseph Williams in Halifax who passed on a vivid description of a Sunday she also had spent in Haworth in July 1746. She discovered the church packed to capacity, with about a thousand worshippers inside, and as many outside unable to gain an entrance. She reported that Grimshaw spent two hours that morning expounding the Lord's Prayer, and although the sermon was so long, it 'came with power'. After the service she found at least a hundred others, unknown to her and mostly to each other, eating at a local inn. But though strangers, all their conversation concerned spiritual matters, and was profitable and serious.

Grimshaw had a deep pastoral concern for every member of his parish. Speaking to John Newton on one occasion about the wide variety of spiritual needs among his congregation, he was able to say, 'By my frequent visits and converse with them, I am acquainted with their several temptations, trials, and exercises, both personal and domestic, both spiritual and temporal, almost as intimately as if I had lived in their families.'[1] Such a detailed knowledge of his congregation was to a considerable extent due to the small societies into which Grimshaw had divided his parishioners from the summer of 1743 onwards. Giving further details of the way he ministered to these groups, Joseph Williams wrote in his diary:

When they come together, after prayer, he gives them a serious exhortation, without taking a text . . . In general he puts them in mind of the depravity natural to mankind . . . the necessity of a thorough change to be wrought in them in order to their being made fit for the employment and blessedness of heaven . . . that they must go to God through Christ, by faith and fervent prayer, and must exercise self-denial and mortification.[2]

[1]Newton, *Letters,* pp. 86–7.   [2]Williams, *Diary,* p. 202.

During the years of the previous curate, Isaac Smith, discipline had become lax in the parish and, as we have seen, when Grimshaw first arrived, he discovered that church attendance was low – Sunday had become a day for business or pleasure. Market day in Bradford had traditionally fallen on a Sunday, providing what might seem legitimate excuse for selling the week's products and buying fresh materials. But it was not long before Haworth parishioners were urged to make alternative arrangements.

With all the authority of an eighteenth-century cleric, Grimshaw expected his parishioners to attend the services of worship on a Sunday and even more so as new spiritual life quickened many who would otherwise merely have attended from duty. Extremes of weather, common enough in that wind-swept village high up in the Pennines, ought not, in Grimshaw's view, to keep any able-bodied believer from attending the means of grace. However profitably the time may be spent, that Christian will in the end be the loser by his reluctance to venture out and meet with other believers. Grimshaw explained his reason for this view in his manuscript collection of his 'Experiences':

When any child of God by reason of extreme cold, snow or rain abstains from his class meeting or from public preaching, though he may and does take care to supply his absence by reading or other religious exercises at home, yet afterwards, he will have the worst of it. He will find more uneasiness by far in his conscience for his negligence than all the distress or harm he could possibly have sustained from the inclemency of the weather . . . The more frivolous is the excuse, the greater is the sin, and the more irksome will be the uneasiness of conscience.

Grimshaw found, however, that it took more than exhortation to change the habits of some of his parishioners. Particularly was this true of certain of the young people who used to enjoy a variety of sports on a Sunday afternoon on the moors above Haworth. On weekdays Grimshaw could enjoy a game of 'football' with them, played with the stones on the moors, but he preached against the practice of using Sunday for such activities.

His words availed little. Finally Grimshaw took to strolling across the moors himself in search of delinquents. Vaulting five-bar gates was no difficulty to their curate, as the young people discovered, and even though they kept a sharp look out for the approach of 'the parson', they were regularly spotted and rebuked, often in public. Sometimes even this proved unavailing and so seriously did Grimshaw consider this violation of the Lord's Day that he would have persistent offenders summoned before the archdeacon's court. A record exists of such a circumstance in 1749 when nine youths from Haworth were disciplined in this way 'for leaping, jumping and practising other disorderly exercises on the Lord's Day and thereby neglecting to attend divine service'.[1]

Another vice which proved particularly difficult to suppress was the habit of groups of young people to resort to a place known as Hoyle-Syke Green, about a mile from the village. There, unseen by any who might report on them, they would engage in undesirable and often immoral activities. After repeated but ineffectual warnings from the pulpit, Grimshaw decided on a more drastic remedy. Setting off one evening incognito, he walked across the moor, until he came upon a large group of young people who were about to join hands and form themselves into a ring. Undetected, Grimshaw joined the circle. But one youth who was standing opposite him glanced at the newcomer's legs. He recognised them as the curate's legs, having had many opportunities to observe those legs as they brought Grimshaw on regular visits to his parents' home. The young man ventured to raise his eyes a little higher. Now he had no doubt. The face into which he was looking was none other than the face of William Grimshaw himself. An urgent message was whispered around the circle, and in a moment all loosened hands and fled in panic, scattering in different directions. Only two remained: those on either side of Grimshaw, who found their hands locked fast in an iron grip. 'Says he to them,' continues the narrator of this anecdote, "I know you, and I know a considerable number of those

[1]Cited by Baker, *Grimshaw,* p. 211.

who have made their escape." He then expostulated with them on the wickedness and folly of their conduct and set them at liberty.'

Subsequently Grimshaw wrote to all whom he could remember who had been present on the occasion, asking them to meet him at the church at a given time. After some hesitation most of the young people complied with the request, knowing no doubt that behind any outward appearance to the contrary, they had in their curate one who cared for their spiritual state. 'Well, what must be done now? What must be done now?' enquired Grimshaw as the abject little group of teenagers entered the room. 'Come, we must pray together.' After praying with them and then speaking sternly of the sinfulness of their behaviour, he concluded, 'I know you, and I know your parents, and I should be sorry to injure you or to hurt their minds. Now if you will promise me that you will never go to Hoyle-Syke Green on a Sunday evening again, I shall drop the matter.' They promised, and so ended a practice which had not yielded to any other more conventional method.[1]

It was incidents such as these which caused Dr Frank Baker to entitle the chapter in his biography of Grimshaw which dealt with discipline within the parish, *A Puritan on the Warpath*. 'No Christian', Grimshaw had written in his 'Experiences', 'ought, can or will give way to any recreation, pastime or diversion whatsoever. He can no more hunt, card, dice, than commit murder or adultery. The Holy Ghost can and does afford us more comfort in one minute than all this world's glories can afford in an 100 years.' In another manuscript he was to include whistling and singing in a trivial manner as conduct unworthy of the Christian.

But set against the background of eighteenth-century 'pastimes', which were often cruel and bawdy, we are not surprised that men of the eighteenth-century revival, serious men, consumed with a desire for God's glory, should condemn such things. If Grimshaw was sometimes excessive in his strictures on the conduct of his

---

[1] C. Radcliffe, letter to Everett, 9 January 1827 (JRULM).

parishioners, this did not stem from the influence of the Puritans. More probably it arose from an over-reaction on his part to his own life-style before his conversion; for during that period cards, dicing and diversions of all sorts had been his constant pre-occupation.

In the personal habits of their curate the Haworth parishioners had a ready example of that disciplined way of life which he encouraged in them. An early account of his life bears this out:

His usual hour of rising was about five; and the melody of his heart rose with him. His first [song of praise] was constantly that excellent doxology:

> *Praise God from whom all blessings flow,*
> *Praise him, all creatures here below,*
> *Praise him, above ye heavenly host,*
> *Praise Father, Son and Holy Ghost.*

He would then join in prayer with his family, those who visited and those who would come. But previously he read the psalms and lessons appointed for the day. After this morning sacrifice he would take an affectionate leave of them, like one who might see them no more, using this kind benediction: 'May GOD bless you, in your souls and in your bodies, and in all you put your hands to do this day! Whether you live or whether you die, may the Lord grant that you may live to him and for him, and with him for ever!' This custom he also observed at night when he took leave of them for rest.[1]

Any staying in the house, together with neighbours and friends, were invited to join in these early morning times of family worship. Elizabeth Grimshaw and the children, John and Jane, now ten and nine respectively, would also be present, with other members of the household, including the two maids who worked at Sowdens, and Jonathan Maskew who farmed the glebe lands. Elizabeth had been unsympathetic towards the work which was

---

[1]Middleton, *Biographia*, vol. IV, p. 405.

engrossing her husband's attention, but in 1746 her attitude began to soften as she too started to seek after a true knowledge of God.

William Grimshaw's watchful concern over the daily lives of his parishioners became a noted characteristic of his ministry. Anxious that all who claimed conversion under his preaching should live consistent Christian lives, he sometimes used unorthodox methods to unmask hypocrisy. The use of disguise to discover the identity of the young people on the moors was one example of this. Another similar anecdote, included in most accounts of Grimshaw's life, can be cited which is probably representative of other such incidents. A man and his wife from the village had made extravagant claims to holiness of life, but Grimshaw was not at all convinced. Rumours had reached his ears that the couple in question were both tight-fisted and unmerciful towards the needy. So borrowing a shabby weaver's jacket and cap, he dressed as a poor beggar in need of a roof over his head for the night. Appearing at the door of his parishioner's house, he asked piteously for a night's lodgings. Not deterred by the man's refusals, the beggar pleaded his destitution and need – but the man remained unmoved and adamant. At that point Grimshaw removed his disguise, and revealed his true identity. It is not hard to imagine the confusion of the man as he received a lecture on 'covetousness and hardheartedness, as would have shaken the nerves of old Charon [the devil] himself'.

While John Newton did not censure his friend for the use of such unconventional means to improve standards in his parish, neither did he commend them for the imitation of others. Grimshaw was acting essentially in keeping with his own character and in response to the rough and undisciplined people among whom he ministered. 'His character, motives and aims were well known and he always acted like himself. What was unstudied and natural in him, might appear affectation in another, and affectation is always disgusting and defeats its own purposes.'[1]

---

[1] Newton, *Letters*, p. 100.

Although Grimshaw was concerned with hypocrisy among those who professed faith, his primary concern for his parishioners' souls was expressed in his ceaseless attempts to warn the ungodly. Fearless of disapproval, he took every opportunity he could to constrain them to consider the vital importance of repentance and faith. Neither did he assume that this was an obligation merely incumbent upon himself. Rather he urged it upon all believers as their God-ordained duty. In a treatise on this theme which he wrote after thirteen years in Haworth, we catch something of the depth of emotion that marked his dealings with non-Christians from the very outset of his ministry:

My neighbour, my friend, my heart longs over you. Your manner of life is actually, openly and evidently such that if not seasonably prevented, it will shortly and certainly terminate in your inevitable, intolerable, eternal ruin and destruction. Allow me therefore, as knowing the terrors of the Lord, to persuade you to repent and turn to the Lord while he may be found. 'Behold now is your accepted time; behold now is the day of your salvation.' There is no repentance, no mercy, no pardon, no salvation in hell; no, not so much as a drop of cold water to cool your tongue, to mitigate your pains, to alleviate your torments for ever. Don't be angry with me, please don't. It's because I love you that I thus address you. Love will not suffer me to see you perish and be silent. It's not my own, but your advantage that I seek. I want you without delay to repent of your sins, 'to seek the Lord while he may be found, to call upon him while he is near' (*Isa.* 55:6-7). Acquaint yourself with him, be at peace with him through his blood, that thereby good may come to you: pardon, peace, grace, heaven, glory, glory for evermore.[1]

In order to restore the backslider and draw the unconverted to repentance and faith, Grimshaw did not hesitate to carry church discipline to its full extent if he deemed it necessary. In accordance with the canons of the Church of England, it was the duty of the clergy to present offenders before the church courts that

[1]Grimshaw, 'The Admonition of a Sinner', unpublished manuscript (JRULM).

they might be charged and then publicly corrected for their misdemeanours. This Grimshaw was prepared to do, that he might reclaim some for the kingdom of Christ.

Documents relating to these offences can still be seen, preserved among papers relating to the York diocese. Such church discipline occurred sometimes two or three times in a year and one example may be cited. Esther Greenwood, a young Haworth woman, was required to appear in 'the Chapel of Haworth aforesaid, upon Sunday, being the twelfth, nineteenth or twenty-sixth Day of November instant in the time of divine service . . . in the presence of the whole congregation then assembled . . . ' She was to come bareheaded, barefooted, and with a white sheet wrapped around her. She would then be required to stand up on the seat in front of the pulpit where she would be formally charged with her offence and then asked to repeat this prayer of confession and repentance after the minister:

Whereas I, good people, forgetting my duty to Almighty God, have committed the detestable sin of fornication with Joseph Wright and thereby have justly provoked the heavy wrath of God against me, to the danger of my own soul and evil example to others, I do earnestly repent and am heartily sorry for the same, desiring Almighty God for the merits of Jesus Christ, to forgive me both this and all other my offences, and also ever hereafter to assist me with his Holy Spirit, that I shall never fall into the like offence again, and for that purpose I desire you all here present to pray with me.

A stiff ordeal for a girl to face, it was probably over-severe, particularly set against modern standards. Although the young man in this case had avoided discipline by joining the army, Esther Greenwood may well have realised that this was imposed for her greater good, and her pastor cared for her eternal welfare. Sometimes Grimshaw would plead for the mitigation of a fine, if one were imposed, or even meet it out of his own resources if he knew the parishioner in question was too poor to pay it.

If a dying parishioner, who had neglected the means of grace, should send for Grimshaw in the time of his extremity and need, he would find his pastor faithful and earnest both in rebuke and warning: 'Now the hand of God is upon you, and you think the devil is ready to take you, and hell open to receive you; now it is, – "Send for Grimshaw",' he would say to such individuals. 'He has talked thus to the most hardened sinners till their beds have shaken under them,'[1] wrote the wife of an itinerant preacher, Joseph Jones, who had spent six months at Sowdens recovering from serious illness.

But severity was always mingled with tenderness as Grimshaw spoke to those nearing death – often to their effectual salvation. Out of the eighteen parishioners he had buried in a certain year, Grimshaw told Mrs Jones he felt confident of the spiritual condition of sixteen of them. No exertion would he spare himself in order to reach the dying, and speak a last word to them before the destiny of their souls was for ever settled.

On many a wild and stormy night, when no-one else would venture out, a lonely figure could often be seen tramping across the moors. It was Grimshaw, taking one last opportunity of ministering at some deathbed. Commenting on this, Henry Venn said: 'He thought his tongue should never lie still in guilty silence, whilst he could speak to the honour of that God who had done so much for his soul. And whilst he saw sinners perishing for lack of knowledge and no one breaking to them the bread of life, he was transported by love to pity them.'[2] As Venn recalled his friend's selfless and unflagging labours, he could only exclaim, 'Witness, ye moors and mountains, how often he was in perils by the way, whilst carrying the glad tidings to some poor cottager who, but for his instruction, would have been as ignorant of Christ as when they were born!'[3]

---

[1]Mrs Joseph Jones, cited in Laycock, *Heroes*, p. 244.
[2]Venn, *Sketch*, p. 35.
[3]Venn, *Christ the Joy of the Christian's Life and Death his Gain* (Leeds, 1763), p. 14.

11

A Bona Fide Methodist

AT THE SAME TIME AS JOSEPH WILLIAMS was battling through snowbound countryside to Haworth in February 1746, John Wesley was also journeying from Bristol to Newcastle, the northern centre of Methodism. Having set out on 17 February, he had taken a week to reach Halifax. On the way he had suffered from both violent mobs and the weather, recording in his journal biting winds, and snow which 'crusted us over from head to foot in less than an hour's time'.[1]

The societies which John Nelson had been forming in Halifax, Birstall and Leeds were growing in numbers, and a visit from John Wesley would have been an encouragement to them. As we have seen, there was a close link between the society in Halifax and the small group of believers in Keighley since the visit of John Wilkinson and it is no surprise that despite the weather Wesley decided to make a first visit to Keighley on his way up the country. When he arrived on 25 February he discovered a society which had grown from its original ten to almost a hundred members – a remarkable increase in a town where the population was only two thousand. If he had not already heard about the curate in nearby Haworth, and the blessing resting upon his ministry, undoubtedly Thomas Colbeck and John Wilkinson would have informed him. But whether Wesley contemplated a

---

[1]John Wesley's *Journal*, p. 233.

visit to Haworth at that time, we do not know, for he merely reports, 'The snow was so deep I could not go through the vales, [and] went the straight way, and came to Newcastle on Wednesday the 26th.'[1]

As the revival in Haworth had not come to fruition until after September 1744, it is not surprising that William Grimshaw had yet to meet the Wesleys. The condition of the roads and the constant demands of the growing numbers of societies would have made any visit from the brothers difficult. But it may also be that a degree of prejudice, arising from Grimshaw's connection with Benjamin Ingham, could explain any reluctance John Wesley might have felt about going out of his way to call at Haworth. By 1746 a warm friendship had been established between Ingham and Grimshaw, and twice yearly from this time onwards Grimshaw used to visit all Ingham's societies, which once again numbered between sixty and seventy. But Ingham's involvement with the Moravians, which had been one cause of the strained relationship between him and Wesley, was decreasing. According to Ingham's co-worker William Batty, by 1746 Ingham was becoming disillusioned with them. But Wesley may not have known this.

1746 was a remarkable year in the north-west of England. William Grimshaw reported on the progress of the revival to John Gillies:

In the year 1746, by this man [Darney] the Lord pushed the work westward. Great numbers in the next parish (Heptonstall) were awakened and brought to a knowledge of Jesus. Lancashire now received the first revival. Pendle Forest, Colne parish, Todmorden, Rossendale, and soon after Haslingden, Rochdale and its parish, were visited by the Lord, and many brought to acknowledge His free redeeming and saving power. This year the work began in Manchester . . .

Subsequently Grimshaw, too, became active in many of these places that he mentions; an early account of his life suggests that

[1]Ibid., p. 234.

from 1747 onwards his influence among these societies which Darney was establishing gave them a measure of stability they would not otherwise have enjoyed.[1]

In 1746 Grimshaw was still reluctant to cross parish boundaries. But as men and women from neighbouring parishes continued to pour into Haworth and find lasting benefit from the preaching, so the requests multiplied for Grimshaw to come to their towns and villages to preach. Hesitantly at first he began to respond to these invitations: 'Nothing but love to the souls of men and a desire of proving a blessing to them, engaged him to preach as occasions offered, in other parishes,' wrote Henry Venn.[2] On occasions the initiative came from Grimshaw. A man by the name of Clegg, who came from Dean Head in Lancashire, was frequently among the worshippers in Haworth. Listening earnestly to the preaching week after week, Clegg had made no profession of faith until one Sunday Grimshaw announced, 'I shall preach at Mr Clegg's on Tuesday next.' As good as his word, he arrived on the appointed day, and both Clegg and his wife were converted not long afterwards. There a small society was formed, and Christian testimony maintained for many years.[3]

But such an activity could not go unopposed by the local clergy who saw the success of the curate of Haworth as a threat to themselves. When Joseph Williams, glad to take up Grimshaw's cordial invitation to visit Haworth any time his business commitments lay in West Yorkshire, returned to Haworth in August of 1746, he also brought news of impending trouble.

On his way he had spent a night in Colne, one of those parishes 'visited by the Lord', as Grimshaw had told Gillies. There at the inn he overheard a conversation which he relayed to Grimshaw. The innkeeper was complaining about a recent visit from the curate of Haworth. He had been 'two hours in his

[1] Myles, *Life and Writings,* p. 19.
[2] Venn, *Sketch,* p. 34.
[3] Clegg died shortly after his conversion and some years later Jonathan Maskew married his widow.

Haworth today

Haworth Church after rebuilding of 1879

Sowdens now

Haworth Moor: 'What has God wrought in the midst of those rough mountains!' *(John Wesley)*

discourse, which was beyond all sense and reason', grumbled the innkeeper. 'He preaches damnation to such a degree', rejoined another, 'it is insufferable.' 'Furthermore', added a third, 'he preaches in barns and private houses and is a great encourager of conventicles.' At this point Williams could forbear no longer. He reported verbatim the exchange that followed: '"Aye," says I, "does Mr Grimshaw preach in private houses?" "Yes, he does," said my chapman [the publican] in an angry tone, "every week, and almost every day." "Why then," said I, "he is almost as bad as the Apostle Paul, for he taught the people publicly and likewise from house to house." To this they answered not a word, but let the conversation drop.'[1]

Williams added that 'the neighbouring clergy, envying his [Grimshaw's] popularity, were caballing and contriving how they might get him suspended'. These were early rumblings of a storm which was to break out with intensity on Grimshaw, Ingham, Batty, Thomas Colbeck and John Wesley himself in the near future, and, significantly enough, Colne was at the centre of the persecution.

In October 1746 Charles Wesley, whose journeys were almost as numerous as his brother's at this time, also visited Keighley. When he reached the town he found an eager congregation soon gathered to hear him preach. His own account of this occasion, preserved in his journal, records that his text was John 3:16. Aware of the potential for the gospel in the place, he commented, 'Here also is the promise of a plentiful harvest.'[2] Doubtless having heard by now of the curate of Haworth whose message and priorities were so similar to his own, Charles Wesley decided to ride the extra miles over the hills to meet him. In his journal for 22 October 1746 he recorded, 'I went on to Haworth; called on Mr Grimshaw, a faithful Minister of Christ.'

Arriving at Sowdens Wesley discovered both Grimshaw and

---

[1]Cited by F. Baker, *Grimshaw,* p. 130, from *Christian History,* 1747, p. 13.
[2]*The Journal of Charles Wesley*, vol. I (London: Mason, 1849, reprinted, Grand Rapids, Michigan: Baker Book House, 1980), p. 432.

his wife ill with a fever, probably one of those virulent infections which so often broke out in Haworth. Alarmed at the acute nature of their symptoms, he was anxious lest Grimshaw's condition might prove fatal. 'We prayed, believing that the Lord would raise him up again, for the service of his church.'[1] He then preached a sermon based on Isaiah 35, clearly chosen to encourage Grimshaw in his weakened condition, and adds, 'All listened; many wept; some received comfort.' A bond immediately sprang up between the two men. Even though Grimshaw was ill, Charles Wesley saw in him an example of spiritual love and zeal. In his journal he noted, 'His soul was full of triumphant love – I wished mine in its place.'[2] Such words were an expression of the highest aspiration for which these early Methodists strove in the spiritual life. The concept of the love of God in the soul embraced within itself every other Christian grace; it was the fountain from which all zeal, all humility, patience and faithful service sprang. Charles Wesley often prayed for it in his hymns:

> *Kindle a flame of sacred love*
> *On the mean altar of my heart.*

Through this visit from Charles Wesley God was preparing Grimshaw to face a further acute trial: Elizabeth did not rally from the fever, dying shortly afterwards. Grimshaw was now left a widower for the second time, and Jane and John were motherless once more. A comment in Charles Wesley's journal also explains why we know so little about Elizabeth Grimshaw; for since her marriage in 1741, this is the first time she had been mentioned in any of the contemporary records.

Although Elizabeth was most probably a religious woman when she married, the work of God at Haworth clearly probed her spiritual experience and found it wanting. Unable to understand or cope with the evidences of new life all around her, Elizabeth became critical and antagonistic towards the work in which her husband was engaged. Small wonder then that so little

---

[1] Ibid. [2] Ibid.

mention is made of her. But all this had changed shortly before her death, for Charles Wesley records in his journal, 'She had been a great opposer, but [was] lately convinced.'[1] God had intervened, and as Grimshaw followed that second sad funeral procession, this time back to Heptonstall, near Todmorden, he had at least one strong consolation: that all had been well with her soul at the last, for his wife had died in the comforts and hope of the gospel.

In January 1747 Charles Wesley was back in Yorkshire, having spent the intervening period itinerating in the north, preaching in villages and hamlets around Newcastle and Gateshead. Now he was on his way south once more. Without hesitation he rode across to Haworth on 22 January to greet 'my dear brother Grimshaw'. To Wesley's surprise he found that instead of allowing him the use of his pulpit Grimshaw had made arrangements for him to preach at a large hall – probably Emmott Hall. Large it might have been, but it was not large enough to accommodate the crowds who were eager to hear Wesley preach, and he was not impressed by Grimshaw's seemingly reluctant support. No doubt the reason for Grimshaw's caution lay in a concern over the effect which such an open support of Charles Wesley might have had on his own ministry. Since the conversations overheard by Joseph Williams, he was well aware that the neighbouring clergy were watching him carefully to find some pretext to accuse him before the archbishop.

That night Charles Wesley slept at Sowdens, but next morning before taking his leave he confronted his friend with 'fearing where no fear was',[2] and pointed out, there was no law, civil or ecclesiastical, which Grimshaw could be contravening by lending him his pulpit. Nor did the Methodist leaders have any intention of breaking away from the Established Church and becoming Dissenters – a possibility which would have alarmed a churchman like Grimshaw. With a conscience as tender as ever, Grimshaw was 'much ashamed at having given place to his threatening

[1] Ibid.   [2] Ibid., p. 440.

enemies'.[1] Never again did he withhold the use of his pulpit from either of the Wesley brothers or from George Whitefield when he came to Haworth two years later. He was now one in heart with the Methodists.

On his way back to Bristol Charles Wesley took the opportunity to visit the societies that William Darney had been forming. Darney's relationship with the Wesleys was a chequered one. Neither of the brothers found him a congenial fellow-worker: his staunch Calvinism troubled them and his doggerel hymns were a trial to Charles Wesley's poetic mind. But he had maintained a loose connection with the Wesleys so that even Richard Viney in his diary for 15 January 1744 describes Darney as one who 'belongs to John Nelson and [the] Mr Wesleys'.[2] Now realising that his spiritual children needed more regular supervision than he was able to supply, Darney was seeking a closer union with the Methodists. Initially he had asked Ingham to take care of them but Ingham had declined and so he proposed to bring his societies fully under Wesley's organisational umbrella.

Three months later John Wesley himself called on William Grimshaw. A brief entry in his journal reads: 'May 1 1747, I read prayers and preached in Haworth church to a numerous congregation.'[3] Clearly there had been no difficulty this time over the use of Grimshaw's pulpit. An immediate rapport was established between the two men, which developed into a rich friendship. A letter written by Grimshaw to John Wesley four weeks later on 30 May 1747[4] reveals that one of the main subjects under discussion during the visit had been the future of William Darney's societies,

[1] Ibid.

[2] 'Richard Viney's Diary', *Wesley Historical Society,* vol. XIII, p. 112.

[3] John Wesley's *Journal,* vol. VII, p. 389.

[4] The level of common interest between Wesley and Grimshaw apparent from this letter suggests there had been previous contacts between them before this date. Although there is no documentary evidence to substantiate this, the fact that Paul Greenwood, one of 'Mr Grimshaw's men', was appointed by Wesley to go to Dublin in the autumn of 1747 could well indicate prior correspondence.

more particularly because 'Scotch Will' was wanting to spend some time in his homeland after six years' absence, which would leave the people without any pastoral oversight. Wesley had agreed to assume this responsibility, and on leaving Haworth had taken time, like his brother, to visit all these scattered groups of believers and had also formed new societies in Darney's circuit. So Grimshaw writes:

The Societies you formed in William Darney's circuit I hear are in a good state. I went amongst those about Todmorden the week after you were there, and to my great comfort found it so. I likewise observed a general disposition in all sorts to hear the gospel. I exhorted twice that day; for I will not have it called preaching. I afterwards gave a short exhortation to a few who happened to come too late to hear either of the former.[1]

This attitude towards his own preaching was no mock humility on Grimshaw's part, but an expression of a meekness of disposition concerning his own ministry, which he expressed on many occasions throughout his life.

He continues his letter by giving a further example of how invitations from other parishes were gradually forcing him to cross parish boundaries with increasing frequency:

At my coming home [from Todmorden] I was met with a letter from a clergyman about fourteen or fifteen miles from hence, and not above two or three from where you preached in Rossendale, before you set off to Manchester. He desired me to come and preach at his chapel on the morrow. I embraced the request, finding freedom in my heart, perceiving that a door is hereby opened, and that the Lord seems to make my way plain before me. I propose to set out today at noon, to walk it, having an agreeable companion to bear me company. I know that the Lord is with me.[2]

As Grimshaw brings his letter to a conclusion we can feel the

[1]Grimshaw to John Wesley, 30 May 1747. For whole letter see Myles, *Life and Writings*, p. 161.
[2] Ibid.

warmth of his developing friendship both with John Wesley and his brother, Charles:

You will not fail to present my tender respects to your brother: the same I desire to all the sincere servants and seekers of the blessed Jesus, your Redeemer and mine. O may we be kept faithful to him to the end: may we ever go forth in his strength . . .To him I heartily commend you and yours. Lord Jesus, sweet Jesus, be with you.[1]

Up until 1747 Grimshaw had rarely ventured beyond the bounds of his own parish except in response to the urgent requests of his hearers. Necessity had driven him to become 'irregular' by preaching in barns and private homes in the vicinity of Haworth, or not far beyond. But now his new friendship with John and Charles Wesley presented him with a far greater challenge: the vision to sally forth regardless of the 'caballing and contriving' of the local clergy, and to bring the message of forgiveness of sins and hope of a better world to come to the masses of the people, wherever he could gain a hearing. But this was no easy step for a man schooled in all the protocol of the Established Church. A second letter to John Wesley, written on 20 August 1747 indicates how hard William Grimshaw had found this to be and how God had dealt with him over the issue.

As with other important spiritual transactions in his life, Grimshaw was able to pinpoint the exact time when God took his apprehensive servant in hand and gave him the spiritual freedom to act in a way which would normally have been against his principles as a churchman. His own description of this experience in this second letter gives an illuminating insight into his mind at the time. He wrote:

But, O dear Sir, I know not what to say; I know not what to do. Sometimes I have made more excursions into neighbouring parishes, to exhort, but always with a Nicodemical fear, and to the great offence of the clergy, which, till lately almost made me ready to sally out no more, but to content myself in my own bounds: till lately, I say; for on

[1] Ibid.

Wednesday was six weeks, from about five o'clock in the afternoon, to about twelve at night, and again for some hours together, I may say, the day following, my mind was deeply affected with strong impressions to preach the gospel abroad; the event I left to the Lord, fearing to be disobedient to what I trust was the heavenly call.[1]

Delivered in this way from his 'Nicodemical fear' Grimshaw was certainly not disobedient to the heavenly call; for at the earliest opportunity he set off on a preaching tour – a tour which he describes in detail to Wesley and which was to be typical of many such excursions throughout the following years. Now he was set on a course of ministry which would govern all his activities for the rest of his life and bring incalculable blessing to the people of the north of England.

The whole visit found me employment for near five days. O it was a blessed journey to my soul! I now, in some measure, begin to see into the import of our Lord's design, by that deep impression on my mind above-mentioned. I am determined, therefore, to add, by the divine assistance, to the care of my own parish that of so frequent a visitation of Mr Bennet's,[2] William Darney's, the Leeds and Birstall societies, as my own convenience will permit and their circumstances may respectively seem to require, all along eyeing the Lord's will and purposes for me. If I find the Lord's pleasure be that I must still launch out further, I will obey; for he daily convinces me more and more what he has graciously done and will do for my soul. O! I can never do enough in gratitude and love to him, for the least mite, if I may reverently so speak, of what his blessings are to me. O, dear Sir, that I may prove faithful and indefatigable in his vineyard! that I may persevere to the last gasp steadfast, immovable, and always abounding

---

[1] Grimshaw to John Wesley, 20 August 1747. For whole letter see Appendix 1.

[2] John Bennet was one of Wesley's earliest itinerant preachers, pioneering the preaching of the gospel in Cheshire and Derbyshire. Writing in 1750 he says, 'My circuit is one hundred and fifty-two miles in two weeks, during which time I preach publicly thirty-four times, besides meeting the societies and visiting the sick'. W. J. Townsend, *A New History of Methodism,* vol. I (London: Hodder and Stoughton, 1910), p. 298. Bennet was one of four lay preachers to attend Wesley's first conference in 1744.

in his work! Do you pray – the same shall be mine for you, your dear brother, and all our fellow labourers.

Not only did Grimshaw give John Wesley an account of God's personal dealings with him in this letter, but he also provided details of the progress of the gospel in Haworth itself. Five years had elapsed since he had begun his ministry and three since the revival had broken out in all its fullness. William Grimshaw could report that far from abating, the work was 'flourishing still more and more; our societies are in general, very lively in the Lord, and several others, though not as yet joined in society are nevertheless come to a sense of the pardoning love of God.' Some were 'under deep concern, or eagerly hungering and thirsting after our Redeemer', and this number included 'two under my own roof just now under true conviction'.[1]

In addition to these two (a girl of eighteen and a boy aged fourteen who were probably in service at Sowdens), Grimshaw confided to Wesley a special token of God's blessing in his own family. Bereft of his wife, he naturally felt a deep concern for his two young children. But now his 'own little girl, between ten and eleven years old' had come under conviction of sin. Nor was this a fleeting childish mood, for Grimshaw continued, 'It is near six months since she first began to show a serious concern for her sinful state.' Perhaps the loss of her stepmother eight months earlier had brought Jane to seek forgiveness and consolation in her father's God.

On the same day that Grimshaw wrote this letter, John Wesley was also writing one to him. As soon as Wesley's letter arrived, Grimshaw hastily replied – a letter that breathes the life and power of the revival which he was witnessing on every side.

You desire a particular account of the progress of the Lord's work here. Indeed, I have the pleasure of assuring you, that I think it never went better, from its first appearance amongst us, than it has done within

[1]Grimshaw to John Wesley, 20 August 1747. The whole letter is of considerable importance as a record of the progress of the revival in Haworth and is included in Appendix I.

these two months. I may say, at Leeds, Birstall, Keighley, Todmorden, Rossendale, Heptonstall, Pendleforest, and in my own parish, the societies are very hearty; souls are daily added to the church; and I may say, multitudes on all sides, (many of whom have been enemies to us and our MASTER'S cause), are convinced of the truth and run eagerly to hear the gospel . . . I think my public exhortations (alias what I call my monthly visitations) were never so visibly blessed, I praise God, for these four years past, as they have been within these last two months. Such a mighty presence of God has been in those visitations, and also in many of our weekly class meetings as I have rarely seen before.

In the light of all this rapid expansion of the work of God, Grimshaw pleaded with Wesley to send him helpers to reap the plentiful harvest – a further indication that Grimshaw now regarded himself as united with Wesley in the spiritual endeavour in which he and his brother were engaged. And in this sense of oneness he included others who were labouring nearby. 'Brother Bennet, Nelson and I . . . are cordially united in carrying on the Lord's work. I hope we believe, and profess and preach one thing – Jesus and him crucified. If you know them, you know me.'[1]

So it was that Grimshaw cemented a warm and lasting relationship with John and Charles Wesley and their fellow workers, and from 1747 onwards could be described as a Methodist himself. In character he was the antithesis of John Wesley: the Yorkshireman was impetuous, lively and unpredictable, and Wesley cool, controlled and orderly. They complemented each other and needed each other in those tremendous days of the eighteenth-century revival. Like all the Methodist leaders, he saw no conflict between Methodism, with its system of societies and class meetings, and the parish church. Methodists met together during the week, and at hours other than the normal services of worship at the parish churches, so that they could continue, in theory at least, in regular communion within the Church of England. In the few cases where the incumbent was in sympathy with the revival as in Haworth, the regular services of the church

[1]Grimshaw to John Wesley, 27 November 1747. Full letter in Appendix 1.

became the Methodists' meeting place. Methodism existed, in Grimshaw's mind, to unite and strengthen new believers and to inject fresh spiritual energy into a church grown moribund and lifeless.

In this endeavour, William Grimshaw could now declare to John Wesley, 'I desire to do nothing but in perfect harmony and concert with you, and beg therefore you will be entirely free, open and communicative to me . . . My pulpit, I hope, shall be always at yours and your brother's service; and my house, so long as I have one, your welcome home. The same I'll make it to all our fellow-labourers, through the grace of God.' William Grimshaw, now aged forty, was indeed a bona fide Methodist.

12

Not Counting the Cost

As William Grimshaw sat writing to John Wesley on 20 August 1747 explaining how he had been delivered from his 'Nicodemical fear' of crossing parish boundaries, he did not mention explicitly that he too had already experienced a taste of that mindless persecution which was so frequently the lot of these early Methodist preachers. He merely contented himself with stating that his excursions into neighbouring parishes had proved 'a great offence to the clergy'. A. C. H. Seymour, who had access to Benjamin Ingham's original journals and diary,[1] describes in some detail in his *Life and Times of the Countess of Huntingdon*, an early persecution in Colne, nine miles west of Haworth, in which Benjamin Ingham, Grimshaw and William Batty were all involved. Although Seymour gives no date for this event, fortunately William Batty, who had good reason to remember the details, records the same episode, and also provides a date: 7 July 1747.

In Grimshaw's letter to John Wesley he mentions that it was six weeks prior to the time of writing that God dealt with him when he had almost decided to 'sally out no more'. Piecing together

---

[1] Seymour also wrote a 400-page biography of Ingham which was unpublished. The manuscript, entitled 'Memoirs of the Life, Ministry and Religious Connections of the Late Benjamin Ingham' is kept in the Cheshunt Foundation, Westminster College, Cambridge.

these two facts, we realise that it was only a day or two after Grimshaw's experiences at Colne that God renewed his faith and courage to venture out again regardless of personal cost or suffering.

In his description of the events of that day, Batty, who had now become Ingham's co-worker sharing both his toils and his sufferings, begins by mentioning that on the way to the house in Colne where Ingham was due to preach they noticed an ominous little gathering at the door of a tavern with the vicar of Colne, George White, in the centre. No sooner had they begun the service and sung three verses of an opening hymn when

the Vicar came furiously into the house with a great mob at his heels; he had a great staff in one hand and the Constable at the other; he rushed thro' the people towards WB [Batty] as he intended to strike, but B Ingham who stood behind him pull'd him up by the coat, and they got into a room where they abode some time, and heard the Vicar and Constable threaten the master of the house with the stocks and although they had no warrant yet they attempted to carry him forcibly away.[1]

Taking up the narrative at this point, Seymour adds that when the householder demanded to know on what authority he was being threatened, the constable at last conceded that he had no warrant and let him go. But by this time the frightened congregation had dispersed. The vicar and the constable then tried to insist that Ingham and Grimshaw should sign an undertaking that they would not preach in Colne again.

When it was understood that Mr Grimshaw, Mr Ingham and Mr Batty refused to comply with any terms, they were violently dragged along the road, the mob flourishing their clubs over their heads, menacing and annoying. They were pelted with mud and dirt, and Mr Ingham's coat torn, and hanging on the ground; thus they were conducted to the Swan Inn, to remain there until dismissed at Mr White's pleasure.[2]

This experience, unnerving in itself, was only a prelude of worse

[1]Batty, 'History', p. 15.
[2]Seymour, *Countess of Huntingdon*, vol. 1, p. 261.

to come. But for a few months all appeared quiet. The local clergy, however, angry at Grimshaw's popularity and his increasing incursions into their parishes tried another method of curbing his activities. In May 1747 Thomas Herring, who had been Archbishop of York since 1743, was promoted to the See of Canterbury. Herring was known to be a moderate and a friend of Methodism, provided it did not take too extreme a form. He had been well-disposed towards Grimshaw, particularly after the latter proved himself Herring's loyal supporter in his stand against the Young Pretender, during the second Jacobite Rebellion of 1745. This made it unlikely that Herring would impeach Grimshaw if any complaints were lodged against him. However, a change was at hand, for in November 1747, the very period when Grimshaw's preaching tours began in earnest, Matthew Hutton was consecrated in York Minster. Now Grimshaw's opponents had the opportunity to air their grievances and put an end to those intrusions into their parishes which had evoked their animosity.

In May 1748, only six months later, Grimshaw was called to account for himself at Wakefield parish church. Remembering full well that his friend Benjamin Ingham had been deprived of his regular ministry in similar circumstances and at the same church, Grimshaw knew he faced the prospect of a comparable outcome. An extract from the interrogation has been preserved, and is one of the better-known anecdotes told of the curate of Haworth.

Hutton: How many communicants had you at your quarterly sacraments, when you first came to Haworth?
Grimshaw: Twelve, my Lord.
Hutton: How many have you now at such solemnities?
Grimshaw: In the winter, four to five hundred, and sometimes in the summer near twelve hundred.
Hutton: We cannot find fault with Mr Grimshaw, as he is instrumental in bringing such numbers to the Lord's Table.

Unable to find fault with Grimshaw on this front, his accusers, prominent among whom was his own vicar Benjamin Kennet, laid a further charge – that of preaching in licensed meeting houses. Under the Toleration Act of 1689, Dissenters were allowed freedom of worship, but all their meeting houses had to carry a licence. Without such a licence they could claim no legal protection but the early Methodists had not yet begun to license their places of worship at this time, preferring the risk of mob violence to being labelled Dissenters. So it was that this second charge could not be substantiated either, though Grimshaw undertook that he would take care never to preach in any building that carried a licence.[1]

But Methodism had an implacable adversary in George White, the 'vicar' of Colne, a courtesy title only for Colne was a chapelry like Haworth. A town growing in importance both in size and industry with a population of three thousand, Colne had become an attractive centre for early Methodist preaching. Benjamin Ingham had evangelised there in 1743 and William Darney had gathered together a society in 1746. When William Grimshaw also began visiting the town that year, White's patience snapped. Not that he was a diligent parish priest himself – far from it, he was notorious for his absenteeism. On one occasion he is said to have read through the burial service twenty times in one night over each of the dead bodies interred during one of his frequent absences.

A Durham boy who had trained for the Roman Catholic ministry in Douai, France, White had soon abandoned his earlier beliefs

[1]Commenting on this question twelve years later in a letter to Charles Wesley, on 31 March 1761, Grimshaw wrote: 'About twelve years ago when Archbishop Hutton was Archbishop of York, amongst other arguments to stop me preaching abroad, he made this one – that I had preached in a licensed meeting house (meaning the Boggart-house at Leeds). And if his Grace could have proved it, (as he upon inquiry into the thing, could not), it is not improbable that he had suspended me. I promised his Grace at that time, that I never would, (though determined to preach abroad) preach in a licensed house; no, nor even in that at Leeds if it should appear to be licensed.' [Boggart House was then the Leeds centre for Methodism]. Cited by Thomas Jackson, *The Life of the Rev. Charles Wesley M.A.* vol. 2 (London: Mason, 1841), p. 190.

and had been accepted into the Anglican communion, Colne being his first appointment. A man of some literary ability, he had squandered his gifts by his addiction to drink and had already served a prison sentence for the debts this habit had incurred. It was to lead to his premature death three years after these events.

In July 1748 this unworthy cleric determined to make another attempt to eliminate Methodism in his parish. His first stratagem was to deliver a sermon on 24 July denouncing these gospel preachers. Basing his harangue on 1 Corinthians 14:33, 'For God is not the author of confusion, but of peace', he tried to prove that such men as Grimshaw, Darney and Benjamin Ingham were 'schismatic rebels' and 'authors of confusion and open destroyers of public peace'. He touched on a theme likely to incite his worldly-minded hearers into action when he insinuated that by mid-week preaching these men were 'causing a visible ruin to your trade and manufacture'. Accusing Methodist preachers of being 'a weak illiterate crowd', White enquired disdainfully, 'Is every bold visionary rustic to be a guide in matters of the highest importance?'[1]

Following this inflammatory sermon, White called for an 'army' of protesters, encouraging men 'to enlist in his majesty's service, under the command of the Rev. Mr George White, Commander-in-Chief . . . for the defence of the Church of England'. All White's 'soldiers' were to gather at the Market Cross at an appointed time where they would be suitably laced with alcohol to inflame their passions. 'Each shall receive a pint of ale advance and other proper encouragements,'[2] promised the vicar.

When John Wesley next visited Haworth in August 1748, he came into a potentially explosive situation. But persecution was no new thing for this intrepid servant of Jesus Christ. He had left Newcastle on 16 August together with Grace Murray, the widow to whom he was engaged, and William Mackford, an itinerant preacher. Arriving at Halifax on 22 August, Wesley had

[1]*Sermon by George White* (Preston, 1748), pp. 11–12.
[2]Batty, 'History', p. 23.

attempted to preach in the centre of the town, but was jostled, covered with dirt thrown at him by the mob, and eventually suffered a deep cut on the cheek from a sharp stone. Only then did he lead his hearers out to a meadow beyond the town where he continued without interruption. Reaching Haworth on 24 August, after first preaching at Keighley on the way, he and his fellow travellers were no doubt grateful for the comforts of Grimshaw's hospitable home after the harassment they had suffered. Crowds soon began to gather as news of Wesley's arrival spread around and he preached in the church at five that evening 'to more than the church could contain'. At five o'clock the following morning he again addressed the people – this early hour was chosen to enable his hearers to attend and also be at their places of employment on time.

After this morning service Wesley and Grimshaw decided to visit Roughlee, just three miles from Colne, in order to encourage members of William Darney's society there. They knew well it would be a hazardous attempt, for two weeks earlier William Batty had again been mobbed near Colne and the angry vicar had then declared, 'I vow to God before they preach in my parish I'll sacrifice ye last drop of blood to root them out.'

But despite this threat, they set out accompanied by Grace Murray and Mackford. They had not gone far before they were met by friends who urged them to proceed no further. They reported that an unruly and drunken rabble was approaching the village from the Colne direction, armed with clubs and any other menacing implements they could find. Even this did not deter Wesley. He knew the risk and was not intimidated. But he commented in his journal as he described that day's events, 'I was a little afraid for Mr Grimshaw, but it needed not; he was ready to go to prison or death for Christ's sake.'[1]

So instead they all urged their horses onwards, planning to reach Roughlee ahead of the mob. Wesley proposed to exhort the people briefly, for he knew they would be expectantly awaiting his

[1]John Wesley's *Journal*, vol. III, p. 369.

arrival, and then set off back to Haworth. In this way he hoped to
avoid a riot, and deprive the rabble of any opportunity to molest
them. All seemed peaceful when they arrived at Roughlee. There
they were joined by Thomas Colbeck from Keighley and William
Batty who had made Roughlee his home since May 1747. Then
Wesley began addressing the gathered crowd. But before he
had been speaking long, the agitated horde of protesters came
swarming down the nearby hill and soon surrounded the company. Headed by the deputy-constable, the rioters interrupted the
service and insisted that Wesley accompany them to Barrowford,
two miles distant, to appear before the constable of Barrowford.
Wesley consented, but this did not deter one man from striking
him across the face, while another hit him over the head with
a stick, and a third brandished his club at him with menacing
gestures.

Grimshaw, Colbeck and Batty followed Wesley, but before
doing so Grimshaw crossed over to Grace Murray, who would
obviously be distressed, and said kindly, 'Sister Murray, I will
have you stay here. We will go and see the end.' Mrs Murray
replied, 'I will do as you think proper,' and for the next two or
three hours she and some of the believers in Roughlee spent the
time in prayer.

Wesley was conducted along the road to Barrowford, led all the
way by a drummer beating on his drum in order to inflame the
mood of the rabble yet more. At last they reached the White Bear
Inn where the local constable, James Hargrave, was waiting. In a
letter of complaint written to Hargrave after these events, Wesley
himself continues the story:

When your deputy had brought me into the house, he permitted Mr
Grimshaw, the minister of Haworth, Mr Colbeck of Keighley and one
more [Batty] to be with me promising that none should hurt them.
Soon after you and your friends came in and required me to promise I
would come to Roughlee no more. I told you I would sooner cut off my
hand than make any such promise, neither would I promise that none
of my friends should come.[1]

[1]Ibid., vol. III, pp. 370-1.

At this the constable's men, no doubt also encouraged by George White, set upon him again, knocking him to the ground. When Wesley regained his feet, he tried to reason with his antagonists for almost two hours. But it was little use:

After abundance of rambling discourse (for I could keep none of you long to any one point) from about one o'clock to between three and four, . . . you seemed a little satisfied with my saying, 'I will not preach at Roughlee at this time.' You then undertook to quieten the mob.

As Wesley, accompanied by the constable, left the inn by the front door, Grimshaw and Colbeck slipped out the back. But they were noticed:

The mob immediately closed them in, tossed them to and fro with the utmost violence, threw Mr Grimshaw down and loaded them both with dirt and mire of every kind, not one of your friends offering to call off your blood-hounds from the pursuit.

When Grimshaw, whose hefty physique was a match for most men, had shaken off his attackers he saw a group of White's men kicking Colbeck as he lay on the ground. Tackling his way through the crowd to defend him, he shouted to the younger man, 'Get out of the way, Tommy, with thy spindle-shanks, let them kick me!' In the event both men were sorely bedraggled by the fracas and Grimshaw lost his wig.

Not content with manhandling the preachers, the angry rabble turned mercilessly on those who had been attending the meeting. William Mackford was severely mauled, while many others were beaten with clubs, and dragged along the ground by the hair, regardless of whether they were men or women. As the people fled, the mob followed them. The road from Roughlee to Barrowford runs parallel to a river flowing in a deep gully some twelve feet below the level of the road. In Barrowford one man was forced to leap from a rock into the water far below or he would have been tossed in headlong. When he dragged himself out, wet and bruised, it was with difficulty that bystanders prevented him from being flung in again. 'All this time,' added

Wesley to Hargrave, 'you sat well pleased close to the place, not attempting in the least to hinder them.'[1]

At last the battered little party turned their horses back towards Haworth, although even as they rode along they could see threatening bands of men waiting for them on the hills. Quickening their pace, they managed to arrive back without further harm. Undaunted by his experiences, Grimshaw was at Wesley's side as the Methodist leader preached at nearby Heptonstall the following evening. But it was a striking contrast with the experiences of the previous day: 'The calmness of the evening agreed well with the seriousness of the people, everyone of whom seemed to drink in the word of God as a thirsty land the refreshing showers.'[2]

John Wesley subsequently wrote his letter of protest to the constable – a step he rarely took – because the sufferings of his companions had grieved him: 'Proceed against us by the law,' he challenged, 'if you can or dare; but not by lawless violence, not by making a drunken, cursing, swearing, riotous mob both judge, jury and executioner. This is flat rebellion against God and the king, as you may possibly find to your cost.' This was a veiled hint that he intended to take legal action against the callous men who had ill-treated the people in this way. This he did; but little justice could be found for the despised Methodists, and the case eventually fizzled out, owing in part to the death of Wesley's principal legal adviser, William Glanville.

Before John Wesley left Haworth after the Roughlee riots, Grimshaw consulted him over the education of his children. John was now twelve and Jane eleven years of age, and, since the death of their stepmother two years earlier, they had been living at Ewood once more with their grandparents, John and Mary

---

[1]It was originally assumed that this letter was addressed to George White, (see *Journal* vol. III, p. 370), but a reference in the MS diary of John Bennet (who was also present on the occasion) makes it clear that it was addressed to James Hargrave, constable of Barrowford. See John Wesley's *Letters*, vol. II, p. 152f.

[2]John Wesley's *Journal*, vol. III, p. 371.

Lockwood. Grimshaw himself spent as much time as he could at Ewood to be with them, but it was twelve miles from Haworth and the arrangement was unsatisfactory. Apart from their education, their father would also have been concerned for the children's spiritual welfare. Jane gave every evidence of a heart tender towards God, but with John he had no such consolation. Perhaps the traits of character which were to cause Grimshaw much distress in later years were already becoming apparent. So he decided to send them to Wesley's Kingswood School in Bristol. As their names appear in the registers for 1748, in all probability they travelled south with Wesley, arriving in Bristol in mid-September.

With John Wesley gone and his children far away, William Grimshaw had one special consolation in September 1748 – his first visit from George Whitefield. Much had happened in Haworth since Whitefield had sailed for America in August 1744. Doubtless through his regular correspondence with the homeland and his friendship with both Ingham and the Countess of Huntingdon, Whitefield had heard of the revival that had broken out in West Yorkshire. When he arrived back in London on 6 July 1748 after four years' absence, he lost no time before he began an itinerary of areas of the country where he knew his spiritual children would be eagerly awaiting him. Writing to Benjamin Ingham six weeks after setting foot in England, he records his movements: 'In London, Bristol, Gloucester and Wales, the glorious Emmanuel since my arrival has appeared to his people.' He then informed Ingham of his proposed travels further afield. 'In about a fortnight I purpose leaving town again, in order to go on a circuit of about five hundred miles.'[1] He was not certain whether he would be able to see Ingham, but in the event he called at Aberford, on his way to Scotland. William Batty wrote in his journal: 'George Whitefield made a visit to B.

[1] Letter from George Whitefield to Ingham, 11 August 1748, cited by Tyerman, *Oxford Methodists,* p. 131.

Ingham; they were hearty together and spoke about accommodating matters with Jn. Wesley.'[1]

None of Whitefield's biographers mention that he also visited William Grimshaw that September in 1748 and preached in Haworth, but Whitefield himself noted the fact in an unpublished journal, probably the one from which John Gillies quotes extensively in his *Memoirs of the Life of the Rev. George Whitefield*.[2] William Myles may also have had access to it when working on his biography of Grimshaw, for he records that Mr Whitefield wrote 'in his Journal':

In September, 1748, I visited Mr Grimshaw at Haworth. In the parish church where this venerable apostle constantly laboured, I administered the Lord's Supper to upwards of a thousand communicants, and preached in the church-yard to six thousand hearers.[3]

In William Batty's account in his 'Church History' there is a suggestion that he and Ingham may well have accompanied Whitefield from Aberford to Haworth. It is more than likely that these men would have discussed the recent riots in Roughlee and Colne and the suffering that the believers in the area were enduring. Perhaps they had heard that George White planned to publish the vitriolic sermon he had preached against the Methodists in July, and were considering what their response should be.

White published his sermon in November 1748 and Ingham wrote to Whitefield suggesting that he should come to the defence of the maligned Methodists and prepare an answer for the press. On 17 March 1749 Whitefield wrote to Grimshaw declining this invitation, in the first of only two letters from Whitefield to Grimshaw which have been preserved. Its warm

[1]Batty, 'History', p. 28.

[2]This journal may well be a continuation of the unpublished journal of Whitefield's journey home from New England *via* the Bermudas from March to July 1748. John Gillies, *Life of Whitefield* (London: 1772), pp. 154–73. The journal is now apparently lost. See comments by Iain H. Murray in preface to *George Whitefield's Journals* (Edinburgh: Banner of Truth Trust, 1960), pp. 14–16.

[3]Myles, *Life and Writings*, p. 37.

tone clearly indicates the friendship already established between them:

What a blessed thing it is, that we can write when we cannot see each other! By this means we increase our joys and lessen our sorrows, and as it were exchange hearts. Thanks be to the Lord Jesus Christ that the work flourishes with you. I am glad your children grow fast; they become fathers soon; I wish some may not prove dwarfs at last. A word to the wise is sufficient. I have always found awakening times like spring times. Many blossoms but not always so much fruit. But go on, my dear man, and in the strength of the Lord you shall do valiantly. I long to be your way, but I suppose it will be two months first . . . . Please tell dear Mr Ingham that I cannot now answer the *Preston* letter, [George White's sermon, published in Preston] being engaged in answering a virulent pamphlet, entitled, *The Enthusiasm of the Methodist and Papist Compared*. Thus it must be, If we will be temple builders, we must have temple builders' lot; I mean hold a sword in one hand and a trowel in the other. The Lord make us faithful *Nehemiahs,* for we have many *Sanballats* to deal with! but wherefore should we fear? If Christ be for us, who can be against us . . . My dear brother, good night. May the Lord Jesus be with your spirit and make you wise to win souls, even as wise as an angel of God![1]

Grimshaw himself then determined to answer the delinquent cleric's attacks on the Methodist preachers. His aim was to dispel the widespread misunderstanding among the people about Methodism and to paint the contrast between the conscientious and self-sacrificing Methodist preachers and the irresponsible behaviour of such churchmen as George White. The result was an octavo book of ninety-eight pages which he published later in 1749, ironically enough using the same printers as the vicar of Colne, Stanley and Moon of Preston. This treatise in defence of Methodism was the only piece of Grimshaw's work to be published in his lifetime. Before the recovery of the manuscripts already mentioned, it had been assumed that this was the only thing Grimshaw had written.

---

[1]Whitefield's *Works*, vol. II (London: 1771), p. 246.

William Myles, who published a biography of Grimshaw in 1806, devoted over half his book to a reprint of the work. Entitled *An Answer to a sermon lately published against the Methodists by the Rev. Mr George White, M.A.,* Grimshaw assigned a third of it to delineating Methodist beliefs and practices that he might dispel any notion that they held unorthodox views. With constant references to the Scriptures, and to the Articles and Homilies of the Church of England, he set forth the main tenets of Methodist belief, which also formed a succinct summary of his own beliefs.

As he had been delivered after a long and painful search from the futile attempt to win the favour of God by his own morality, it is not surprising that Grimshaw should include statements which demonstrate the total corruption and bondage of man's will since the fall, and his inability to contribute in any way to his own salvation:

What a dangerous mistake those people are under, who believe and are taught as the *modern language* of but too many of *our pulpits*, that *conversion* is nothing more than a turning from a *bad* to a *good* life, and that if they do their best, striving to *live as well as they can*, the Lord will forgive their sins and save their souls. This notion or doctrine . . . is utterly contrary to the Holy Bible, 39 Articles, Catechism and Liturgy of the Church of England, and the *principles of our dissenting brethren.*

Referring to such teaching as 'this free-will merit mongering heresy', Grimshaw states,

I refuse not to declare it to be my own opinion that this doctrine of the devil has well-nigh filled all the churches in the nation within these few years . . . God who would not have the death of sinners nor the kingdom and gospel of his dear Son to be totally abolished amongst us, raised up the Methodists on purpose to reclaim and preach up the same, to restore the church to her primitive purity and revive her Homilies and Articles out of the dust, and to purge her of that epidemical vice and wickedness which is everywhere observable where free-will heresy prevaileth.[1]

[1]Myles, *Life and Writings,* p. 88.

Having set out the Methodist principles at length, and touched on every aspect of the scriptural doctrines of salvation through the merits and death of the Son of God, Grimshaw then attacked the errant vicar of Colne both with sarcasm and scorn. These faithful Methodist preachers, he pointed out, had been caring for White's neglected flock 'night and day . . . without a penny from your purse whilst you boarded at Chester Castle' (i.e., in prison because of debts incurred from excessive drinking). He then pressed home his attack, deprecating the vicar's 'late riotous conduct, heading a lawless rabble of irreligious dissolute wretches, under the name and title of Commander-in-Chief, spiriting them up to the perpetration of many grievous outrages and inhumanely treating and abusing numbers of poor inoffensive people'.[1]

Grimshaw's *Answer* was more than a match for the vicar of Colne. Luke Tyerman commented, 'The one [White] was a braggadocio, the other [Grimshaw] was a giant; and with a giant's knotted club, he belabours the pompous priest with anything but the gentleness of a carpet knight.'[2] The work never became popular reading, but one of its lasting values is found in its description of Methodism:

Methodism, so called by way of reproach, is a complete system of gospel-truths, and a perfect summary of reformation-principles . . . Notwithstanding the general opposition made to it on all sides, it daily gains ground. Its progress, considering how few years it is since its first appearance, is surprisingly extensive. It has all the marks and indications of a divine work. It ascribes the total of man's salvation to the mere free grace of God, the sole merits of Christ and the operation of the Holy Ghost. It makes faith the instrument, Jesus's blood the cause, and the Spirit the discoverer of our justification. It attributes our sanctification to this heavenly paraclete . . . It is everywhere spoken against.[3]

[1] Ibid., p. 113.

[2] L. Tyerman, *The Life and Times of John Wesley,* vol. 2 (London: Hodder and Stoughton, 1880), p. 17.

[3] Myles, *Life and Writings,* p. 148.

George White himself soon returned to his alcohol, dying in 1751 after another period of imprisonment for debt. But there is a tradition, mentioned by John Newton, that when he faced his last extremity and death seemed imminent, it was William Grimshaw that he sent for to come to his aid.

13

ANECDOTES FROM HAWORTH DAYS

MOST GREAT MEN HAVE SUFFERED at the hand of the anecdotalist. For some, their admirers have so inflated their gifts that they have appeared more than human, while for others, detractors have destroyed their reputation by exaggerating their misdemeanours; and for all, recollections passed on by word of mouth have become distorted in the retelling, until it is hard to distinguish between truth and fiction.

William Grimshaw has suffered more from his detractors than from his admirers. The existence of popular legends and mis-representations about him is perhaps one reason why he has not enjoyed the respect and interest of Christians, concerned to learn of their spiritual heritage. To call him 'Mad Grimshaw', a label coined in derision to describe not only Grimshaw but any whose preaching demanded a heart response, was scarcely damaging. But to assert, as did Robert Southey, that he actually suffered bouts of insanity in his unregenerate days;[1] or to state, like J. H. Overton, a usually reliable historian, that he was 'eccentric to the very verge of insanity'[2] is surely irresponsible, for no evidence

[1] Robert Southey, *Life of Wesley*, vol. 2 (London: Longmans, 1846), p. 263.
[2] J. H. Overton, *The Evangelical Revival of the Eighteenth Century* (London: Longmans, Green & Co., 1891), p. 60. Overton expresses a modified view in *The English Church in the Eighteenth Century* where he says 'The eccentricities of "Mad Grimshaw" have probably been exaggerated; for one knows how when a man acquires a reputation of this sort every ridiculous

whatever exists to support such assertions. None of his contemporaries, who worked together with him in the revival, have left any comment which might suggest that he was regarded as an eccentric.

Less serious, but also damaging, is an anecdote about Grimshaw which arose from the common practice of the day for churchwardens to leave the church during the singing of the psalm before the sermon, in order to round up any who were loitering in the streets or taverns, and escort them into the church.[1] Church attendance was still compulsory by law[2] and taverns were illegally open during church service hours, though both laws were generally ignored. Grimshaw, however, could not always rely on his churchwardens to do their duty.

A colourful anecdote has survived that illustrates just such a situation. It was told by John Dean, who lived near Colne and described himself as 'an ear and eye witness'. On this occasion in 1759, Grimshaw sent two of his churchwardens to check up on parishioners idling their time away in the public houses. A long time seemed to elapse and yet they had not reappeared; the psalm was over and the people were waiting. Grimshaw himself then left the lectern and walked out of the church in search of his church-wardens. An uneasy whispering broke out in the congregation as the people speculated about what might have happened. At last there came the sound of heavy footsteps approaching, and a rustling in the porch. In came the churchwardens, 'bearing the insignia of their office, but moving onwards with reluctant step and downcast looks like criminals on their way to the bar in a court of justice'. Immediately behind them came Grimshaw who boomed 'in a voice sufficiently stentorian to reverberate through the remotest corners of the church: "For shame! for shame! What think you! The churchwardens who went out to detect others and

---

story which happens to be current is apt to be fathered on him.' vol. II (London: Longmans, Green & Co., 1878), p. 176.

[1]Hardy, *Incumbent*, p. 58.

[2]This remained the case until 1830.

prevent them from sinning, I have found in the inn drinking a pint of ale! For shame! For shame! For shame!'" These last words were uttered at intervals as he mounted the steps to his pulpit.[1]

As the result of such an incident it is likely that Grimshaw felt obliged to check the streets and public houses himself, for Newton, writing almost forty years later, has left this description:

It was his frequent and almost constant custom to leave the church, while the psalm before the sermon was singing, to see if any were absent from worship, and idling their time in the churchyard, the street, or the ale-houses, and many of those whom he so found, he would drive into the church before him.

This story, undoubtedly true, must be set against the background both of the times, which were turbulent and often lawless, and also of the customs of the day. But exaggerations and fictitious details have been added to Newton's account which Spence Hardy, writing in 1861, mentions in his biography of Grimshaw, though only to dismiss as 'probably a piece of irony or a myth'.[2] These included the singing of Psalm 119 to allow Grimshaw plenty of time to tour the three taverns close to the church and the use of a horsewhip to drive his parishioners into worship.

These embellishments, which have been included in most subsequent biographies of Grimshaw, can be traced directly to the novelist Mrs Elizabeth Gaskell, who introduced them into her popular *Life of Charlotte Brontë*, published in 1857. May Sinclair, in a preface to the *Everyman's Library* edition of this book, commented concerning Mrs Gaskell, 'She was not always careful to sift the evidence before her. She jumped to conclusions.' More of a novelist than a biographer, Mrs Gaskell would enliven her narrative with hearsay accounts which she had

---

[1]Everett, 'Curate of Haworth'. Grimshaw was not a teetotaller. His anger was directed in this instance against the sin of hypocrisy.

[2]Hardy, *Incumbent,* p. 58.

not taken care to verify, and add details created by her fertile imagination. May Sinclair continues by questioning 'whether a novelist is the best biographer, for a biographer must be the humble servant of facts.'[1]

As she paints the background to Charlotte Brontë's life and attempts to show the influences that moulded her thinking, Mrs Gaskell provides a brief description of Grimshaw. She then adds: 'He sometimes gave out a very long psalm (tradition says the 119th), and while it was being sung, he left the reading desk, and taking a horsewhip, went into the public houses and flogged the loiterers into church. They were swift who could escape the lash of the parson by sneaking out some back way.' Elaborating further, she refers again to 'good Mr Grimshaw's stout arm and ready horsewhip'.[2]

Neither William Myles, writing in 1806, nor James Everett, who took painstaking efforts to gather together all local traditions for his biography, mentions this use of a horsewhip. In her recently published definitive work on the Brontë family, one of Juliet Barker's primary aims has been to expose the myths behind some of the long-cherished traditions concerning the Brontë sisters which were first circulated by Mrs Gaskell in her biography of Charlotte Brontë. But she also seeks to correct the damaging comments contained in the book about Patrick Brontë, Charlotte's father. Mrs Barker reveals that far from being an austere, bigoted and unreasonable man, as Mrs Gaskell represents him, he was a warm evangelical Christian, a friend of Charles Simeon and also of members of the Clapham Sect. If Mrs Gaskell could so misrepresent facts concerning a man she had not only met but who she knew would actually read her work, it is not hard to imagine that she could yet more readily add imaginative details when there was none to correct the record.[3]

[1] Mrs Gaskell, *Life of Charlotte Brontë* (London: Dent, Everyman's Library, 1966), Preface.

[2] Mrs Gaskell, op. cit., pp. 16, 17.

[3] Juliet Barker, *The Brontës* (London: Weidenfeld and Nicolson, 1994). It is a pity that while correcting the myths introduced by Mrs Gaskell concerning

With the high prestige 'the parson' enjoyed at that time, Grimshaw's mere appearance on the scene would be enough to produce a swift reaction, without any resort to physical force. Newton confirms this, by adding another anecdote immediately after telling of Grimshaw's habit of checking up on the ale-houses. 'A friend of mine,' he narrates, 'passing a public house [in Haworth] on a Lord's day morning, saw several persons making their escape out of it, some jumping out of the lower windows, and some over a low wall. He was at first alarmed, fearing the house was on fire, but upon enquiring what was the cause of the commotion, he was told that they saw the parson coming. They were more afraid of their parson than of a justice of the peace. His reproofs were so authoritative, and yet so mild and friendly, that the stoutest sinners could not stand before him.'[1]

Having cleared Grimshaw of the use of a horsewhip in the above circumstances, we must add that Everett relates an anecdote which may have given rise to Mrs Gaskell's account, for it includes the use of a horsewhip, but on a different occasion. Apparently a group of unruly youths had been taking delight in jostling and assaulting some of Grimshaw's parishioners as they gathered to attend a prayer meeting in a village near Haworth. After the second or third incidence of such harassment, the leader of the meeting reported the situation to Grimshaw, for even the local constable could not be relied on to help the Methodists. Grimshaw replied that if it should happen again, he was to be notified. Once more the same ruffians set upon the people; so on the next occasion, Grimshaw, disguised in a greatcoat, joined the youths. Because it was dark, they did not recognise the burly figure of the curate, as he urged them ever onwards from the back of the group. Gradually he inched the gang nearer and nearer to the lighted doorway of the cottage where the meeting was to be

---

the Brontës, Mrs Barker repeats uncritically the 'horsewhip' story, not realising that this too was a figment of Mrs Gaskell's imagination. See p. 91.

[1]Newton, *Letters*, p. 94.

held. Then with one final heave, he pushed the last young man forward into the confines of the room and slammed the door. Still blinking in the bright light, the youths scarcely realised what was happening when their new companion suddenly produced a horsewhip from under his greatcoat and 'dealt round its utmost virtue on the astonished clowns until his vigorous arm was tired.' Having thoroughly subdued the miscreants, Grimshaw then fell on his knees and pleaded with great earnestness for their souls.[1]

Another anecdote is often told to illustrate the respect which Grimshaw had gained in the parish – a respect not accorded automatically to all Haworth's curates. We read of a man who was riding with all speed to fetch a midwife for his wife who was in labour. It happened to be a Sunday and to his consternation his horse lost a shoe. As time was at a premium, he hastened to the blacksmith to ask him to shoe the animal without delay. 'No, no,' replied the blacksmith, 'I cannot shoe your horse on the Lord's Day, even if you pay me double.' Realising the anxious husband's predicament, the blacksmith agreed to assist the man if the minister gave permission. Together they went to seek out Grimshaw, who, on learning the nature of the case, readily gave consent for the horse to be shod.

When James Everett decided to write a biography of William Grimshaw early in the nineteenth century, he had one major asset of which he took full advantage. He knew that there would be some still alive in Haworth and the surrounding area who would retain clear memories of Grimshaw and whose recollections of his preaching, habits and personal characteristics would lend interest and authority to his work. With this in mind he wrote to many Methodist leaders, lay preachers and Christians requesting help in gathering together such information. In addition, he set off himself to walk around the area and question elderly people he might meet, to piece together a more complete picture of his subject.

Writing when he had almost concluded the work, Everett says,

[1]Everett, 'Curate of Haworth'.

'I visited the place in 1826. And though 60 years had elapsed since his eyes were closed in death, his presence was still visible – his voice audible. He seemed to meet us at every point, like a sword turning every way to guard the way of the tree of life ... Think as you would of the felicity of the people in his being succeeded by pious men [Patrick Brontë was the curate at the time], Grimshaw would again obtrude. Everything bears the imprint of his name, bears the stamp of his character, zeal and labours.'[1] Everett discovered that wherever he went in Haworth, it was the same: 'Stop an aged person, utter the name of Grimshaw – it operates like a charm – the tongue of the dumb is instantly set loose. Introductory tales are rehearsed or early facts of which they were eye or ear witnesses are recounted.'[2]

Among the recollections Everett collected is an account, also told by John Newton, of an old blind woman who lived about two and a half miles from Haworth. She had made 'high sounding professions of superior attainments in religion', but Grimshaw was not convinced that her daily life matched up with her professions. Calling unexpectedly on her on one occasion, Grimshaw found the old woman spinning at the door of her cottage. Instead of speaking, he touched her with his cane. Imagining it was some mischievous lad, the old woman remonstrated loudly. Grimshaw touched her again and then again. Unable to contain herself any longer, the old woman jumped up and 'swore by Him who made her that she would knock him down'. Upon this display of anger and blasphemy, Grimshaw revealed his identity and rebuked her for hypocrisy.[3]

Another anecdote involving an old woman reveals Grimshaw's determination to buy up every opportunity to bring the gospel to his parishioners. Meeting her on the moors as he rode along on one occasion, he asked her whether she had ever heard a gospel sermon preached. 'No,' replied the woman, she had not. 'If you have never heard one before, you shall hear one now', was

---

[1]JEN. [2]Ibid.
[3]Newton, *Letters*, p. 100. Everett dates this incident in 1749.

Grimshaw's prompt reply, as he exhorted her to faith and repentance.[1] And yet another similar anecdote demonstrates his kindliness. Overtaking the stooped figure of an old woman as he crossed the moors to Colne, he reined his horse to a halt and asked her where she was going. 'To Colne, to hear Grimshaw,' came the reply. When he commented on her infirmities, which made her progress slow and painful, she replied that her soul was there already and she was determined to make her body follow. At this Grimshaw offered to take her behind him on his horse, and we can imagine her surprise when she arrived and discovered his identity.[2]

As little was written on Grimshaw until many years after his death, the reliability of any anecdote can never be finally ascertained. The only criterion we have by which we may judge a story, narrated after so great a lapse of time, is its compatibility with all we know of the general character of Grimshaw himself. An anecdote which can easily be credited is included by Spence Hardy, but told in greater detail by Everett. Again it relates to a cottage prayer meeting held in an area known as The Marsh, about a mile from Haworth. Dating it in 1752, Everett's informant narrates that once again those who attended the meeting on a Sunday evening were being constantly molested by youths. Again the people appealed to Grimshaw. This time he put on an old woman's cap, and peered out stealthily from behind the door of the house where the meeting was being held. Seeing the lace-capped face, the youths began their taunts and jibes. Each time 'she' appeared they grew more daring. At last one youth, bolder than the rest, declared, 'If that woman puts her head out again, I will seize her.' The next time the lace-capped face appeared the youth lunged forward, but found himself held in an iron grip, and struggle as he might, he could not extricate himself. Bringing the offender into the cottage, Grimshaw revealed his identity and soon the young man, whose name was Paul Beaver, was obliged

[1]JEN.   [2]Hardy, *Incumbent*, p. 224.

to reveal the names of his companions and all the gang were required to appear at the church the following day to ask for pardon. After that there was no more trouble.[1]

One of the local pastimes, which had become an occasion for much evil, proved beyond even Grimshaw's powers of rebuke – it was the Haworth Wakes. Held twice a year, these occasions included stalls for the sale of small items and the auctioning of cattle. But a steady deterioration had taken place, and in Grimshaw's day they were largely given over to horse-racing on the moorland plateau above Haworth known as Penistone Flats. Small bets and gambling were the order of the day. This was in contravention of an Act of Parliament in 1740, aimed at controlling such events by legalising only those races which carried prizes of £50 [over a year's salary for most] or more. The Haworth Wakes were therefore illegal and Newton describes the scenes which took place on these occasions as 'exhibiting the grossest and most vulgar riot, profligacy and confusion'.[2]

Repeatedly Grimshaw warned, pleaded, and remonstrated against such practices within the confines of his parish. His prestige, due partly to his position as curate, was so high that the propagators of these events listened politely, whereas a less respected man might have been rough-handled for such interference. But still they persisted with their customary arrangements. At last Grimshaw resorted to the only power which none could withstand – the power of prayer. Earnestly he sought God that he would intervene and put an end to the Wakes. He may have feared his prayers were unanswered, for as the time for the races came round, all the people assembled as was their custom. But before they could begin, threatening black clouds began to darken the sky. Then torrential rain cascaded down, sending the contestants scurrying through the downpour muttering, 'This man has power with God.' Not for one hour, or even for one day, but throughout the entire three-day period of the races, the rain

---

[1] Ibid. and JEN.   [2] Newton, *Letters*, p. 103.

poured down relentlessly, washing out the entire event. 'Old
Grimshaw has put a stop to the races by his prayers,' the organis-
ers complained sorrowfully. Forty years later this dramatic event
was still remembered and spoken of in Haworth.[1]

A final anecdote, again recorded by both Hardy and Everett,
must be included. Grimshaw owned a cow at one time; she was a
fine animal, without a trace of a cattle disease which blighted
some of the Yorkshire herds during Grimshaw's later years in
Haworth. Doubtless she kept the household at Sowdens supplied
with milk and butter – so that Grimshaw could have his favourite
dish: onions boiled in milk. But gradually he discovered that the
natural pride and affection he felt for his cow was turning into an
obsession. In fact, thoughts of his cow filled his mind when he
tried to pray. Even worse, he realised to his alarm that when he
went up into his pulpit to preach, the animal was still in the back
of his mind.

There seemed only one solution to the problem: he must sell
his cow. When a would-be purchaser came to look at Grimshaw's
cow, he inspected her carefully. She seemed an excellent beast; so
why should Grimshaw wish to sell her? Perhaps she had some
hidden defect. So he began to question Grimshaw closely. 'Ah,'
said Grimshaw sadly, 'her fault, which is a fault to me, will be no
fault to you. She follows me into the pulpit.' And so the cow was
sold. Grimshaw had demonstrated that he understood the true
meaning of Christ's words, 'If your right hand offend you, cut it
off.'

Numerous other anecdotes circulated about the ebullient curate
of Haworth – some credible enough, but others improbable, at
least in the form in which they have survived. Many to whom
Everett wrote asking for information about Grimshaw replied,
adding further accounts of his activities during his twenty-one
years in Haworth. Everett sifted through the material and selected

[1]The meterological journal of the *Gentleman's Magazine* for 1759 records
unusually heavy rainfall in the north of England from 12–17 October 1759.
This would have been the time when the Haworth races were normally held.
Cited by Baker, *Grimshaw*, p. 214.

some recollections for inclusion in his biography others he rejected, clearly realising that they had either become distorted by time or had originated from those who resented the spiritual disciplines that the revival brought to Haworth. Here and in other places we have included some of the more reliable anecdotes that have survived of William Grimshaw's ministry and characteristics.

14

DAYS OF THE SON OF MAN

FROM 1748 ONWARDS GEORGE WHITEFIELD took every opportunity he could to visit Haworth. In his letter to William Grimshaw, on 17 March 1749, he had said, 'I long to be your way, but I suppose it will be two months first.' In the event it was September before he was able to fulfil this desire, but the occasion was memorable, even to Whitefield who was accustomed to witnessing great crowds gathered to hear him preach. Writing to a friend after his visit to Yorkshire, which had included a visit to Benjamin Ingham, he says, 'I preached four times at Aberford, four times at Leeds and thrice at Haworth, where lives one Mr Grimshaw. At his church I believe we had above a thousand communicants, and in the churchyard above six thousand hearers. It was a great day of the Son of Man.'[1] Describing the same occasion to the Countess of Huntingdon, Whitefield wrote, 'Never did I see more of the hand of God in any of my journeys than this. At Mr Grimshaw's I believe there were above six thousand hearers. The sacramental occasion was most awful [awesome].'[2]

A brief glance back to the twelve communicants whom Grimshaw had discovered in Haworth when he first began his ministry seven years earlier, highlights the contrast which the

[1]Whitefield to Captain W—, *Works* vol. 2 (London: 1771), p. 282.
[2]Luke Tyerman, *The Life of George Whitefield,* vol. 2 (London: Hodder and Stoughton, 1876), p. 234.

revival had brought. By 1743, the number of communicants had grown to fifty or sixty, as Grimshaw had informed Archbishop Herring, but by 1748, as we have seen, he could report to Archbishop Hutton that twelve hundred were attending the communion services – a number which confirms Whitefield's estimate.

In 1743 Grimshaw had given a somewhat unworkable undertaking to Archbishop Herring that he would endeavour to stop administering the sacraments to communicants from other parishes. This was in compliance with the twenty-eighth Canon Law of the Church which required all worshippers to be 'sent home to their own parish churches and ministers, there to receive communion with their own neighbours'. Clearly such a commitment was impracticable in the situation in which Grimshaw found himself and he, in common with other early Methodists, eventually waived this regulation and welcomed all to join with his own parishioners on these occasions.

Each month, and sometimes more frequently, these communion services were held,[1] and normally Grimshaw himself would preach unless either of the Wesley brothers or George Whitefield were in the area. The Church of England parish system, exercising little discipline over the spiritual credentials of those who partook of the Lord's Supper, contributed to the large number of communicants, for, according to its twenty-sixth Canon Law, no one was to be excluded except 'notorious offenders' and 'schismatics'. But the effect of the revival and the searching nature of Grimshaw's preaching minimised the likelihood of unconverted people partaking. So much was this the case that John Wesley, commenting on the numbers attending the communion services, stated that 'there was scarce a trifler among them'. Grimshaw's own high regard for such services formed another safeguard against 'triflers'. Henry Venn, in his comments on Grimshaw, asked rhetorically, 'Which of you ever received with

[1]Grimshaw's 'Diary' shows evidence of communion services most Sundays during certain periods. ·

him the Holy Communion without perceiving it was an exquisite feast of joy to his own soul?'[1]

William Myles has preserved for us further details of the way in which Grimshaw conducted these services. Not content with merely using the set form of words provided in the *Book of Common Prayer*, Grimshaw often 'broke out in the most lively, pious and animating exhortations and enlivened the whole service with hymns suited to the occasion so that the people enjoyed a heaven upon earth and returned to their habitations blessing and praising the Lord for his mercy and love'.[2] Little wonder they delighted to be there. Mrs Joseph Jones, who spent six months convalescing at Sowdens, also described these occasions: 'At the sacrament, in singing the psalm or hymn, his voice has been so raised, it seemed more than mortal . . . There has scarce been a dry eye among the communicants; whose number was seldom short of a thousand.'[3]

Unlike the open-air Communion Seasons to which Whitefield had become accustomed on his visits to Scotland, these services were held within the church itself. Beginning at 9 o'clock in the morning, William Grimshaw would conduct the first service. When the building was filled to capacity, there would be preaching and singing followed by a first administration of the Lord's Supper. At the conclusion the worshippers would file out of the church and others would take their place. The second service then began. Sometimes the church would be filled with communicants three or even four times over. But this did not mean that the earlier congregations had returned to their homes – far from it, the joys and fellowship of the day had only just begun. If a visiting preacher were present, he would address the thousands who thronged the graveyard from some gravestone or vantage point outside the church.

After his visit to Haworth and the surrounding areas in September 1749, Whitefield travelled on to Newcastle for a brief

---

[1]Venn, Funeral Sermon, p. 12.   [2]Myles, *Life and Writings,* p. 26.
[3]See Laycock, *Heroes,* p. 244.

visit but a week or two later was back in Yorkshire. On 25 October 1749 Whitefield wrote to Lady Fanny Shirley (aunt of the Countess of Huntingdon), from Ewood reporting the blessings that attended his preaching wherever he travelled in the area: 'I have now I think preached about thirty times in Yorkshire . . . Congregations have been very large, and a solid, convincing and comforting influence hath everywhere attended the word.'[1] And to another member of the nobility he reported, 'Will it not rejoice you very much, honoured madam, to hear the glorious Emmanuel is riding on in the chariot of his gospel conquering and to conquer. Every day people flock to hear the word, like doves to their windows. I have preached about thirty times in Yorkshire.'[2]

One evidence of 'the glorious Emmanuel's' conquering power lay in the conversion of Captain and Mrs Gallatin. A naturalised Swiss nobleman, Bartholomew Gallatin was a captain in the English army. He and his wife led an unsettled life as they were constantly on the move. But in 1749 they were quartered in Manchester, where Whitefield preached on his way south once more. They both heard him and Mrs Gallatin was converted. Writing about her to Lady Fanny Shirley, Whitefield reports, 'Mrs Gallatin at Manchester goes on well and is not ashamed to confess him, who I trust has called her out of darkness, and made her partaker of his glorious light.'[3] Captain Gallatin too was deeply affected, as Whitefield later informed the Countess of Huntingdon, 'I conversed for about two hours with the Captain on the nature and necessity of the new birth. He was affected and I hope it was blessed.'[4] But by the following year he was able to write to the Countess of Huntingdon about 'kind Colonel Gallatin', and to say, 'I hope he will prove a good soldier of Jesus Christ.'

A tall woman of striking appearance, Mrs Gallatin (sometimes called Lady Gallatin by her contemporaries), was diffident by

[1]Whitefield, *Works,* p. 285. [2]Ibid., p. 286.
[3]Ibid. [4]Ibid., p. 288.

nature and throughout her life struggled against spiritual fears and lack of assurance, though her conversion was genuine enough. Possibly Grimshaw had accompanied Whitefield to Manchester and had met her in October 1749, but if not he certainly met her the following year, when he began a correspondence with her which he hoped would sustain and steady her in all the changes and uncertainties of her circumstances. When the Captain and his wife were posted to Musselburgh in Scotland late in 1750, they found little to encourage them spiritually in the area where they were stationed, and, as a result of this experience, they invited John Wesley to visit Scotland. This he did for the first time in April 1752.

In June 1750 George Whitefield was back in Yorkshire once more. Anticipating this further visit, William Grimshaw took the step of having two pewter flagons made to contain the extra communion wine that would certainly be needed. These were intended to hold a supply sufficient to refill the silver cup in regular use during the service. Both these flagons may still be seen: one in the vault of York Minster and the other in the Brontë Museum in Haworth. They are twelve inches in height and hold about four pints each. Both flagons have an inscription on the side which breathes the spirit of life and devotion so apparent when they were first brought into use. One carries a stanza from a hymn by Isaac Watts:

> *Blest Jesus, what delicious Fare!*
> *How sweet Thine entertainments are!*
> *Never did Angels taste above*
> *Redeeming Grace or dying Love.*

The other bears all the hallmarks of one of Charles Wesley's verses, but could equally have been composed by Grimshaw himself:

> *In JESUS we live, In JESUS we rest;*
> *And thankful receive HIS dying bequest;*
> *The Cup of Salvation, HIS Mercy bestows,*
> *And all from HIS passion our happiness flows.*

Around the base of the flagons is Grimshaw's name and also those of his church wardens with the date 1750.

But in spite of the thronging crowds partaking of the Lord's Supper on these 'high days', as Grimshaw himself was to describe them, he never lost an individual pastoral concern for the communicants. He knew all his Haworth parishioners, their circumstances, problems and spiritual state. The majority of those who came from outlying areas were also the fruit of his ministry over the years. So when Thomas Colbeck, so signally used by God in Keighley, came forward to partake of the elements, Grimshaw, knowing that Thomas often felt condemned because of his sins, tweaked his ear gently and said as he handed him the cup, 'And for thee too, Tommy.'

The warm spiritual affinity established between Grimshaw and George Whitefield brought the latter back again to Haworth in October 1752 after his return from a short trip to America in 1751. Once more the people flocked to join in worship and to hear him preach. Writing a description of this visit to Yorkshire, Whitefield rejoiced over the manifest work of God in which he had shared. 'I have scarce known whether I have been in heaven or on earth. At Leeds, Birstall, Haworth, Halifax, etc. thousands and thousands have flocked twice or thrice a day to hear the word of life. A gale of divine influence hath everywhere attended it.'[1]

To this occasion also belongs an anecdote not published before which illustrates the effect of Whitefield's preaching on the consciences of his hearers. As he mounted some higher ground, probably a gravestone, to address the waiting assembly of men and women crowded into every corner of the expansive Haworth graveyard, he noticed a small group of soldiers, laughing and behaving in a facetious manner at the far end of the graveyard. Raising his voice, Whitefield called out to them: 'Fellow soldiers, fellow soldiers, fellow soldiers, come near!' Impelled by the authoritative note in his call, the men made their way through the multitude until they were standing near the preacher. Then

[1]Ibid., p. 448.

addressing them directly, Whitefield described the conduct of another rough group of 'fellow soldiers' – those soldiers gathered at the scene of Christ's crucifixion. He told them of a soldier who had pierced the side of the Son of God with a spear. The depth of pathos with which he presented the wounded Saviour to these hardened men broke them down until they wept aloud.[1]

These were indeed 'great days of the Son of Man'. But, as we have seen, they were not free from persecution and trial. A day or two before Whitefield's earlier visit to Haworth on 3 June 1750, William Batty notes in his 'Church History' that Grimshaw had been preaching as far afield as Ingleton in the North Yorkshire Dales where he was mobbed by a vicious and mindless crowd. Nearer home he had suffered abuse from the rabble in Yeadon and Guiseley, north of Leeds. Here both the rector and his curate, men of similar ilk to George White of Colne, inflamed the crowds to perpetrate acts of violence on such messengers of Christ as Grimshaw, Darney and Jonathan Maskew. On one occasion when Darney was preaching, the curate of Guiseley rushed into the house followed by a mob of agitators. 'Give me your name, give me your name,' he demanded. 'Is your name Grimshaw?' Someone in the crowd called out, 'No, it is Scotch Will!' Then there was general confusion, and a cry of 'Pull him down, pull him down,' sounded from many voices. Only with difficulty did Darney escape injury.

The advice which William Grimshaw gave to young Thomas Mitchell, whom he had encouraged in his earliest attempts to preach, and Paul Greenwood who had worked with him during the early years of the revival in Haworth, clearly sprang from his own experience. Writing an account of his own life, Thomas Mitchell recorded the encouragement he had received from 'the example and advice of good Mr Grimshaw'. He then added:

One time Paul Greenwood and I called at his house together and he gave us a very warm exhortation which I shall never forget. He said, 'If you are sent to preach the gospel, all hell will be up in arms against you.

[1]JEN.

Prepare for the battle and stand firm in the good ways of God. Indeed you must not expect to gain much of this world's goods by preaching the gospel. What you get must come through the devil's teeth, and he will hold it as fast as he can. I count every covetous man to be one of the devil's teeth. And he will let nothing go for God but what is forced from him.'[1]

Not only did William Grimshaw encounter persecution from unruly mobs during the early 1750s but he also faced the acute personal trial of the death of his young daughter, Jane. As we noted, John Wesley took the two Grimshaw children with him in September 1748 to be educated at the Kingswood School in Bristol. The school, begun by Whitefield in 1739 for the education of the children of the Kingswood miners, had been passed over to Wesley in 1740. He had opened a 'New House' in June 1748, intended for boarders only, principally the children of his itinerant preachers. And to this New House John and Jane were taken. The girls' wing of the school was short-lived, with Jane Grimshaw being the only pupil whose name has survived in the records.

Judged by modern standards, the rules were stringent: parents had to agree that no girl could return home during the course of her education. They were to be taught 'Reading, Writing and Sewing; and, if it be desired, the English Grammar, Arithmetic and other Sorts of Needlework'.[2] Girls were occupied from early in the morning until eight at night, and on Fridays, if they were in good health, they were expected to fast until 3 p.m. – a fact which reflects Wesley's High Church background. The strict regime of devotion and study is reminiscent of Susannah Wesley's own 'school' in which she supervised the education of her family, and which must have also influenced John Wesley's thinking. As we have seen, no recreational time was to be provided for the girls, for Wesley unwisely maintained that, 'She who plays when she is a Child, will play when she is a Woman.'[3]

[1]Thomas Mitchell, in *Early Methodist Preachers,* vol. I, ed. Jackson, p. 247.
[2] John Wesley's *Journal,* vol. III, p. 357.   [3]Ibid.

Although the regulations at Kingswood were so strict, it was staffed by men and women of known Christian character, and provided John and Jane Grimshaw with a better education than they could have obtained in Haworth. Only one small school existed in the village, with a curriculum restricted to basic English instruction. Catering for forty children, it was financed by an annual endowment of £18 which proved insufficient to staff the school. So for two short separate periods Grimshaw found himself unavoidably involved in educating the children of Haworth – an additional burden to his already demanding agenda

Grimshaw observed John Wesley's regulations and did not attempt to bring his children home during their time at Kingswood. There is evidence, however, that he visited them in Bristol in July 1749. But with her father far off, Jane did not seem to thrive and soon after this visit she was taken ill, possibly during some winter epidemic. She died on 14 January 1750, at the age of twelve. She had been fifteen months at Kingswood.

But God had been preparing the child for a better home. In a letter to his father which arrived in Haworth two weeks after Jane's death, John Grimshaw described his sister's last days. One of Wesley's itinerant preachers, John Bennet, was visiting Haworth when the letter came and he preserved a record of its contents in his diary entry for 27 January 1750. John had told his father that his 'sister Jenny, for some time before she was taken sick, seemed very pensive and thoughtful'. During her actual illness she 'bore up wonderfully, and when she grew very weak her mistress, Mrs Francis, going into the room, heard her speaking in a low voice.' Thinking that Jane was praying, she hesitated to interrupt her. But quite suddenly, the child had called out in clear tones:

> *He hath loved me, I cried,*
> *He hath suffered and died*
> *To redeem such a rebel as me.*

And only moments later Jane had died.[1]

[1] John Bennet, manuscript diary (JRULM).

News travelled slowly and Jane had already been buried for two weeks before news of her death reached Haworth. Bennet records that Jane was 'very near and dear unto him' but added that her father had been consoled in the knowledge of the child's faith expressed at her dying. Charles Wesley, who with his wife Sally was living in Bristol at the time awaiting the birth of their first child, had also noted Jane's death in his journal for that Sunday in January 1750: 'The Spirit helped our infirmity at Kingswood sacrament. A daughter of our brother Grimshaw's was just departed in the Lord; being perfected in a short space.'[1]

As soon as he could make arrangements, Grimshaw undertook the long journey down to Bristol. Charles Wesley greeted his friend cordially when he arrived a week later, and was particularly able to sympathise with his friend because only the previous day he and Sally had lost their own expected child. He commented in his journal for 4 February, 'I brought my friend Grimshaw home with me, comforted for his happy daughter.'[2]

After his bereavement Grimshaw decided to take John back home with him. The lad who was almost fourteen had shown no marked inclination to study, and so his father must have decided it would be better to have him in Haworth. There he planned to apprentice him to a master weaver, one of his parishioners, John Greenwood, a good and godly man, whose influence on young John Grimshaw could be only beneficial.

By the age of forty-two William Grimshaw had already experienced three painful bereavements. Writing at about this time to Mrs Gallatin, who had also been bereaved, he was able to look beyond this earth to the inhabitants of the heavenly city and exclaim, 'Our loss is their everlasting gain. Yet a little while, a few pulses more, and we shall overtake them, and share with them, and the rest of the church triumphant, in the eternal glories of heaven.'[3]

George Whitefield was not the only one to visit Haworth during

[1]*Journal of Charles Wesley*, vol. II, p. 67.
[2]Ibid.   [3]Ibid.

these years; Charles Wesley, whose travels since his marriage had become less wide-ranging, still managed the occasional visit to the north. With him Grimshaw probably enjoyed a closer friendship and compatibility in thought and purpose than with any other. In September 1752 Charles Wesley arrived in Leeds and invited a number of preachers to meet him there. Grimshaw was among the number. William Darney also arrived, but without invitation, and was not admitted. In Grimshaw Darney had found a friend and patron who constantly pleaded his cause with both John and Charles Wesley, but on this occasion even Grimshaw could not secure his admission to this private conference.

After several preaching engagements in the area, Charles Wesley rode across to Haworth. We can almost sense the keen anticipation that he felt as he hurried to join Grimshaw again. In a section of his journal now apparently lost, he recorded:

I hastened to Haworth. I never saw a church better filled: but after I had prayed in the pulpit, the multitude in the churchyard cried out that they could not hear, and begged me to come forth. I did so and preached on a tombstone. Between three and four thousand heard me gladly. At two I called again to double that number, 'Behold the Lamb of God, which taketh away the sin of the world!'

Anxious to see and hear the preacher, the people clambered onto graves and walls or any other vantage point they could find. Some would even perch on the church roof or cling to the tower; others climbed onto the roofs of neighbouring houses, or lacking such agility, contented themselves with listening at nearby windows. 'The church leads and steeple were filled with clusters of people and all as still as night. If ever I preached the Gospel, I preached it then. The Lord take all the glory,' recorded Wesley.[1]

Before he left Yorkshire Grimshaw arranged for Charles Wesley to preach in a large field near Ewood Hall where he frequently stayed when he was preaching in the area. As soon as

---

[1]Missing portion from C. Wesley's *Journal*, Sept. 15, 1752, cited by Jackson, *Life of Wesley*, vol. I, p. 586.

he had concluded the service in Haworth, Wesley records, 'I took horse immediately, and followed our nimble guide, Johnny Grimshaw, to Ewood. His father came panting after us.' The following day memorable preaching services were held when many thousands gathered. Wesley wrote of that occasion, 'Such a lively people I have not met with, so simple, loving and zealous. I could gladly have stayed to live and die with them.'[1]

During September 1753 George Whitefield was in Haworth once more, finding a Sunday spent with William Grimshaw and his eager parishioners a strong attraction. He wrote to the Countess of Huntingdon enthusiastically about the occasion, 'Last Saturday I returned from Leeds ... what the glorious Emmanuel gave us to see and feel is quite inexpressible. What a sacrament at Haworth! We used thirty-five bottles of wine.' The original copy of a letter from Grimshaw to Mrs Gallatin describing the same occasion can still be seen at the John Rylands University Library of Manchester. Dating his letter 19 September 1753, Grimshaw says,

We have lately had Mr Whitefield in these parts, and since, I suppose, you have had him at York. Here, and in general everywhere about us he had more numerous congregations than before. In my church he assisted me in administering the LORD's Supper to as many communicants as sipp'd away 35 Bottles of Wine within a Gill. It was a High Day indeed – a Sabbath of Sabbaths!

'Great days of the Son of Man' was the description which Whitefield had used of such times in Haworth and the surrounding areas. Many more similar days, some even more remarkable, were still to come. Such joys must have compensated in full measure for the persecution and even the personal sorrows which were Grimshaw's experience at this time.

[1]Ibid.

15

'The Great Haworth Round'

'William Grimshaw used his body with less compassion than a merciful man would use his beast,' wrote Henry Venn.[1] It was an accurate description of Grimshaw's exertions for the kingdom of God during the 1750s. With few family commitments now remaining after the bereavements he had suffered, he flung himself into a ceaseless round of travelling and preaching. All his domestic needs were cared for by his housekeeper, Mary Shackleton, commonly known as Molly, who, with the maids who lived at Sowdens, also undertook to provide hospitality for the numerous passing preachers and guests whom Grimshaw delighted to entertain.

From 1747 onwards he had been itinerating regularly into neighbouring parishes regardless of consequences; in his letter to John Wesley on 20 August 1747 he had described the first of these itineraries – a prototype of that preaching circuit which was to earn the name of the 'Great Haworth Round':

Last week I struck out into Lancashire and Cheshire, Mr Bennet bearing me company. We visited the societies in Rochdale, Manchester and Holme, in Lancashire; and Booth-bank in Cheshire. At the same time we made a visit to Mr Carmichael, a clergyman at Tarvin, near Chester ... from thence we came back by Booth-bank to Manchester, visited the society a second time and there we parted. I called and spent part of

[1]Venn, *Sketch,* p. 35.

two days with William Darney's societies, particularly those in Todmorden, Shore, Mellor-barn, Rossendale, Bacup, Crosstone, Stoneshawfate, Crimsworth-Dean; everywhere the Lord was manifestly with us: great blessings were scattered and much zeal and love, with great humility and simplicity, appeared in most people everywhere. The whole visit found me employment for near five days. O it was a blessed journey to my soul! . . . O, dear Sir, that I may prove faithful and indefatigable in his vineyard! that I may persevere to the last gasp steadfast, immovable, and always abounding in his work! Do you pray – the same shall be mine for you, your dear brother, and all our fellow labourers.

God granted that petition and up until the final weeks of his life Grimshaw was constantly on the move, 'faithful and indefatigable', regardless of health or weather, scarcely sparing time to eat adequately. Venn continues: 'For the course of fifteen years or upwards he used to preach every week fifteen, twenty and sometimes thirty times, besides visiting the sick and other duties. He thought he would never keep silence while he could speak to the honour of that God who had done so much for his soul.'[1]

And from August 1747 Grimshaw had been able to assure Wesley:

I desire to do nothing but in perfect harmony and concert with you, and therefore beg you will be entirely free, open and communicative to me. I bless God I can discover no other at present, but every way a perfect agreement between your sentiments, principles, &c of religion as you conceive mostly conducive to the welfare of the church, the private benefit of her members, and, in the whole, to the glory of the Lord.

So, joined in heart and purpose with John Wesley, William Grimshaw had also adopted his carefully developed system of evangelisation which already bore all the hallmarks of that worldwide organisation forever associated with Wesley's name.

No development in that system was pre-planned but each aspect originated from some necessity that faced the early

[1]Ibid.

Methodists. The use of the name *Society*, to describe the gathered groups of men and women awakened to their spiritual needs, was taken from a concept familiar to John Wesley, both from its use by the Moravians, but more so because of the *Religious Societies*. These became popular from 1671 onwards as a result of the work of an able German preacher, Dr Anthony Horneck, who ministered in the Savoy Chapel, London. Awakened by his preaching, a number of young men asked Horneck if he would meet with them on a weekly basis to discuss spiritual issues. The idea developed and similar groups sprang up mainly in and around London. Horneck drew up rules for these Religious Societies, including one which stipulated that only matters of Christian living were permissible as topics for discussion, as opposed to theological issues. This work of God led to an increasing concern both for the state of the nation and the unevangelised masses, and eventually societies such as the *Society for Promoting Christian Knowledge*[1] were formed. Horneck's work was popularised at the end of the century through the writings of Dr Josiah Woodward whose book *Account of the Rise and Progress of the Religious Societies in the City of London*, first published in 1699, went through several editions. At their height there had been more than forty or more of these societies but by Wesley's time only a handful remained.

In 1739, therefore, John Wesley adopted the term, using the name *United Societies* to describe the emerging Methodist assemblies. But because membership of these early societies depended only on a declared intent to *seek* forgiveness of sins and a true knowledge of God, John Wesley soon found he had to introduce a means for closer fellowship amongst regenerate members. *Band meetings* were therefore introduced early in the revival. At these weekly gatherings men and women meeting separately would discuss their problems and temptations and encourage each other in the faith.

As the work in Bristol grew, Wesley soon realised he would

[1]Formed 1698.

need a *preaching house* where the society could gather for worship and fellowship and in 1739 the first such building was erected in Bristol and called the New Room. But by 1742 there was still a considerable debt to be paid off on this project, so it was suggested that all members of the society should be divided into groups of twelve, and each member of a group or *class* should contribute a penny every week to defray this expense. *Class leaders* or *stewards* were appointed to collect the money; but as it soon proved impracticable for the stewards to visit each member in his home, the classes began to meet weekly.

This arrangement brought with it a degree of accountability and discipline – for the stewards were also asked to check on the spiritual state of the individual members of the class – and in addition it provided a system of finance which under-girded the developing activities of Methodism. *Class meetings* were gradually to supersede *band meetings,* though in many places both existed side by side.

Class tickets were issued to every member of a society, often by Wesley himself, or in the Haworth Round by Grimshaw.[1] These tickets bore the name of the member and the date of issue on one side and on the other some symbol or logo: a Bible, an angel, an anchor. They had to be renewed quarterly, renewal depending on the spiritual standing of the applicant. If he had lost his concern to live in a godly manner, his ticket would be forfeited, and with it the right to attend his class meeting or the quarterly *love feasts* – a simple communal meal. An entry in John Bennet's diary for 30 April 1748 shows Grimshaw undertaking this task of examining ticket holders: 'Found Mr Grimshaw, W. Darney and P. Greenwood assembled together with many others in a little house near the town [i.e., Haworth]; Mr Grimshaw examined every particular person touching the state of their souls.' Such a knowledge of every member of a society involved Grimshaw in regular visits to the societies at least four times each year.

[1] John Whitaker of Otley was a member of a Methodist society for seventy years and regarded it as a high honour that he had received his first class ticket from Grimshaw himself. *Methodist Magazine,* 1827, p. 225.

To maintain a constant spiritual care and oversight of the numerous converts of the revival, Wesley had created a system of *rounds* across the country. Either he or his brother, Grimshaw or one of the other itinerant preachers, would travel these rounds on a regular basis, visiting and encouraging all the societies. By 1746 there were six rounds in existence; Haworth was included in a vast northern round made up of Yorkshire, Lancashire, Cheshire, Derbyshire, Nottinghamshire and parts of Lincolnshire. For this round Grimshaw assumed responsibility under the overall authority of John Wesley from 1747 onwards. Although the round was subdivided several times over as the revival progressed, at this time Grimshaw attempted to cover the whole area. Little wonder then that in his letter dated 27 November 1747, he begged Wesley to send up preachers from Cornwall to help him.

The want of preachers here at present is very great. That the harvest in these parts is very large and the labourers are few, is very manifest: why it is so, the Lord of it only knows ... But, dear Sir, are there such plenty of helpers in Cornwall? Send us one or two of them without further entreaty ... New and numerous classes have been joined lately. Were not matters thus with us, you may easily suppose I should not be so urgent with you for assistance.[1]

Responding to this appeal Wesley commissioned helpers from Cornwall such as Thomas Meyrick to leave all, travel north and help Grimshaw who had divided the round, estimated at eight thousand square miles, into smaller circuits. These he was to visit regularly together with such men as John Bennet, William Darney, Paul Greenwood and Thomas Meyrick.

The introduction of *Quarterly Meetings* – another of the characteristic developments of Methodism, first mentioned in the notes of the Methodist Conference of 1749, can be traced to Grimshaw's suggestion and was implemented in the Haworth Round in 1748. The idea came in response to the need to coordinate all the scattered societies in any region. Similar to a

[1]Grimshaw to John Wesley, 27 November 1747, cited by Myles, *Life and Writings*, p. 168.

present-day conference of church officers, it drew together representatives of all the societies in a given round, and provided an opportunity for discussing problems, changing class stewards if necessary and distributing funds. An old circuit book dating from October 1748, probably the oldest in existence, has been preserved. Bound in vellum and yellow with age, it is written in Grimshaw's handwriting and preserves details of this initial Quarterly Meeting which was held near Todmorden. Grimshaw listed all the names of class stewards in different circuits of the Haworth Round, from Cockermouth in the north to Birstall in the south. Such a meeting would require a steward to keep a regular account of all the donations collected from the various classes and a record of how it was allocated. This too fell to William Grimshaw adding to his heavy load of responsibility. Most of the donations were used to help the itinerant preachers, some of whom had little other source of income. And so we read:

		£	s	d
Oct. 14, 1748 [sic]	Gave Wm. Darney	0	1	7
July 11, 1748	Wm. Darney's wife	1	10	0
Jan. 10, 1749	A pair of Boots for W. D.	0	14	0

But the most demanding call on William Grimshaw's time and strength lay in visiting the growing number of societies in his extensive round: groups of men and women aroused to their need through the work of the Methodist preachers. Surrounded by intense spiritual darkness and finding no help from the local parish churches, these young converts would have found such pastoral visits of paramount importance. In his letter of July 1754 to Dr John Gillies, Grimshaw lists many places where the revival had broken out:

About the year 1748, I think, the Lord was pleased to visit Cheshire, and there was a great awakening near Macclesfield, and in Stockport, Astbury, Alpraham [fifteen miles east of Chester], Chester, &c. Great things hath the Lord done in these places ... I should have mentioned before the work at Hull, Pocklington, Rotherham, Sheffield and scores of other towns and villages.

In all of these places, excluding Lincolnshire which he admits was too far distant from him, the arrival of Grimshaw on his white horse would be a familiar and welcome sight among these groups of young believers.

Grimshaw divided his vast 'parish' into distinct areas and followed a well-planned itinerary in order to include as many societies as possible in his schedule. During the winter months, when rain and snow made many roads impassable, he was usually itinerating within a fifteen to twenty mile radius of his home. Sunday was always spent in Haworth engaged in the services of his own church, and Monday was usually devoted to matters of concern arising from the ministry on the previous day. So from Tuesday to Saturday he would devote his time to visiting the societies, usually returning home each night. If his travels were in the Halifax area, he would base them around Ewood, spending the night there. Ewood Hall had been left by Sarah's parents to young John Grimshaw, and was therefore rapidly becoming a Methodist centre.

Over the years Grimshaw developed two fairly regular circuits, which he covered in alternate weeks. One schedule was considerably fuller than the other, which led him to speak playfully to John Newton of 'my idle week' and 'my busy week', but these descriptions were misnomers for all his weeks were packed with activity. A careful study of his diary, which he began in 1755 but failed to keep up for long, gives some evidence of these two circuits which Grimshaw tried to follow. Tracing his activities from 5 October 1755 – a Sunday – we read:

Oct. 5th – Today has been a high & a happy Day; The Word was blessed in the great congregation & the Lord, I hope I may say, made HIMSELF known to us in the breaking of Bread. We had a sweet and lovely Feast. HIS Banner over us was love. Glory be to GOD in the Highest!

Oct. 6th – Today I have had no cause to complain, tho' not one of my liveliest Days. I preached at Cullingworth, Denham [Denholme, 5½ miles west of Bradford] & Over Town [possibly Upper Town,

Oxenhope – 1 mile from Haworth] with indifferent freedom – Blessed be the LORD!

Oct. 7th – Today I preached at Rush Hills [2^1/$_2$ miles west of Haworth] Preaching House; and went out collecting some relics of the Subscriptions for the Rebuilding of the church. I had a middling Day. Blessed be God!

Oct. 8th – I preached at Baledon [Baildon], Menstone [Menston] & Otley. I met and exhorted the societies in each place and was very happy all Day in my soul. O my Soul, praise the LORD!

Oct. 9th – I preached at Otley [15 miles north-east of Haworth], Addingham, Silsden, Sutton and Newsham [Newsholme, 15 miles north-west of Haworth] – It was a blessed Day to me, & I hope to many. I had much of the LORD's presence in me, and with me.

Oct. 10th To Day I preached at Newsham [Newsholme] – and Scoles [Scholes, 1 mile from Haworth] – I had much of the Lord's presence, but this evening I have trifled and some heaviness is on my spirits. O LORD, be THOU my Keeper, & so will I praise THY name!

Oct. 11th – I had this day a solid Sense of the Divine Presence – Glory be to GOD!

Oct. 12th – This is a high Day – The LORD was in the midst of the camp. Mr Whitefield[1] read prayers in the Morning and preached twice to a very numerous Audience (some 1000s of people) & assisted me in administering the LORD's Supper to a great number of communicants. GOD gave Mr Whitefield great Power in Preaching, & sent a gracious rain upon HIS Inheritance. Praised be the LORD!

Grimshaw records preaching fourteen times that week, mainly to the north of Haworth, and this can represent his 'idle week'. The week following was not typical as he spent some time with Whitefield in Keighley, Halifax and Heptonstall. But an example of a 'busy week' can be found from June 21–28 the following year. Here Grimshaw mentions twenty-three occasions on which he had preached, and although he does not say where he went, it is probable that he travelled south and west to include Bradford,

[1]This 1755 visit was unknown to Whitefield's biographers.

Todmorden, Halifax and Bacup – places which figure frequently in the diary. Three days of that week read as follows:

21. Preached four times – It was a rich day surely – Glory be to GOD!
22. Preached five times – a rich day indeed for myself, I hope and others – Glory be to GOD!
23. Preached four times – Visited two sick persons – A good Day – Glory be to GOD!

All this was achieved in spite of appalling road conditions. Many 'roads' remained impassable in winter even for carriages, while men and horses had been known to drown in potholes on the Great North Road. In summer they were little better, some proving no more than ditches filled with rubble. Even when roads were tolerable travellers were at risk from bandits and highwaymen. On occasions Grimshaw's sturdy horse could not carry him to some remote moorland village. Then he would undertake the journey on foot: and his was a familiar figure often to be seen tramping alone across the wild terrain.

One road was an exception; this was the Roman road from Lancashire *via* Illingworth and Haworth to Boroughbridge which was widened and repaired by Act of Parliament in 1735 and financed by a turnpike trust. More turnpike roads were gradually introduced as the century progressed and Grimshaw, with understandable self-interest, was a keen advocate of the system. For one such road leading from Bradford through Haworth to Colne, he and his son John were both named among the two hundred trustees in a 1755 Act of Parliament. This involved them in a duty to check that the work was accomplished. Grimshaw himself invested £100 in a trust for maintaining the road, to be repaid by the tolls levied on travellers.

In the summer when travelling conditions were easier, he would range further afield. A letter to Mrs Gallatin on 31 August 1751 catches something of the extent of his journeys and the resulting pressure on his life:

Glory be to God, I have been so busied for some time in the gospel work, which flourishes wonderfully in these parts, that I have not had much leisure or thought about writing letters. Yours, therefore, which I received the favour of some time since, I hope you will excuse my not answering sooner. This morning I preached the sixtieth time since August came in. I have lately visited Derbyshire, Cheshire and Lancashire and various parts of the country. I preached in the latter end of July in the new [preaching] house ... at Manchester. The house was full, and many out of doors. At Chester also to a numerous audience out of doors. In short we have large congregations some scores of miles around, and new doors opening daily.

Details like these make us the more surprised to read in John Newton's otherwise useful biography of Grimshaw a statement such as this: 'I believe he seldom passed the boundaries of his own county and not often those of his immediate stated services. He was not like the peacock that spreads its plumes and admires himself . . . but rather like the pheasant, which although a beautiful bird, is content to live unseen and unnoticed in its native woods.'[1] Such a comment can only be explained by the fact that Newton was less familiar with Grimshaw and with the extent of his labours than has sometimes been assumed, and also because he was writing over thirty-five years after Grimshaw's death.

During the better weather Grimshaw could often be found in places far distant from Haworth. Scattered throughout local circuit books and contemporary records are references to his visits. Sheffield, forty miles away, was one of the most southern places where he would call. Although it had become part of the Cheshire Round, separated from the Haworth Round in 1748, Grimshaw often included it in his itineraries. Wesley had placed it under the care of John Bennet, who was still at this point one of his most valued associates,

In the Fulwood area of Sheffield an enterprising young convert, Mrs Woodhouse, fixed on the scheme of draping a white sheet across some prominent bush on the top of an adjacent hill whenever Grimshaw, Bennet, either of the Wesleys or George Whitefield arrived in the area. At the sight of the white sheet the

[1] Newton, *Letters,* p. 119.

people of Sheffield began streaming down the hillsides to the home of the Woodhouses, once an alehouse but now a preaching centre, to hear the words of life.[1]

Not far from the Welsh border, some seventy miles from Haworth, lay the old city of Chester. Here too Grimshaw would call on his pastoral travels. In August 1751 he was there and in April 1753 was back again, this time after a visit to Bolton on a ministry of reconciliation. John Bennet, who had frequently travelled with Grimshaw, had pioneered a fruitful work in Cheshire, establishing a society in Bolton. But in October 1749 he had distressed John Wesley by marrying Grace Murray, the widow to whom Wesley was engaged, and this only a day or two before Wesley himself was due to marry her. Grace Murray, who had been housekeeper at Wesley's Newcastle children's home, appears to have been encouraging both men in their hopes of winning her at the same time. But at Charles Wesley's insistence the matter was concluded by her marriage to Bennet.

Despite these circumstances, Bennet and Wesley had continued to work together until 1751 when Bennet had taken land in Bolton and had built a preaching house for the society there. This led to a quarrel with Wesley over the contents of the trust deed and by 1752 Bennet had left the Methodists, becoming an Independent. In 1753 he built Duke Chapel in Bolton where he became pastor of the sixty believers who had left the Methodists with him. Writing to Mrs Gallatin of these things on 12 April 1753, Grimshaw reports:

Last week I was in Manchester and Bolton with Mr and Mrs Wesley.[2] In both places the work of God prospers greatly especially in Manchester. There are two hundred and fifty in society there, and this summer must enlarge the preaching house as much again as it is. In Bolton differences heal ... several revolters in the rupture occasioned by Mr Bennet are returned to us, but he himself has quite left us. In Chester there is a wonderful stirring up. All around us in general we have numerous congregations.

[1]Everett, *Methodism in Sheffield,* 1823, p. 104.
[2]Wesley had subsequently married Molly Vazeille in February 1751.

Not only was Grimshaw a familiar visitor among the societies far south of Haworth, such as Stockport, near Manchester and Glossop in Derbyshire, he was an equally welcome figure among the northern societies. He knew the believers in Hartlepool on the east coast and must have visited them as early as 1748, for in 1749 he encouraged George Whitefield to include the town in his northern tour. In an old circuit book in Osmotherley, six miles from Northallerton in North Yorkshire, we find the following entry for 19 July 1752: 'For William Grimshaw and William Darney, 1s 3d.' This must have been the sum paid for the expenses of these two preachers. Nearby Helmsley, where Dr Richard Conyers ministered from 1755 onwards, was another place visited from time to time by the tireless evangelist from Haworth. Kendal received occasional visits and also Ingleton, though here Grimshaw had faced physical abuse from the crowds in 1750. From the warm and familiar tones of his letters to the believers in Newcastle, the northern centre of Methodism, it is likely that he had occasionally even ventured the hundred or more miles to meet them.

So great was the confidence which John Wesley placed in William Grimshaw that in the conference held in Bristol in August 1749 he had nominated him as his successor with over-sight for all the affairs of Methodism. On him would devolve the appointment of Methodist preachers and their designation to different areas throughout the country. In all legal documents from 1750 onwards Wesley named him a trustee of properties built or acquired for Methodist worship. This fact accounts for Grimshaw's concern and personal involvement in issues affecting Methodism far beyond the limits of his own circuit – extensive as it was. His attendance at Wesley's annual conference whenever it was in Leeds, or occasionally in Bristol if there were important matters to discuss, would also make Grimshaw a familiar figure in Methodist circles throughout the country.

But such journeys as these called for exceptional physical strength, and William Grimshaw knew well that few possessed his strong constitution. In defence of his brethren who were not able to undertake such labours, he once declared at a Quarterly Meeting of the local Methodist Association, 'I am not everyone and everyone is not me. For my part, I could take my saddle bags on my shoulders and take a sufficiency of linen for my journey and walk every mile of the circuit' [some three hundred at that time], but he went on to convince those who expected others to do the same, that some would find such exertions beyond their powers.[1]

Henry Venn could write of Grimshaw, 'In sixteen years he was only once suspended from his labour by sickness, though he dared all weathers upon the bleak mountain.'[2] Newton, who pleaded in a letter to John Wesley that his own health, broken as it had been by his earlier trials, would not permit such exertions,[3] adds a testimony similar to Venn's, commenting that even when he was well into his fifties, Grimshaw had the strength and vigour of a young man. 'He was a stranger to sickness and pain, nor was there any visible abatement either of his mental or bodily powers.'[4]

Despite all his travels and concern for believers far distant from his own immediate parish, Grimshaw did not neglect his own people. On the contrary, as we noted, he asserted to Newton that he had a detailed knowledge of the circumstances and trials of each person under his spiritual oversight.[5] But he was not an entire 'stranger to sickness and pain' as Newton had suggested. A careful examination of his letters, particularly as the 1750s progressed, reveals days of weakness, pain and even a premonition of early death, though he was hardly fifty years of age.

Whatever his physical condition, Grimshaw had an inward compulsion to serve his God while opportunity remained, and it drove him relentlessly onwards, night and day. Confirming the

[1]JEN.
[2]Venn, *Sketch*, p. 35.
[3]Newton to John Wesley, November 1760, cited by Tyerman, *Life of Wesley*, vol. II, p. 365.
[4]Newton, *Letters*, p. 133.
[5]Ibid., p. 87.

fact that he did indeed suffer periods of ill health, Mrs Joseph Jones wrote: 'He never stuck at any weather, or suffered it to hinder his labour. In the coldest weather he never complained of cold, but thanked God for whatever he sent. He was sometimes very much afflicted in body, but bore it with invincible patience.'[1] He allowed himself little respite from his labours and could certainly have echoed his friend Charles Wesley's aspirations:

> *I would the precious time redeem,*
> *And longer live for this alone:*
> *To spend and to be spent for them*
> *Who have not yet my Saviour known.*
> *Fully on these my mission prove,*
> *And only breathe to breathe thy love.*

A graphic description of the way Grimshaw conducted his itinerant ministry has survived from the pen of William Crabtree, a young man converted through his preaching who later became the pastor of the first Baptist chapel in Bradford. After describing Grimshaw's extensive travels in all the surrounding areas, he continued,

He divided the country into districts, taking one regularly each week. His usual manner was, upon entering the house, after having with uplifted hands pronounced a blessing upon the people assembled, to fall down upon his knees and pray with great fervency, and then preach with a plainness and pungency peculiarly adapted to his hearers, for a convenient space of time.[2]

Dismissing his congregation, he would hurry on to the next village or to another house in a distant part of the same village, providing it was large enough to accommodate all the people who had gathered. Sometimes Grimshaw's hearers were not expecting him. If he saw a cottage door open, he might enter and give a brief exhortation to the people as they sat at their work, weaving,

[1]Laycock, *Heroes,* p. 244.
[1]Everett, 'Curate of Haworth'.

spinning, dyeing the wool fabrics. Then he would continue on his way.

We are left wondering when Grimshaw found time for meals or other refreshment in his seemingly ceaseless round of activity. Often, and probably to the detriment of his health, his nourishment was scant and eaten hastily as he journeyed from place to place. One friend remembered the day he called at his home when on his way to some distant preaching engagement and he begged a little oatcake – probably the first thing he had eaten that day. The friends urged him to spread a little butter on it. 'Oh no!' says he, 'a bit of bread at one house, and a little butter at another.' And so he went on his way. On another occasion he called at a home where some friends were just preparing the dinner. Knowing he would be welcomed, Grimshaw went to the pot and helped himself to a potato; then he went to the salt cellar and sprinkled a little on his potato, saying cheerfully, 'A potato and salt are too good for me.'

Yet another has recorded that Grimshaw never disdained to eat with the lowliest and poorest of men, accepting with gratitude the simplest provisions they could share with him. His favourite food, as we have seen, was an onion boiled in milk, and if he were offered bread and butter in addition, he would consider he had eaten sumptuously. One day, in the heat of summer, he was overcome with thirst, and stopping at a cottage not far from Haworth, asked if he could have a drink of milk. The householder replied, 'We have no butter-milk, but we have some whey which my family will not drink.' 'Let me have some,' requested Grimshaw, and after quenching his thirst, exclaimed, 'Oh, this is good!' adding, 'If I had to do with your family, I would make them drink it.'[1]

Mrs Joseph Jones continues in her account of Grimshaw's life: 'In labours he was most abundant and indefatigable. He never preached less than twenty times a week. I have known him preach twenty-eight times. Once he told me he had preached thirty-one

[1] JEN.

times. Indeed, his whole life was scarcely anything else than preaching, prayer and praise.'[1] But Grimshaw viewed his exertions in a different light. Writing to William Romaine in 1762 he could say, 'When I come to die, I shall have my greatest grief and my greatest joy – my greatest grief that I have done so little for JESUS; and my greatest joy that JESUS has done so much for me. My last words shall be: *"Here goes an unprofitable servant!"'*

---

[1]Laycock, *Heroes,* p. 244.

16

EVERY MOMENT TO GOD'S GLORY

'THIS DAY I GIVE MYSELF UP TO THEE, a living sacrifice, holy and
acceptable unto thee . . . In thy service I desire and purpose to
spend all my time, desiring thee to teach me to spend every
moment of it to thy glory.' This prayer, which formed part of
a solemn written covenant made by William Grimshaw on 4
December 1752, was abundantly answered, even though he
himself could never feel he had rendered enough service to the
God he loved and to whom he owed the incalculable debt of his
own salvation.

Grimshaw made at least thirteen personal covenants or dedi-
cations of himself to God, each at some critical moment in his
spiritual experience. The first, as we have seen, was in 1738
when he was earnestly seeking salvation and an answer to his
spiritual perplexities; and again, he had covenanted with God on
8 August 1744, a few weeks before the experience which he
described as 'that wonderful manifestation of thyself unto me',
and which transformed his ministry. And now again, in the
middle of incessant activity for the kingdom of God, he spent
time in prayer and fasting to transcribe and sign this longest of his
covenants and the one which he was to renew at regular intervals
for the remainder of his life.

How Grimshaw became familiar with this practice of covenanting with God we are not now in a position to say. Perhaps the
believers in Rochdale whom he met during his brief curacy in

Littleborough introduced him to it. But it is evident that all the covenants he made sprang directly either from his quest for rest of conscience or from his desire for progress in his conflict with indwelling sin and the life of godliness.

Biblical in origin, the practice is far less common today than it has been at any time since the sixteenth century. The concept of men and women pledging themselves to each other and to God has often played an integral part in religious life, particularly in days of persecution, and examples of it can be found even before the Reformation. The Waldensians, hounded to and fro on the mountains of Italy, would covenant together before God as a declaration of loyalty to one another and to the faith they held dear.

Scotland could be called the Land of the Covenant in a unique sense. Between 1556 and 1683 thirty-one public covenants were ratified, declaring the people's right to purity in faith and worship. But the practice of personal covenanting with God was also common in Scotland during that period. Like Jacob at Bethel, the individual believer would covenant to give himself unreservedly to God, promising to walk with him in obedience and love, to shun sin and serve him all his days. In exchange he would engage God to be his God, to save him from condemnation, keep him through life, uphold him in death and bring him at last to his eternal glory.

Specimens of a few such covenants made by believers dating from the sixteenth century onwards have been preserved for us. Sometimes these moving declarations of faith and intent were written on the fly-leaf of some old book, or perhaps in a Bible or some private journal or even on a scrap of paper. Gradually the custom became more widespread and when Dr Philip Doddridge published his best known work *The Rise and Progress of Religion in the Soul,* in 1745, he advocated this practice of covenant-making as a way to gain a stronger assurance and as a stimulus to godly living. In addition, he provided a long sample covenant which Christians might adopt as their own.

William Grimshaw's covenant of 1752, deliberately following

this pattern recommended by Philip Doddridge,[1] suggests he had recently been reading the work. The spiritual usefulness of such transactions with God, particularly when accompanied by a season of prayer and fasting, would have appealed to Grimshaw in the light of his own previously established practice. Choosing to use Doddridge's wording throughout, he only adapted and modified it here and there to meet his personal circumstances and heart condition:

And now once more, and for ever, I most solemnly give up, devote and resign all I am, spirit, soul and body, to thee and to thy pleasure and command, in Christ Jesus my Saviour, this 4th December, 1752; sensible, O Lord, of my vileness and unworthiness, but yet that I am thy pardoned, justified and regenerated child.

Inscribed on parchment, signed and dated, the covenant contained over fifteen hundred words and combined in itself all the passionate desires of his soul after God, with his longings to serve him more effectively.

Deeply aware of his sins, he first confessed that, 'My base corruptions and lusts have [in] numberless ways, wrought to bring forth fruit unto death; and if thou wert extreme to mark what I have done amiss, I could never abide it.' In tune with his own express desire to use every moment in God's service, he then prayed, 'Use me, O Lord, I beseech thee, as an instrument of thy glory; and honour me so far as either by doing or suffering thy appointments, I may bring praise to thy name and benefit to the world in which I live.'

Anticipating the day when he should end his earthly course, he continued, 'When I have done, borne, and endured thy will upon earth, call me hence at what time and in what manner thou pleasest; only grant that in my dying moments, and the near approach of eternity, I may remember this my engagement to thee, and may employ my latest breath in thy service.' Then, in

---

[1] Philip Doddridge, *The Rise and Progress of Religion in the Soul, Miscellaneous Works* (London: William Ball, 1839), p. 117.

the nature of a covenant, Grimshaw engaged his God to come to his aid in his dying hour: 'When thou seest me in the agonies of death, remember this covenant too, though I should be incapable of recollecting it: look down upon me, O Lord, thy languishing, dying child. Place thy everlasting arms under my head, put strength and confidence into my departing spirit, and receive it into the embraces of thine everlasting love.'[1]

Grimshaw closed this covenant with words of his own which indicate the momentous significance it held for him: 'I solemnly subscribe this dedication of myself to the forever-blessed Triune God, in the presence of angels and all invisible spectators, this fourth day of December, 1752.' In addition, and in accordance with Doddridge's suggestion, he purposed to renew this covenant four times each year, on the last Friday of January, April, July and October for the rest of his life.

Only twenty months were to elapse before Grimshaw made another, though much shorter covenant. Discovered in one of his Bibles, written on the blank page between the Old and New Testaments, it was dated 4 August 1754. Packed into a few terse lines, it contained all the same spiritual aspirations found in the longer covenant:

Often have I, and once more do I, totally devote – most solemnly surrender by this sacred book of God, and forever give up to God in Christ my Head and Lord, my body, soul and spirit – and all I am and have and may be, in the fullest sense of St. Paul's exhortation Rom. 12:1, 2. And I nothing doubt, but that, as I have hitherto found by many years experience in Christ, that His grace is sufficient for me; so I always shall be enabled to do all things through Christ which strengtheneth me. So help me, O Triune God.

William Grimshaw Minr. of Haworth August 4th 1754[2]

Grimshaw's desire to spend all his energies wholly in the

---

[1]Grimshaw's covenant with God, quoted by Myles, *Life and Writings*, p. 190. Full text in Appendix 2.

[2]W. W. Stamp, *Historical Notices of Wesleyan Methodism in Bradford* (1841), p. 30.

service of God is amply demonstrated in the fragments of his diary recovered early in the nineteenth century, then lost from view again for a further hundred years. Unfortunately some of the diary is defaced and much is missing: only the portion covering the first two months in which Grimshaw kept this diary, from 14 September 1755 until 3 November that year, appears to be complete. Nothing else remains apart from June 1756, which is almost complete, and a few days in March 1757.

Begun on 14 September, his forty-seventh birthday, Grimshaw expresses his regret that he had not attempted to keep a diary before. Briefly surveying his spiritual life up until that point, he writes:

In all these Periods of Life, I have gone through manifold Trials and temptations, which wou'd take many large Volumes – Notwithstanding which, I have been, Glory be to God, wonderfully preserved even until this day – I have sometimes thought to [keep a diary] but hitherto never did. Of late I've sometimes thought it was too late, as my days seem to be far spent, to begin such a diary – But . . . I begin Now – THIS DAY being my BIRTHDAY – I renewed my resolutions . . . as also my Vow & Covenant in the most solemn Manner to be in all possible respects thro' His Grace the LORD's for Ever.

Starting with a Sunday two weeks later, we may accompany Grimshaw for a further week of his life:

Sep. 28th [1755] – To Day GOD has been with me, especially in the Great Congregation, and at the Holy Sacrament – surely His Mercies never fail them that fear HIM.
Sep. 29th – I preached to Day at Lees and Hainworthshaw. Lord JESUS be praised, I have cause to believe THY presence was with me and the People – My Soul was this Day refreshed, I have felt THEE near me all Day – I spent I hope a profitable time with Mr Ingham – Praise the LORD O my Soul, for all His Benefits.
Sep. 30 – To Day THOU, LORD hast been with ME, but I've trifled in my conversation, nor have I improved the golden moments of it either as to my Spiritual or temporal concerns, as I should have done. LORD, I abhor myself for it. Be THOU merciful to me a sinner.
Oct. 1st – To Day I must laud the LORD for his goodness to my soul, I

preached at High Binns, at Denham Park & at Oakes. I hope the LORD blessed the Report at each place. Praise the LORD, O my Soul!

Oct. 2nd – Preached at Oakes again, at Holdworth & at Mixenden and visited and exhorted two sick persons. My Soul was happy. I enjoyed a sweet Mien of Heart. – Praise the LORD for this Day.

Oct. 3rd – This morning with great power and plainness I preached at Sowerby Street to a large congregation, and in the Even: at Ewood – I had a very wandering mind this day and could meditate but little, and therefore I count this a barren Day; For little Meditation makes a barren Heart. My Leanness, My Leanness!

Oct. 4th – Today I preached at Fearny Lee [&] Snaboothe; At the former place with much power at the latter with less, and afterwards at Sowdens, as I thought, with still less, tho' my LORD, I believe bless'd the message at every place. My soul, blessed be HIS Name, was much in Communion with the LORD tho' sometimes troubled with wandering thoughts.

To spend 'every moment to God's glory' as Grimshaw well knew was a goal ultimately unattainable on earth, involving far more than a mere round of ceaseless activity. It was a demanding spiritual exercise which required a regular and diligent discipline of life. The means Grimshaw employed in his own endeavour to reach such a standard can be gleaned from a letter he wrote to believers in the societies in Newcastle. 'Let me prescribe to you a method how to live one day well,' says the curate of Haworth. And in case they should think he was urging on them too high a standard of Christian living, he assured them that he too tried to make it his pattern of life – 'Nor will I presume to lay a burden on your shoulders and not touch it with my own fingers':

As soon as you awake in the morning, employ half an hour in five things: Bless God for the mercies of the night past; pray for the blessings of a new day; examine well your own heart; meditate upon some spiritual subject; and lastly, plan the business of the approaching day. Then rise at four o'clock, but never later than five if well.[1] While you put

---

[1]Without electricity these people would often have had seven or eight hours sleep by this time.

on your clothes, pray or praise mentally, but suitably to your state. Then spend another half hour in secret meditation, praise and prayer. After this call your family together, read a chapter, and as you have ability and leisure, expound it to them, then sing a hymn and conclude with prayer.

Pray always before and after meat: thus take the curse from off your victuals, and bless God for the benefit of them. Begin, proceed in, and lay by work, thus: Begin with that which should never cease – *prayer in your mind*. While you are at your work, meditate, praise or pray; or converse religiously with those about you. This will not hinder, but further your labour. As often as you can retire a few minutes to prayer, at *nine* o'clock in the morning, and *three* in the afternoon. It would be well to spend a little time in prayer with your family, immediately after dinner. In the evening constantly observe the same order of devotion as in the morning. At going to bed, revise the thoughts, words and actions of the past day. What appears amiss, beg pardon for. What is well, bless God alone for; and never close your eyes with any unforgiven sin upon your conscience . . . Never neglect this or some other method of walking with God.[1]

Mrs Joseph Jones, who had ample opportunity to observe Grimshaw's way of life, suggests that he did indeed strive to put such a cycle of spiritual duties into effect.[2] But he often grieved that he had wasted both time and opportunities. On 30 September 1755, as we have seen above, he had complained of 'trifling' in his conversation and not 'improving the golden moments', and on 14 October, the day after he had accompanied Whitefield to Keighley and enjoyed 'great Liberty in my funeral Discourse', he could protest sadly,

To Day I have trifled – I have loitered it away in doing little, or I fear, but little to GOD's Glory – Let it not come into the Number of my Months – Be ashamed O my Soul before the LORD for so embezzling thy golden Moments.

[1]Grimshaw, To the societies in Newcastle, 27 January 1761, cited by Myles, *Life and Writings*, pp. 186-7.
[2]Laycock, *Heroes*, p. 245.

William Grimshaw's diary reveals a man of sensitive conscience, deeply aware of his sins – sins that some might think
inconsequential – but sins nevertheless that clouded his communion with God and brought him into distress. Having come
home to Sowdens after an exhausting day on 16 October 1755
when he had been accompanying Whitefield as he preached
first in Halifax, and then again in the evening at Ewood Hall,
Grimshaw admits, 'I was angry with our Maid at night. Lord, hast
THOU not pardoned me!' But a sense of forgiveness did not
always come so easily. Three days later on 19 October, he
complains that his soul 'was brought into much heaviness'. The
following day he confesses, 'To Day I laboured under the Weight
of last Night's sin. Lord deliver my Soul. – I know THOU wilt not
cast me off for ever.' But he still felt troubled the next day, fearing
he had 'provoked the LORD again' and lamented bitterly, 'Surely
may I not fear hell. O how heavy is My soul! Will the LORD be no
more entreated? I will not let THEE go. Surely THOU wilt forgive.'
But the next day it was the same again, 'Oct. 22nd, To Day I
laboured under the Divine frown. I exhorted 5 or 6 families Young
and old to seek & follow the LORD & preached once . . . ' At last
we read, 'Oct. 23rd, I felt my soul more cheerful. I preached with
tolerable liberty at Heptonstall. Did the Quarterly day business
and met the Sowdens Class. I hope am restored – Glory be to
GOD!'

Commenting on this cycle, common in the believer's
experience, of giving in to temptation, followed by a sense of
the withdrawal of God's favour, Grimshaw was to write in his
manuscript 'Experiences':

When we give way to a temptation, as there is always a consenting of the
will, so there is an immediate gloominess and trouble that covers the
soul; this is the veiling of God's countenance, which is greater or less as
the consent is greater or less; and will cause us accordingly greater or
less sorrow in repentance, and a longer or a less interval before we are
received to pardon, favour and beauty of God's face again.

Although on all essential matters of doctrine and practice

Grimshaw was united in heart and mind with John Wesley, his knowledge of his own heart and his daily conflict with temptation left him profoundly uneasy with the teaching which Wesley and his followers propounded concerning 'sinless perfection' or 'perfect love' as Wesley preferred to term it. In 1756 Wesley set out his own position on this vexed issue in a letter to one who was about to publish a treatise against Christian perfection. In it he explained, 'When I began to make the Scriptures my study (about seven-and-twenty-years ago), I began to see that Christians are called to *love God with all their heart and to serve him with all their strength; wh*ich is precisely what I apprehend to be meant by the scriptural term Perfection.'[1] And to another he wrote, 'But is there not *sin* in those that are *perfect?* I believe not; but, be that as it may, they feel none, no temper but pure love, while they rejoice, pray and give thanks continually. And whether sin is *suspended* or *extinguished*, I will not dispute; it is enough that they feel nothing but love.'[2]

But Grimshaw did feel inward sin and could not in all honesty declare that he felt 'nothing but love'. His sensitivity of conscience led to fluctuations in his spiritual experiences, which he confided to the pages of his diary. His frequent use of vows and covenants as weapons in the warfare against such indwelling sin reflect this constant struggle. So we read on 2 June 1756, 'A Grievous temptation – Gave Way – Broke my vow – Renewed it in a most solemn Manner – LORD, grant I may never violate it more.' And again on 24 June, 'A Dreadful Day! Sorely tempted, and sorely gave way. In a most solemn Manner renewed my Vow'.

Looking back on such periods of spiritual conflict, Grimshaw was to distinguish more clearly between temptation and sin. In his 'Experiences' he wrote:

In all sorts of temptations also whatsoever, as you commit no sin by them so long as your hand or heart, will or desire consent not, nor

---

[1]Wesley's *Letters*, vol. III, p. 157.
[2]Ibid., vol. IV, p. 213.

comply therewith: so long as you feel an enmity, detestation and hatred against them, or, let me add, not the least desire after them, you are innocent.

But, he continues, the believer must exercise constant vigilance. 'When you first see a temptation, look up to God in a word of prayer, and you shall immediately be delivered. Sometimes it will return again and again, perhaps a dozen times in the space of five minutes . . . ' Nor could he ever relax in this battle against sin. 'The Christian's war is perpetual and without a truce,' he declares in another manuscript, but the outcome was not in doubt: 'His victory is certain and his crown glorious. If his hand be wounded, his heart is safe. And though he is sometimes foiled, yet he is never vanquished.'[1] Temptations resisted and overcome can even be turned to profit in the Christian life:

The more we are tempted, the faster we are rooted and established in the faith. At first young Christians are ready to faint under them, as bullocks unaccustomed to the yoke; but in process of time, they learn their profitableness, and are not so desirous to be rid of them (for no cross, no crown) but desire that they may always have strength to bear, resist and overcome them.[2]

As we read portions of Grimshaw's diary and his other writings, we meet his more human side. Here is a man who was frequently cast down by a sense of failure, and yet whose quality of spiritual life demonstrates the power of God to transform and sanctify. Some have queried whether his use of covenants and vows to God as a weapon in the daily conflict against temptation and sin was in fact more of a hindrance than a help – it seemed at times to increase his sense of despair when he fell short of his own avowed intent. This may be the case and it is possible that he himself came to realise this, for after 1758 there are no further

---

[1]Grimshaw, unpublished manuscript, 'The Nature, State and Condition of a Christian' (JRULM).

[2]'Experiences'.

records of new covenants, although he continued to reaffirm his covenant of 1752 four times each year until his final months of life.

'In thy service I desire and purpose to spend all my time . . . every moment of it to thy glory,' Grimshaw had declared in that covenant on 4 December 1752. How far he succeeded in that aspiration can best be judged from the testimony of those who knew him and had worked with him. 'Mr Grimshaw', said William Romaine 'was the most laborious and indefatigable minister of Christ that ever I knew, and I believe one of the most so that ever was in England since the first preaching of the gospel.'[1]

---

[1]William Romaine, cited by Erasmus Middleton, *Biographia*, vol. IV, p. 407.

17

YEARS OF CONSOLIDATION

'I BLESS THE LORD HIS WORD STILL SPREADS AND FLOURISHES on all sides of us,' wrote William Grimshaw to Mrs Gallatin on 10 May 1754. These words could sum up the steady progress of the work of God in the Great Haworth Round during the 1750s. Writing to Dr John Gillies two months later, Grimshaw added, 'The Lord Jesus still carries on his work in the heart in a still, serious, affecting way, and I trust with as great success as ever since it began . . . In most places where the gospel has been purely preached, it still flourishes, congregations increase, and doors are continually opening. Come and help us is the common cry.'[1]

Vast congregations continued to pour into Haworth each Sunday, and particularly when either John or Charles Wesley or George Whitefield happened to be in the area. With Grimshaw assuming responsibility for organising the Methodist circuits and the duties of the itinerant and lay preachers in Yorkshire, John Wesley's visits became less frequent than formerly. But in June 1752 he was back in the area, though his visit had not been pre-planned. When he had arrived at Whitehaven to board his ship for Ireland, he discovered that the captain had sailed without him. Turning back he travelled into Lancashire and Grimshaw took horse to meet him at Todmorden. Here the Todmorden

[1]Grimshaw to Gillies, *Historical Collections,* p. 508.

circuit book records that Grimshaw handed over the sum of six shillings from the circuit towards Wesley's expenses.

For a week from 8 June the two travelled the round together, preaching wherever there was an opportunity. They visited Roughlee, scene of their sufferings at the hand of George White and his drunken mob four years earlier, and found 'a large, serious and quiet congregation', the vicar of Colne having died the previous year. But it proved to be a frustrating tour for Wesley, fraught with problems. Not only had he missed his ship to Dublin, but twice the horses he had been riding had fallen lame; and when he purchased yet another horse he discovered, when he arrived at Manchester to collect it, that it had been 'borrowed'. This meant a journey to Chester to recover his animal. At last he managed to sail to Dublin on 13 July.

The following year John Wesley was back again and records in his journal for 30 May 1753 the crowded congregations in Haworth. As we have seen, George Whitefield also came in the autumn of 1753 and had helped Grimshaw to administer the sacrament to the ever-increasing number of worshippers. It had been 'a high day' indeed, but these great gatherings also accentuated the continuing need for more space in the Haworth parish church.

The problem was evident once more in April 1755 when John Wesley preached at Haworth shortly before an important annual conference of Methodist leaders to be held that year in Leeds. Noting his movements in his journal, Wesley wrote, 'April 27, 1755. It rained till we came to Haworth: notwithstanding which a multitude were gathered together at ten. In the afternoon I was obliged to go out of the church, abundance of people not being able to get in.'[1] More than ten years previously Grimshaw had applied for permission to enlarge the church. Now it became imperative that work should begin.

Although authorisation for the alterations had been granted in 1743, raising the necessary funds had proved the main cause of

[1]John Wesley's *Journal*, vol. IV, p. 114.

the delay, for, apart from a small proportion of the cost, it had all to be raised from the Haworth parishioners, most of whom were poor. The situation had altered considerably in the ten years that had elapsed since then: funds had been accumulating, some donated by other parishes, but now as a Methodist leader Grimshaw could also appeal for financial help from a far-flung circle of well-wishers. Most could only contribute small sums, but these would mount up, and friends such as Captain Gallatin and his wife and the Countess of Huntingdon were doubtless able to contribute more generously.

Work on the building began in June 1755, and involved increasing both width and length of the existing structure, making the enlarged church almost square in shape, with twin aisles. The walls were also to be raised by over twenty-two feet to accommodate galleries. The pulpit was to be moved to the centre of the south wall and placed between the third and fourth windows. Additional pews were to be installed with a probable seating capacity of 525 seats.[1] Elsewhere there would remain plenty of standing room as was common in churches at that time.

Most of the work was completed within four months, but Grimshaw himself was not happy with the introduction of extra pews, as it would inevitably limit the numbers who could crowd into the church. He only consented on the condition that pew holders would allow those who were standing to enter the pew if at all possible. Pew rents formed one of the main sources of church income[2] and would finance the building of the galleries; although these were not in fact erected until after Grimshaw's death.

An anecdote has survived, told by John Dean, who described himself as 'an eye and ear witness', which indicates that Grimshaw was far from pleased at the erection of the heavy boxed pews in the church. On one occasion, just as he was about to begin to

[1]For further details of planned enlargement, see Baker, *Grimshaw*, p. 184.

[2]Figures are extant from 1791 for the annual cost of renting a pew in Haworth parish church. The cheapest was one guinea while the most expensive recorded was £15 for three seats in the front pew of the north gallery.

preach, he caught sight of an old woman standing near one of the pews, unable to find a seat. 'For shame! For shame!' he called, [adding the name of the pew holder] 'Don't you see that old woman standing there in the aisle ready to drop? Open the pew door and let her in!' The pew holder complied instantly, and it may well have been that he had not noticed the old lady standing there, for the sides and door of the pews were high.

The American humorist, Bret Harte, visiting Haworth shortly before the highly disputed demolition of Grimshaw's 1755 church took place in 1879, left the following vivid description:

As a shrine-breaking American citizen, I suppose I ought to go in for change, under the name of improvement and rebuilding; but if any word of mine could keep the old church intact – could fix forever to posterity its grim hard unloveliness; could perpetuate the old church-yard . . . could preserve the religious discipline of those uncomfortable stiff-backed pews; could secure a mortgage on that bleak lonely outlying moor beyond . . . the hilly street and unsympathetic inn . . . I'd say it.[1]

Grimshaw's diary for the last few months of 1755 indicated that he personally had to shoulder the responsibility for many of the material decisions and details of the new building. On 15 September, we read, 'I preached at Barcroft , the LORD own'd us – We had, I hope, a solid edifying meeting. I then assisted the trustees the Remains of the Day in letting the pewing of the Church. My soul was kept at peace all Day.' A week later he records, 'Sep: 22nd – This day I wrestled with the Lord for Pardon. I hope found it and renewed my Vow most religiously and solemnly. Paid Humphrey Wood for glazing the East, West & North Sides of our Church.' Clearly feeling the pressure of all these extra duties, Grimshaw then makes a rare reference to his health, 'In the evening should have attended the Haworth class, but was prevented by great Pain in my Head. – LORD, what is man!'

But welcome assistance was at hand, for at the Methodist

[1]Bret Harte, cited by Turner, *Haworth*, pp. 163–4.

conference in May of that year, John Nelson himself was appointed to the Haworth Round to take some of the burden from William Grimshaw. United in mind with Grimshaw over issues which were currently causing a degree of dissension among Methodists, John Nelson's presence in the area would have been a consolation. A letter from Nelson to Charles Wesley describes the spirit of unity and love he discovered as he started working more closely with Grimshaw: 'I am now in Mr Grimshaw's Round, and I find my soul blessed in speaking to the people. All the preachers that I conversed with seemed to be more united in love than ever I saw them before . . .'[1]

By October 1755 the enlarged church was ready for use and the first of Grimshaw's friends to preach in it was George Whitefield. In his diary for 12 October 1755, Grimshaw notes that Whitefield preached twice to 'a very numerous audience (some 1000s of people)' – a fact which suggests that even the new premises could not meet the requirements of such occasions.

Not surprisingly, the following year Grimshaw put into effect an expedient to meet this problem; for in 1756 we have the first mention of the scaffolding pulpit, familiarly known as 'Mr Whitefield's pulpit', erected between the third and fourth windows on the south side of the church. Doubtless Grimshaw had conceived the idea earlier when he had his pulpit moved to the south wall between the same two windows. This would enable the preacher to emerge from the church through a window and from the vantage point of the raised platform address the patient crowds thronging the churchyard.

Appropriately it was Whitefield himself who was also the first of the visiting preachers to preach from the scaffolding pulpit on 8 August 1756. Having arrived in Leeds the previous Sunday, he spent a fortnight travelling around the area, preaching in Bradford, Birstall and Tadcaster, until he almost lost his voice, but could record, 'Though hoarse, the Redeemer helped me to

---

[1]Complete letter in Laycock, *Heroes,* p. 159.

speak so that all heard.'[1] On some of Whitefield's preaching tours in Yorkshire the Countess of Huntingdon and Lady Margaret Ingham accompanied him as he travelled around. In all probability an astonishing but undated episode, preserved by A. C. H. Seymour in his *Life and Times of the Countess of Huntingdon*, took place at this time[2] for we know that both these ladies were present on the occasion. Although Seymour does not specifically mention Haworth as the place where the event took place, the account itself makes the location evident. Describing the circumstances Seymour writes:

As Mr Whitefield mounted the temporary scaffold to address the thousands spread before him, he was observed to engage in secret prayer for a few seconds. Then casting a look over the multitude, elevated his hands and in an energetic manner implored the divine blessing and presence. With a solemnity peculiarly his own, he announced his text – *'It is appointed unto men once to die and after this the judgment.'* After a short pause as he was about to proceed, a wild terrifying shriek issued from the centre of the congregation. A momentary alarm and confusion ensued. Mr Whitefield waited to ascertain the cause, and besought the people to remain still. Mr Grimshaw hurried to the spot, and in a few minutes was seen pressing through the crowd towards the place where Mr Whitefield stood. 'Brother Whitefield (said he, with that energy which manifested in the strongest manner the intensity of his feelings, and the ardour of his concern for the salvation of sinners), you stand amongst the dead and the dying – an immortal soul has been called into eternity – the destroying angel is passing over the congregation, cry aloud, and spare not!' The awful occurrence was speedily announced to the people. After a lapse of a few moments, Mr Whitefield again announced his text. Again a loud and piercing shriek proceeded from the spot where Lady Huntingdon and Lady Margaret Ingham were standing. A thrill of horror seemed to spread itself over the multitude when it was understood that a *second* person had fallen victim to the king of terrors. When the consternation had somewhat subsided, Mr

---

[1]Whitefield, *Works*, vol. III, p. 189.

[2]An alternative date for this incident could be October 1760 when both Whitefield and the Countess of Huntingdon were in Yorkshire.

Whitefield gave indications of his intention of proceeding with the service. The excited feelings of many were wound up to their highest point. All was hushed – not a sound was to be heard – and a stillness like the awful stillness of death spread itself over the assembly, as he proceeded in a strain of tremendous eloquence to warn the Christless sinner to flee from the wrath to come.[1]

Two months later Whitefield was back in the area and Charles Wesley was there too, on his last recorded visit to the north of England. Arriving at Leeds towards the end of September, Wesley spent much of the time preaching, visiting society leaders and old friends. On 7 October he rode to Aberford, west of Leeds, hoping to see Benjamin Ingham. But he discovered that his friend had just set out on a four hundred mile tour of all his societies, comprising some thousand or more believers. In December 1755 a number of his converts had seceded from the Church of England, and Ingham had felt obliged to call together the leaders of his societies and draft the basis for a new association, with its own statement of faith, rules and organisation. Similar to Methodism in structure, these independent groups were to be known jointly as the *Inghamite Societies*.

Disappointed at missing Ingham, Wesley was delighted when Grimshaw arrived the same evening at nearby Seacroft. 'Soon our dearest brother Grimshaw found us and brought a blessing with him,' recorded Wesley in his journal. Grimshaw spent the night in Seacroft with Wesley and enjoyed the rare opportunity of spending time together the following day. 'I continued until one in conference with my worthy friend and fellow labourer – a man after my own heart! . . . with such may my lot be cast in both worlds!' wrote Wesley in his journal.[2] Together they set off to a preaching engagement after which Wesley returned to Leeds and Grimshaw home to Haworth, for it was already Friday evening and Whitefield was expected there on Sunday.

Once again on 10 October 1756 Whitefield preached on the

---

[1]Seymour, *Countess of Huntingdon*, vol. I, pp. 265–6.
[2]Charles Wesley's *Journal*, vol. 2, p. 123.

scaffolding pulpit after he had helped Grimshaw administer the sacrament to the numerous communicants within the church. To Lady Huntingdon he wrote later that month describing the events of those days: 'I have been in honest Mr Grimshaw and Mr Ingham's round, preaching upon the mountain to many thousands . . . The sacrament at Mr Grimshaw's was most awful [awesome].' Charles Wesley himself preached at Birstall on the Sunday that Whitefield was in Haworth and records good-naturedly, 'My congregation was less by a thousand or two through George Whitefield preaching today in Haworth. Between four and five thousand were left to receive my warning from Luke 21.'[1]

An independent account has survived of this occasion when Whitefield was preaching in Haworth. A young man of twenty-one, Samuel Whitaker, who had been under conviction of sin since he was a lad of seventeen, heard that Whitefield was due to preach and mingled with the thousands gathering in the church-yard that Sunday. He records the circumstances and the sermon which he could never forget:

The Rev. George Whitefield was expected to preach at Haworth Church, but the place being too small, a scaffold was set up in the yard, and he preached from Zechariah 9:12, 'Turn you to the strongholds ye prisoners of hope, even today do I declare that I will render double unto you.' I got among the crowd, nearly under the scaffold, and it was the most affecting time I ever experienced. He spoke as if he was privy to all my thoughts, words and actions, from the tenth year of my age.

Not long afterwards Whitaker was converted and became a Wesleyan lay preacher for the next sixty years.

The following night all three met again in Leeds for a watch-night service, described as an occasion of 'solemn power' by Charles Wesley. At Whitefield's insistence, Wesley had preached first, followed by Whitefield. 'Few, if any went unawakened away,' added Wesley. A week later Wesley also preached from the

[1]Ibid., p. 124.

scaffolding pulpit. Recording his visit to Haworth after spending the week preaching in the area, he wrote in his journal, 'The church which had been lately enlarged could scarce contain the congregation, who seemed all to tremble at the threatenings or rejoice in the promises of God.' After celebrating the communion – an occasion when Wesley writes, 'We had a blessed number of communicants and the Master of the feast in the midst' – he discovered that following a short interval he was expected to preach again, first in the church and then from the makeshift pulpit outside where thousands were standing waiting. Wesley continues: 'Then I mounted a scaffold and lifting up my eyes, saw the fields white unto harvest . . . The churchyard which will hold thousands was quite covered over . . . God gave me voice to reach them all . . . ' But no sooner had he finished preaching than he found he would have to start over yet again. 'I do not remember', he confessed, 'when my mouth has been more opened or my heart more enlarged.'[1]

After spending four more days together, travelling around the societies and preaching, the two men parted. Wesley recorded in his journal for 21 October 1756, 'I parted with my right hand, my brother and bosom friend, Grimshaw,'[2] little knowing as he wrote those words that it was probably the last time the two ever met.

A tablet in the Haworth Methodist Church commemorates five visits made by George Whitefield to Haworth. In fact there were many more, for few years passed between 1748 and 1762 when he did not visit Haworth at least once and sometimes twice. Frank Baker, whose doctoral thesis on Grimshaw was published in 1963, estimates that Whitefield could have visited Haworth as many as seventeen times. Certainly, the fact that the scaffolding pulpit became known as 'Mr Whitefield's pulpit' suggests that this is likely to have been the case.

That old Haworth churchyard witnessed scenes in those days far beyond anything the present-day stream of sight-seers could

[1]Ibid., p. 127.　　　　　　　　[2]Ibid., p. 129.

guess. Packed into every corner, perched on walls, gravestones and tower, those eager hearers strained to hear the words of life. On one occasion, Whitefield caught sight of a figure clinging to the tower. 'Man,' he called out, 'I have a word for thee.' Startled at being singled out in this way, the man listened with close attention, and was later converted and joined the Methodists. There were lighter moments as well. Once when Whitefield and Grimshaw emerged together from the church window onto the platform, Grimshaw found that someone had provided a pillow to act as a Bible-rest on the makeshift lectern. 'What,' cried Grimshaw in astonishment, 'do you think we come here to sleep?' And matching his actions to his words, he flung the pillow far into the crowd.

Sometimes even Whitefield himself discovered a word of rebuke directed at him by his friend, the curate of Haworth. So impressed had he been by the powerful spiritual work enacted by God amongst the people of Haworth and the surrounding areas, that he allowed himself to speak unadvisedly of it in one of his sermons. After he had rebuked the sins of the ungodly, he suggested that most of the congregation before him scarcely needed such admonitions for they had long enjoyed the benefit of an able and faithful preacher; they were so well-taught that their spiritual life was evident to all. Grimshaw sprang to his side in an instant. 'Oh Sir,' he interrupted, 'for God's sake, do not speak so! I pray you, do not flatter them! I fear the greater part of them are going to hell with their eyes open.'[1]

Even though many evidences of the power and blessing of God rested upon Grimshaw's life and ministry, his clerical opponents never ceased to seek opportunities to silence the curate of Haworth and to prevent his activities beyond the borders of his own parish. As we have seen, Archbishop Hutton's antagonism melted away when he learnt of the effectiveness of Grimshaw's ministry. So when Archbishop John Gilbert succeeded Hutton in 1757, Grimshaw's enemies tried once more to stir up trouble.

[1]Newton, *Letters*, pp. 121–2.

After listening to their complaints the archbishop decided to attend a service at Haworth, before which he took the opportunity to raise all the same vexed issues with Grimshaw: crossing parish boundaries and preaching in private homes. But he added a further accusation. 'I hear', he said, 'that your discourses are very loose and that you can and do preach about everything.' But he was a fair-minded man and so continued, 'That I may judge for myself, both of your doctrine and manner of stating it, I give you notice that I expect you to preach before me and the clergy present in two hours hence, and from the text which I am about to name.'

To the cleric's astonishment, William Grimshaw looked out of the vestry door and saw the expectant people waiting patiently for the service to begin, and responded, 'My Lord, why should the congregation be kept out of a sermon for two hours ... I will begin immediately!' After the set prayers, Grimshaw mounted his pulpit, and led the congregation in extempore prayer. Forgetting his august and captious hearers, he pleaded at the throne of grace for the God of mercy to look in pity on the people, and in particular wrestled in prayer for the archbishop himself until the whole congregation was melted down and few, apart from his hardened critics, could restrain the tears. After he had preached with liberty on the text selected by the archbishop, he closed the service and dismissed the congregation. Crowding round afterwards, Grimshaw's antagonists strained their ears to hear what the archbishop would say to curtail the activities of the curate of Haworth. Taking Grimshaw by the hand, the archbishop said in a trembling voice, 'I would to God that all the clergy in my diocese were like this good man.'[1]

This brought to an end these active attempts to silence Grimshaw. The later 1750s were therefore years of consolidation of the work of God begun so gloriously soon after Grimshaw had arrived in Haworth. They were also years of steady expansion as

---

[1]From A. Strachan's *Life of George Lowe*, cited by Ryle, *Christian Leaders*, p. 128.

the effects of the revival spread far beyond that small Pennine community. Politically the situation in the nation at that time was a cause of deep concern to Grimshaw and the other Methodist leaders, for in 1755 the Seven Years War, which had long been threatening, at last broke out. Grimshaw feared this was the judgment of God on the land for its sins and writing to Mrs Gallatin in June 1756 he expresses these concerns and also his determination to devote all his strength to the work of God while opportunity remained.

I wish my dear Major all health, much happiness of his new com-mission, and at the end a glorious heaven. My sincere respects to him. Times are like to be perilous. No wonder, for iniquity abounds. The sword is drawn. O! that seeing God's judgments are out in the earth, the inhabitants of it may learn righteousness.

In these parts I hope, the Lord's work prospers. The harvest truly is great, but truly the labourers are few . . . I keep preaching as usual, glory be to my Lord, and I hope not without a blessing to souls. Lord, grant I may never faint . . . I hope I shall not be long before I write again to you. Write soon. Sweet Jesus, my dear, dear, very dear Master, bless you and my Major. Pray for me, and I'll pray for you. [1]

[1]Complete letter in Laycock, *Heroes,* p. 164.

18

GRIMSHAW'S UNPUBLISHED WRITINGS

IN SPITE OF THE DEMANDS ON HIS TIME AND ENERGY, needed in maintaining both the care of his parish and the responsibilities of the Haworth Round, William Grimshaw found time to write three treatises. This was in addition to his one published work – his answer to the vicar of Colne's attack on Methodism. The most important of these three was one entitled 'The Admonition of a Sinner',[1] probably written in 1755. Extending to forty-four closely written pages, this treatise was designed to awaken Christians to the important duty of reproving outward and obvious sin wherever they might encounter it and of warning unbelievers of their plight if they did not repent and turn from such sin.

When John Wesley was eighty-five years of age he preached a sermon entitled 'The Duty of Reproving our Neighbour'. As he looked back across fifty years he recollected, no doubt with some nostalgia, the zeal and fervour that had marked the early days of the revival. And this one particular characteristic stood out in his mind: the courage with which many of the pioneer preachers had rebuked sin wherever they saw blatant expressions of evil among the people. 'I never heard or read of any considerable revival of religion,' said the fearless old preacher, 'which was not attended by a spirit of reproving. I believe it cannot be otherwise . . . All the

---

[1]Grimshaw, 'The Admonition of a Sinner' (JRULM).

Methodists, so called, in every place, were reprovers of outward sin.'[1]

One name which would have sprung to Wesley's mind as he thought back on those days would have been that of his friend William Grimshaw whose diligence in this duty had been an effective means of promoting the work of God in Haworth. Describing this aspect of his life, another wrote of Grimshaw, 'He used great plainness and simplicity in his conversation with all men, sparing neither poor nor rich, but boldly reproving all as necessity required.'[2]

So in writing 'The Admonition of a Sinner' Grimshaw was proposing guidelines for others which arose directly both from his understanding of the Scriptures and from his own experience and practice; for he had left no method untried in his attempt to curb manifest expressions of wickedness in his parish. Like Isaac Smith, Grimshaw had found many of his parishioners hardened against all his efforts. William Darney had also pinpointed this same obstinate resistance to the gospel among certain sections of the people in Haworth. In part of a long poem describing the progress of the revival, he contrasted the locals with those from other areas:

> *But while the strangers do receive*
> *the blessing from above;*
> *There's many near the church that starve*
> *for want of Jesus' love.*
> *They do content themselves like swine*
> *to feed on husks and dirt;*
> *For all their pleasure is to sin*
> *and live in carnal sport.*[3]

---

[1]Wesley's *Works,* Sermons, vol. 2 (London: Wesleyan Conference Office, 1872) p. 303.

[2]Mrs Joseph Jones, Laycock, *Heroes,* p. 246.

[3]For whole poem, consisting of 104 stanzas, see William Darney, *A Collection of Hymns* (Leeds: 1751).

So when other methods proved ineffectual, Grimshaw would be direct and ungarnished in his approach to those he knew to be guilty of immoral conduct. His words might cause offence but they went like arrows to the mark. On one occasion he was in a shop, when in came a man who he knew had been guilty of adultery, not just once, but many times. Without a moment's hesitation, and in front of all in the shop, Grimshaw exposed the man's sinful course of life: 'The devil has been very busy in this neighbourhood,' he announced, 'I can touch the man with my stick who lay with another man's wife last night: the end of these things will be death, the ruin of body and soul for ever.'[1]

Three further examples of situations in which Grimshaw was fearless in his rebuke, where others might well have acted differently or remained silent, must suffice as illustrations. The first concerns a stonemason who lived near Ewood Hall where Grimshaw spent much of his time while his children were young. At this period he would conduct a service at Ewood on the Saturday night and again early on Sunday morning before riding the twelve miles back to Haworth ready for the morning service. The stonemason was regularly at these services and being a good singer would raise the tune and lead in the singing. One Saturday night he was absent. On enquiring the reason, Grimshaw learnt that the mason had fallen into his old habits and was too inebriated to attend. But next morning he was back as usual. Grimshaw gave out his own favourite hymn:

> *Come, ye that love the Lord*
> *And let your joys be known.*

But seeing the stonemason preparing to raise his voice and lead the singing, Grimshaw lifted his arm for silence. Shaking his fist in the offender's face, he admonished in broad Yorkshire, 'Sing if ta dare!'

Grimshaw showed the same resolution when among the nobility. When the young Earl of Huntingdon, whose rejection of

[1] Myles, *Life and Writings*, p. 51.

his mother's faith was so heavy a burden to the Countess, tried to draw Grimshaw into speculative argument over his unbelieving principles, Grimshaw, declined, saying: 'My Lord, I do not refuse to argue because I have nothing to say, or because I fear for my cause. I refuse because argument will do you no good. If you really needed any information, I would gladly assist you. But the fault is not in your head but in your heart, which can only be reached by divine power. I shall pray for you, but I will not dispute with you.' The young earl afterwards admitted that he was more impressed by the honesty and firmness with which Grimshaw dealt with him than by any arguments he might have advanced.

On another occasion Grimshaw reproved a woman whose admiration for the talents of a certain preacher blinded her to his lack of grace. 'Madam,' he admonished sternly, 'I am glad you never saw the devil. He has greater talents than all the ministers in the world. I fear if you saw him you would fall in love with him, as you have so high a regard for talents without sanctity. Pray do not be led away with the sound of talents.'[1]

But Grimshaw himself knew well that to reprove sin in his parish would immediately invite unpopularity and often antagonism. He regarded such consequences, however, as part of the price he must pay to please his God and to discharge his spiritual duty to the souls of the people. In the second of his unpublished works, 'The Believer's Golden Chain', he wrote, ''Tis the part of a good man to reprove, though his reproofs are not taken in good part. It is better to lose the smiles of men than to lose the souls of men. We must not suffer wicked men to walk in the devil's ways without reproof.' But this duty, he insisted, was not just the responsibility of the preacher. Every Christian had a God-given obligation to call the attention of friends and colleagues to the sins which would bring their souls under the displeasure of God. 'He can be no true friend to you who is a friend to your sins, and you

---

[1] Hardy, *Incumbent*, p. 98.

can be no friend to yourself, who are offended at him who tells you of your sins.'[1]

This responsibility to rebuke sin, incumbent on every believer, had become increasingly important in Grimshaw's thinking during the 1750s. As we have seen, a serious political situation was developing between Britain and France and the threat of all-out war seemed to be gathering momentum. This hazardous situation, which did indeed lead to the outbreak of the Seven Years War in 1755, coupled with a number of natural disasters several years earlier, led Grimshaw to form a gloomy prognosis both for the country and for the Church of Jesus Christ. In his thinking, the nation, so favoured in recent years by the work of revival manifest on every side, was now under threat of imminent judgment for her sins and lack of repentance. These fears either sprang from or were heightened by a spiritual experience which Grimshaw had early in 1752.

He describes it in some detail in his 'Experiences':

On Saturday, February the first, a little after nine o'clock of this morning, I had it most strongly impressed on my mind that the vial of God's wrath is almost full, and he will shortly pour it out in some grievous judgment or other upon this nation, and upon this parish in common with, if not more grievously than on many other places of the land, for the sin and wickedness of it in general; but especially for her contempt and disregard for the gospel.

Such a premonition led him on to an increasingly serious awareness of his duty to warn, rebuke and exhort the people with added urgency that if possible such judgments might be averted. 'O that the gospel trumpet might continue to sound in our kingdom,' he exclaimed in the next sentence. 'O that the impending ruin our iniquities will involve us in may thereby and by speedy repentance be prevented, but I am not too much persuaded that it will. I am almost persuaded that the present sinners and gospel-despisers will be the greatest sufferers in the approaching

[1]Grimshaw, 'The Admonition of a Sinner'.

calamitous judgment and that therefore the same is not far off –
Repent, O England, Repent! O ye saints, cleave so much closer to
the Lord, as you see this day of sorrow to the nation approaching!'[1]

In the light of this experience Grimshaw redoubled his efforts
to stir up in other believers an awareness of their responsibility
to warn people of their imminent spiritual peril, unless they
repented of their sins. Particularly was this the case when he discovered that his friend Charles Wesley also shared this sense of
impending calamity – regarding it as a possible harbinger of the
approaching end of the gospel age. Such was the background that
led Grimshaw to write 'The Admonition of a Sinner'.

Clearly intending this work for publication, Grimshaw begins
with an introductory letter to his prospective readers, followed
by a preface and a foreword. In the letter he acknowledges a debt
to Richard Baxter, who had written on a similar theme in *The
Saints' Everlasting Rest*[2] and pleads for the serious attention of
Christians to this duty, now so pressing in the light of these
impending judgments of God:

I entreat you, therefore, as you care for the honour of God, as you
desire the prosperity of his spiritual and heavenly kingdom, as you wish
the salvation of poor but precious souls, as you covet the salvation of
your own, as you would be clear of the blood of all men and as you will
answer for it at the dreadful day of judgment, that you seriously
consider the nature and necessity of this duty, and spare no pains nor
omit any opportunities or occasions of discharging it.

Taking for his starting point the words of James 5:20, 'Let him
know that he which converteth the sinner from the error of his
way shall save a soul from death and hide a multitude of sins',
Grimshaw divides his treatise into three main sections: *The Duty
Considered, A Duty Shamefully Neglected* and *Encouragements
and Motives in the Path of Duty*. Each section he also subdivides,

[1]'Experiences'.
[2]Richard Baxter, *The Saints' Everlasting Rest* (London: Kelly, 1834),
pp. 130–50.

as he elaborates on his subject. In a highly readable style, he develops his arguments until the urgent and imperative nature of his theme fills the reader with a sense of shame at his own neglect of this duty and a desire to fulfil his responsibilities with greater boldness and conviction. No sensitive Christian can avoid the force of his arguments.

But there is no undue harshness in his words; rather he comes alongside his readers, diagnoses their problems and suggests reasons why they may be reluctant to rebuke the sins of others, and ways in which they may become more God-honouring in this duty. If Christians really believed what the Word of God declares concerning the reality of hell, 'surely we could not hold our tongue, nor look them [our unbelieving friends and family] in the face without tears'. Rather than cowardly restraint, 'Let us weary sinners out with our loving and earnest entreaties,' he exhorts. 'It is one main way to save souls, and though it may seem very painful at first, yet practice will not only make it easy, but delightful too.'

The motive for reproving sin was all-important in Grimshaw's eyes. To engage in any rebuke of the shortcomings of others merely out of a sense of duty was an inadequate or even selfish motive. 'When we reprove anything reprovable in another, we must take special heed that in so doing we are not selfish rather than truly Christian-hearted.' Simply to ease the conscience, or to speak out of a fear that one might otherwise incur the disfavour of God, is not a commendable motive. 'Rather', he wrote, 'let us be careful to have a view chiefly to the glory of God and our brother's benefit and 'tis enough.'

Again and again, Grimshaw suggests ways in which unbelievers might be approached and challenged:

Say to him plainly, Neighbour: I fear for your estate. Surely, if you were a Christian . . . you would be a new creature, old things would have passed away; all things would have become new. You would have new thoughts, new words, new company and a new conversation. But alas, you seem altogether a stranger to the great work of regeneration . . . you can curse, swear, drink, commit adultery. You are inordinately attached to the world, and drowned in its cares. All your talk is about it . . . Look to your state in time; you must be born again and live to Christ, or be damned for ever.

In the final section of this treatise he deals on the one hand with the grievous consequences of failure in this duty, and on the other with the joys that flow from its faithful discharge. The work takes on Grimshaw's own distinctive style: racy, bold and effective. After demonstrating the painful regrets the Christian may face on his deathbed for his negligence in exhorting unbelievers, he then speaks of the joys awaiting him in the life to come when he meets those whom he has effectually warned and turned into the path of righteousness.

Countering the objection that in heaven believers may not know whether or not their friends and children still on earth have been converted, Grimshaw has an answer:

May not the angels carry the news to them? They brought good tidings to men of a Saviour born in Bethlehem for our redemption; they sang on that happy occasion . . . and no doubt, with the like joy they carry the good tidings of the conversion of sinners to the saints at rest. They may even tell them their names, whose relations they are and where they live.

So believers at rest in heaven

will be as glad to hear of it as the angels themselves; glad to be informed that such in the flesh who were their relations, whose sins were probably so wicked and so vicious, as to have caused them much grief and dread of their damnation, are now in the way of Zion, and glad, exceedingly glad, at the prospect of shortly seeing such, especially their relations whom they once despaired of ever seeing there.

We may sense a degree of longing in these words, arising no doubt out of Grimshaw's own personal burden for his son, John. Having lost his own mother at the age of three and his stepmother when he was ten, John's childhood had been unsettled, much of it being spent at his grandparents' home at Ewood Hall. The pressures on his father's time would also have made normal home life difficult. As we have seen, John had been sent to school at Kingswood in Bristol at twelve years of age, but his education terminated abruptly after Jane's death. Apart from these difficulties, a streak of fecklessness seems to have characterised this young man, increased no doubt by the sizeable inheritance into which he came at the age of twenty-one. His mother's parents had settled all their estate on John and Jane while they were still children. A dozen or more properties in the vicinity of Luddenden were bequeathed to John, and when Jane died, her portion, comprising a farm, an adjoining cottage and £100 in cash, was added to John's already substantial legacy.

With so much wealth coming to him, the youth had little incentive to master a trade, and soon idled away his time, becoming more and more addicted to drink. Seeing in his own son the same traits of character that had set Grimshaw himself on the path of spiritual ruin, it is not hard to imagine that the father did all in his power to reclaim his son. The pain and shame reached its height when John fathered an illegitimate child – a sin for which Grimshaw had often had cause to discipline others in the parish, as we have seen. He must have wondered if he would ever see the answer to his prayers, exhortations and tears. Such thoughts were clearly uppermost in his mind as he wrote of the believer's joys in heaven when their unconverted children were eventually brought to salvation.

Yet for John Grimshaw there was no ultimate excuse for his godless ways. Not only had he witnessed his young sister's believing life and death, but he had seen in his father's manner of life an eloquent testimony to the energising power of true religion. Such consistency of life, as Grimshaw himself pointed out in his 'Admonition of a Sinner', was essential in a Christian who wished to be effective in this important duty of rebuking sin:

If we instruct others in what they are to believe and do to escape hell and obtain heaven, and yet appear not to be circumspectly holy ourselves, but apt to comply with the ways of the world, our instructions, admonitions and reproofs will avail them little . . . Let our lives therefore be strictly exemplary if we would reclaim others and would bring them to Christ, and by him, to heaven.[1]

Throughout this treatise Grimshaw's deep love for the souls of others shines out constantly as the compelling motive. As he considers the present condition and future state of unbelievers he cannot refrain from exclaiming:

Did we really believe that our dear, but poor, ungodly parents, wives, children, brothers or sisters might certainly lie in the fiery pit of hell for ever, if not converted before death, how could we refrain from striving day and night to deliver them from the danger of so deplorable an end? It could not be. So inestimable, so precious are they in the eye of him that made them, that to prevent their otherwise inevitable, intolerable damnation and to procure their eternal salvation, he graciously sent his Son, his only begotten Son into the world, to assume our nature, and to become obedient to death, even the death of the cross. These considerations, if deeply laid to heart, would surely make us solicitous for the welfare of poor sinners, and through the help of God to spare no pains for their conversion.

Cruelty and inhumanity to men's bodies is a most damnable sin. What must it be to their souls, which are immensely more valuable? Alas! we, while here, neither see nor feel what their souls do when they are in hell, for want of our faithful admonition. Little do we know what many a poor wretch, who was once our neighbour, acquaintance, relation now endures in hell upon whom we never bestowed one hour's advice to prevent his destruction. Could we do it now it is likely we readily would, but alas, it is too late. The season is past. As death left them, judgment will find them. The devil has them, and must have them for ever. In hell fire they are, and there must be for ever. O that this consideration may rouse us to beware the alike unmerciful behaviour to poor sinful souls in the future![2]

Grimshaw called a second treatise, already mentioned, 'The Believer's Golden Chain'. Full of epithets, antitheses and striking

---

[1] 'The Admonition of a Sinner'.

[2] Ibid. For a full treatment of this work see Paul E. G. Cook, 'William Grimshaw and The Admonition of a Sinner', Westminster Conference Papers, 1995.

metaphors, it was written neatly in an octavo-sized notebook, roughly bound between boards and consisted of twenty-seven pages. After defining the essential characteristics of a Christian, Grimshaw describes the 'golden chain' which he would have him wear around his neck as 'an ornament of grace'. It consists of twenty links, every link a jewel of encouragement or advice for the believer as he presses towards his goal. For each Grimshaw provides a succinct, memorable and often epigrammatic title, summarising the whole paragraph before he expands it in some detail.

So for the first link Grimshaw advises, 'Hear the best Men; Read the best Books and keep the Best company.' And for the second gem in the believer's necklace he suggests, 'Think and Meditate much of the Four Last Things – Death, Judgment, Hell and Heaven'; for the third, 'Set the watch of our lips by the Sun of Righteousness.' Expanding on this Grimshaw changes his metaphor and writes, 'Live in print, and keep the copy of your lives free from blots and blurs, that all may see the example clearly.'

In many of the links Grimshaw indulges in a play on words to make the point more memorable. So he advises in the tenth link, 'Do good in the world with the goods of the world.' His prose demonstrates a poetic turn of mind and a sense of rhythm and balance. 'Acquaint yourselves with yourselves. No man begins to be good till he knows he is bad. Nor can he relish the sweetness of God's mercies who never tasted the bitterness of his own misery ... A man may be acquainted with the grace of truth who never knew the truth of grace.'

Often the preacher in Grimshaw overtakes the writer, particularly when he considers the eternal destiny of the souls of his readers:

Time ere long will be to you time no longer. Opportunities are for eternity, but not to eternity ... Your time is short and your work is great. You have a Christ to believe in, a God to honour, a soul to save; a race to run; a crown to win; a hell to escape and a heaven to gain. If you lose your time, you lose your souls ... Today is better than tomorrow.

Today is thy living day; tomorrow is thy dying day. Now if ever, now for ever, now or never, up and be doing lest thou be for ever undone.

By the twentieth link Grimshaw has abandoned his attempt to speak exclusively to the Christian. Under the title 'Set out for God at your Beginning and hold out with God unto your Ending', he pours out his anxiety and concern for those who neglect their souls, and particularly the young: 'As there are none too old for eternity, there are none too young for mortality,' he warns. The open worldliness often expressed among the younger generation grieved him; possibly he remembered his own wasted youth:

My beloved, it is sad that we should live so long in the world and do so little good: or that we should live so little in the world and do so much evil Think not to dance with the devil all day and sup with Christ at night . . . The flower of life is of Christ's setting, and shall it be of the devil's plucking? Will you hang the most sparkling jewel of your young years in the devil's ears? If God's day be too soon for thy repentance, thy tomorrow will be too late for thy acceptance.

Like 'The Admonition', this treatise was probably prepared for publication, but Grimshaw's third and final manuscript was considerably shorter and possibly designed to be a lecture. Entitled 'The Nature, State and Conduct of a Christian', it had nine closely written octavo-sized pages. Unintentionally these pages with their six-fold picture of the character of a true believer, provide us with a self-portrait of their writer. As in the preceding manuscript, we have first a definition of a Christian:

The real Christian is a member of Christ, a child of God and an heir of the kingdom of God. He is endowed with the Spirit, washed in the blood and clothed in the righteousness of JESUS CHRIST. All his sins are forgiven. He has the witness, the divine unction in himself. He can cry ABBA, FATHER, and through the merits of his blessed SAVIOUR, confides in the promises, relies on the faithfulness and depends upon the all-sufficiency of GOD. He is justified freely, accepted by God favourably and sealed with the Holy Spirit of promise.

Then follow six brief sketches of the Christian. He is a penitent but pardoned man, a humble man, a patient man, an honest man, a faithful man and a happy man. Clearly these were the ideals which Grimshaw set before himself as he aspired after growth in grace and likeness to Christ. Some we have already noticed: his sense of sin; 'he daily repents because he daily offends'; some we will see later as we trace his zeal and humility. But here we notice his fourth description that 'The true Christian is an honest man.' Integrity and upright dealings, both in business and personal relationships, Grimshaw saw as an essential quality in a godly man.

He is simply and sincerely upright, and this begets such a confidence in him as often wrongs him . . . His word is his bond and his yea his oath . . . With him it is not *This I saw not*, but *this I said*. All his dealings are square and above board. He tells the faults of what he sells and restores the unforeseen gain of a mistake in reckoning . . . His ear is the sanctuary of his absent friend's name and of his present friend's secret.

Grimshaw's honesty in business dealings may be illustrated by the fact that when many of the local cattle developed a cattle murrain, and anxious farmers tried to sell off their animals without disclosing that their herds were affected with the disease, traders would come to Grimshaw and ask him to act as the honest broker, certifying that the animals they were buying were free from infection.

Perhaps the most evocative picture of the believer and the one that reminds us most strongly of Grimshaw himself is the final one – 'The true Christian is a happy man' – for happiness, springing from spiritual joy, was one of Grimshaw's outstanding characteristics. A village artist painted the only known portrait of Grimshaw, which was later unprofessionally doctored to restore its faded colours. The result has produced a rather heavy-featured, dull-looking image. This is not in keeping with the testimony of those who knew him who maintained that joy sparkled in his eyes, lighting up his whole face, which – at his own confession – was not the most handsome. Describing this portrait Spence Hardy writes:

There is a heaviness and doltishness about the features as we have them now, which rather speaks of one who loves glebe and greed, than of one whose merry smile made known how he loved a pleasantry, and whose elevated look told of the soul of fire, now radiant in his own parochial temple, and then flashing in the midst of the wild moor or in some distant part of the land, and constantly burning to promote the glory of God.[1]

This joy, so notable a feature of Grimshaw's personality, sprang from an inner contentment with the providence of God in his circumstances whatever they might be. Describing the happy man, he wrote, 'Upon him all smaller crosses fall as hailstones upon a roof, and as for greater calamities, he can accept these as tokens of love . . . He can make his cottage a palace and his croft a kingdom when he lists.' Such a Christian, according to Grimshaw, is one who rightly evaluates this earth in comparison with the glory to come and is able to live cheerfully in the prospect of joys stored up for him:

His eyes are so fastened on heaven, that no earthly object can remove them; yea, his whole self is there before his time . . . He is so caught up in these heavenly contentments, that he looks down with disdain upon the earth as the place of his banishment . . . He is well provided for both worlds. He is sure of peace here and glory above and therefore enjoys a light heart and a cheerful face.[2]

It only remains to ask why none of these manuscripts was ever published. Possibly the reason was finance. Grimshaw's limited income and almost prodigal generosity often left him in embarrassing circumstances. The time needed to organise and raise the necessary subscriptions to see the work through the press could also have been another reason why he laid it to one side. In the case of 'The Admonition', he may have been deterred by the fact that John Wesley had republished an abridged version of Richard Baxter's *The Saints' Everlasting Rest* in 1754 as volume thirty-seven of his *Christian Library*. Grimshaw may well have felt that

[1]Hardy, *Incumbent,* p. 214.
[2]"The Nature, State and Conduct of a Christian'.

the points he was making had been better expressed by Baxter, to whom he was indebted for some of his material, as he himself acknowledged in the introduction to his own work.

After his death the manuscripts were held in the family until about 1820 when they were given to James Everett. Everett kept them for forty years and then sold them to Luke Tyerman in 1862, along with his unique collection of original letters from the Wesleys, Whitefield, John Fletcher, William Romaine and much other material from the previous century. By that time it is likely that there would not be sufficient interest in Grimshaw's work to merit the expense of publication and they were transferred to the Methodist archives probably at Tyerman's death. The rediscovery in the 1960s of these manuscripts, together with Grimshaw's account of his personal reflections called 'Experiences gather'd by Conversation with my own & the Souls of others' and fragments of his diary, have provided a more direct knowledge of their author.

19

THE UNRESOLVED TENSION: CHURCH OR DISSENT

A DEGREE OF TENSION WAS BUILT INTO the basic structure of Methodism from the outset: a tension between Church and Dissent. None of the first leaders of Methodism had any desire or intention of separating from the Church of England. A profound fear of showing sympathy towards Dissent – itself largely in a state of spiritual decadence – coupled with a basic suspicion of anything that might indicate a movement in that direction, was common among all churchmen. Any suggestion that Methodism should become a unit distinct from the Established Church was viewed with consternation, even dismay, by most Methodist leaders. Writing in 1789 at the age of eighty-six, and at the close of his long ministry, John Wesley declared his personal position: 'I never had any design of separating from the Church of England. I have no such design now ... I declare once more, that I live and die a member of the Church of England and that none who regard my advice and judgment will ever separate from it.'[1]

William Grimshaw held the same view – if anything, he was more rigid in his allegiance to the Church than John Wesley, and his attachment was only exceeded by Charles Wesley whose views on the subject were probably a major reason why he withdrew to a large extent from an itinerant ministry after 1756. But

---

[1]Tyerman, *John Wesley,* vol. III, p. 634.

from the moment that John Wesley began to introduce features into the early Methodist movement which could be described as 'irregular', he had set out on a road which would eventually lead to a separation. Unordained preachers, crossing parish boundaries, field preaching, class meetings, financial backing for the preachers, preaching houses for Methodist gatherings; all these contained within them an influence which would ultimately bring about a break with the Established Church. The old bottles could not contain the new wine for ever.

When William Grimshaw began to recognise this he shrank back from the inescapable consequences of the work to which he had so freely given all his energies and spiritual strength. An early indication of problems to come had occurred in 1752 when, as we have seen, John Bennet seceded from Methodism and became an Independent pastor. Grimshaw had hastened to Bolton to attempt to bring about a peaceable solution to the disquiet and to minimise the disruption among the believers there. In the event he was able to write to Mrs Gallatin in March 1752, 'The differences occasioned of late by Mr Bennet . . . will not be so harmful to the churches as I a while ago feared they would be. Let us pray for the unity and peace of Jerusalem.'[1]

The issue of receiving the sacrament from the hand of their local vicars and curates in their own parish churches was one of the most insoluble and recurring problems to face the early Methodists. Confronted by clergy who were bitterly opposed to their beliefs and sometimes active in persecution, the converts of the revival naturally urged their local Methodist preachers to administer the sacrament to them in their own preaching houses. Some of the preachers, prepared to suffer privation and physical abuse for the sake of the souls of the people, felt that both they and those to whom they ministered should not be denied this privilege.

This led to an increasing measure of unrest among the preachers – men whose sterling work formed the lifeblood of Wesley's

[1] Letter to Mrs Gallatin, 14 March 1752.

organisation. Clearly the issue would have to be addressed when
the 1753 conference met in Leeds. William Grimshaw was
present on that occasion, together with many of his faithful
fellow-workers in the north of England: John Nelson, Joseph
Jones, Jonathan Maskew, Thomas Colbeck; about thirty men in
all. An attempt was made to strengthen the commitment of these
preachers to the Established Church and to restrict them to a
ministry of preaching and exhortation. But in 1754 another crisis
erupted when Charles Perronet, one of Wesley's lay preachers
and brother of the better-known Edward Perronet,[1] took the
step of officiating at a communion service attended by fellow-
preachers and members of one of the London societies.

John Wesley was concessive over the question of lay preachers
officiating at communion services, but his brother Charles
allowed all his High Church background to overcome his reason
and attempted to raise the strongest opposition to such conduct.
He found in Grimshaw a willing seconder although the problem
did not arise in Haworth, where the people enjoyed days of
spiritual blessing whenever the communion was celebrated
among them. Eventually it was decided that the whole question of
the relationship of Methodism to the Established Church must be
thoroughly discussed at the conference due in May 1755. Both
the brothers came north in April and spent time in Birstall
together studying the issues. As we have seen, John Wesley came
on to Haworth and spent time there preaching in the church and
later discussing these matters with Grimshaw.

Grimshaw expressed his own views in a letter to Mrs Gallatin
written on 2 May 1755, immediately prior to the conference –
views which he would undoubtedly have put forward at the
conference.

As to the Lay Preachers' new scheme, I've no relish for it, nor is it
expedient, but rather evidently clogging our Connection with several
grievous difficulties. Their main design, as I understand, is to take
upon them the office of administring the Lord's Supper. But this, as

---

[1] Edward Perronet wrote the hymn, 'All hail the power of Jesus' Name'.

I conceive, is not expedient; because few of the clergy deny this sacrament to our people. Nor is the reception of it from a carnal minister's hand any objection thereto, or any obstruction to the communicant's blessing, provided he receives in faith.

As to the difficulties attending their design – such an attempt cannot be countenanced without a manifest rupture with the Established Church. We must then be declared Dissenters. The clamour and resentment of the clergy will then, and deservedly, be great against us; the work of God which has hitherto been greatly blessed in our hands, I fear will then be greatly impeded . . . and for my part, should this scheme take place I must leave the Methodists; for I am determined to live and die in close communion, a member and minister of the Church of England; for though I can by no means endure the doctrines and deportment of the clergy in general, yet I have no reason to quarrel with our Church. Her Articles, Homilies, Catechism, Liturgy, etc. for the main are orthodox and good. Methodism in substance is the same. I can harmoniously, as matters have hitherto been carried on, be a minister of our church and a Methodist preacher, and thus I could wish to live and die. But if my fellow labourers must needs be innovating, I must adhere to the former capacity and decline the latter. Mr Wesley is now among us, I have conferred with him upon this affair, and he is as much against it as I am.[1]

The conference at which these things were debated was the largest yet held. On 6 May 1755 at least sixty-three preachers gathered in Leeds to discuss the matter. The two Wesleys and Grimshaw were the only ordained men present, although Ingham, who had relinquished his close connections with the Moravians in 1753, was admitted for part of the conference. The main question before the delegates was tersely worded, 'Ought we to separate from the Established Church?' The issue of unordained men dispensing the sacraments was secondary to this larger question and dependent upon it. No details of the discussions have survived; but the concessive position taken up by the preachers who were prepared to forego their wishes for the sake of the harmony of the whole movement, clearly eased the

[1]Complete letter in Laycock, *Heroes,* p. 149.

situation for John Wesley. In his *Journal* he summarised the conclusions they had reached: 'Whatever was advanced on one side or the other was seriously and calmly considered; and on the third day we were all fully agreed in that general conclusion, that (whether it was *lawful* or not) it was no ways *expedient.* '[1]

William Grimshaw was satisfied with the outcome of the conference but he knew that in reality this was only a truce and anticipated that these matters would recur in the future. Several more of the preachers did in fact separate from Methodism that year and become Independent pastors, including John Edwards of Leeds and John Whitford from Bolton, both of whom had worked with Grimshaw in the Haworth Round in 1753. When he wrote to Mrs Gallatin some months later, Grimshaw added a note to his letter about these things: 'The design of administering the ordinances &c. by our preachers got seemingly quite quashed at the Leeds Conference. Though since there appears an intention of reassuming it there, insomuch that a rupture is expected in these Societies in a little time.'[2]

Charles Wesley's attitude was more extreme. Although he had conceded in a letter to his wife, Sally, 'All agreed not to separate: so the wound is healed – slightly,'[3] he was in fact unhappy about the situation and left the conference abruptly without telling anyone, saying he would never attend another – a threat which he did not put into effect. His brother wrote to him the following month in a strain of puzzled exasperation.

Did you not understand that they all promised . . . not to administer even among themselves? I think that a huge point given up; perhaps more than they could give up with a clear conscience. They showed an excellent spirit. When I (not to say you) spoke once and again . . . I admired their spirit and was ashamed of my own. The practical conclusion was, 'Not to separate from the Church'. Did we not all agree in this? Surely, either you or I must have been asleep, or we could not

---

[1] John Wesley's *Journal*, vol. IV, p. 115.
[2] Letter to Mrs Gallatin, 15 September 1755.
[3] Jackson, *Life of Charles Wesley*, p. 79.

differ so widely on a matter of fact. Here is Charles Perronet raving because his friends have given up all; and Charles Wesley because they have given up nothing; and I in the midst staring at one and the other.

The tension had eased, but Grimshaw was right to regard it as only a truce. Charles Wesley did everything in his power to keep the issue alive. Everywhere he went he campaigned on the matter, urging his hearers to cleave fast to the Established Church and its sacraments. He enlisted the support of Samuel Walker, whose ministry in Truro in Cornwall had been powerfully used by God to the conversion of many hundreds of men and women. But, unlike Grimshaw, Walker had never become 'irregular', and had never ventured beyond parish bounds, or made use of lay preachers.

Samuel Walker, with little understanding of Methodist problems, wrote to John Wesley proposing his own solution. The more able of Wesley's lay preachers should seek ordination at the hands of their bishops while the others should give up the itinerant ministry and become 'readers' or 'inspectors' of the different societies. They should then content themselves with reading sermons to the people and providing spiritual guidance only. Walker's suggestion, impractical in any case for few bishops would ordain ex-Methodist lay preachers, was entirely repudiated by John Wesley, who objected that it would leave most of his people without ministry. He would rather separate from the Church than take such a retrograde step.[1]

Clearly the whole question would have to be discussed again and the next conference, fixed for September 1756 in Bristol, was the forum for this further debate. William Grimshaw attended, even though the journey would have taken him four or five days, for he felt the issues were of great moment, both for himself and Methodism. The conclusions of this conference were the same as in 1755, and Wesley summarised them in his journal saying, 'We largely considered the necessity of keeping in the Church . . . and

[1]See Tyerman, *John Wesley,* vol. II, p. 209.

there was no dissenting voice. God gave us all to be of one mind and of one judgment . . . My brother and I closed the Conference by a solemn declaration of our purpose never to separate from the Church, and all the brethren concurred therein.[1]

The anomalous position in which these early Methodists were placed, with their Church loyalties at variance with the new work of the Spirit of God taking place all around them, is demonstrated again by Grimshaw. Having declared that he was determined to live and die in the Established Church, in 1758 he began to build a Methodist preaching house in Haworth for his people. Despite all his protestations to the contrary, he anticipated, as he was later to warn Charles Wesley, that when he had died the Methodists among his people might not be able to obtain the ministry they needed in the parish church and would require their own place of worship.

A legacy of £140 left by the widow of Henry Thornton of Leeds to build such a preaching house gave Grimshaw the necessary funds to start. Land in West Lane was leased from the Lord of the Manor, Joseph Midgley, and the work progressed rapidly between May and September 1758. But even this legacy did not provide enough finance to complete the project and Grimshaw found himself needing at least £80 in addition. Most of the deficit he funded out of his own meagre stipend. It caused him considerable embarrassment and on one occasion his state of 'debitis', as he called it, was a source of some anxiety.

One somewhat bizarre detail comes to light in Grimshaw's correspondence with Mrs Gallatin in connection with the financing of his preaching house. In common with some others in his day, he saw nothing intrinsically wrong in taking part in the State Lottery. This was held annually until it became illegal in 1826. Tickets, which were partly loans to the treasury, cost £10 each, a considerable sum of money in those days. £6 of this was to be put towards the purchase of Government Stock, as a form of investment, while the remaining £4 was used to help finance the 6,000

[1] John Wesley's *Journal*, vol. IV, p. 186.

prizes on offer. These in turn were to be used to purchase further stock. Additional tickets could also be bought not linked with any Government investment in hope of gaining a lucrative prize, not unlike the modern National Lottery scheme. Perhaps, thought Grimshaw, he might come up on the lottery and so bale out his little preaching house from its load of debt!

So in a postscript to a letter dated 2 November 1758 he asks Mrs Gallatin, who was living in London at that time, to purchase '2 quarters of shares and two quarters of chances' on his behalf from a certain stockbroker who had advertised lottery tickets. Grimshaw did not explain his motive for entering the lottery and was not entirely satisfied that he was doing the right thing, and so adds a further postscript to his letter: 'If you know of any sin in offering to buy any part of a ticket or tickets, we are open to conviction . . . If there be no harm in it, as indeed we see none, we desire the favour of the purchase.'

Grimshaw succeeded to a small extent in his venture, though Mrs Gallatin, who had also entered, did less well in hers. Justifying himself for having taken part, he then explained his need 'to reduce a debt which is occasioned by building a preaching house in this town'. As he commiserated with Mrs Gallatin over her failure to make much financial gain, he added, 'I could have rejoiced if better success had attended your own tickets', but concludes, 'We know the lot is of the Lord; He, blessed be his name, hath done what seemeth him good . . . .' However, it was an experiment Grimshaw did not think he would be repeating, and therefore concluded, 'I think, as you do, it is much if I venture again; though thanks be to the Lord for that small prize.'[1]

In addition to his financial concerns, another problem was also causing Grimshaw uncertainty at this time: the question of remarriage. Twelve years had passed since Elizabeth's death and Grimshaw, who was nearly fifty, must have often felt his loneliness

---

[1]Letter to Mrs Gallatin, 19 January 1759, Laycock, *Heroes,* p. 191. John Newton also used such means in an attempt to raise funds, until he found himself £70 in debt.

acutely. Possibly he had met someone suitable – we do not know; but on 5 August 1758 he decided to resolve the matter by the casting of a lot. This was a means for determining problems which John Wesley had once used, a means also favoured by Benjamin Ingham and the Moravians. So having a gold coin from Portugal known as a Joannes, Grimshaw decided to use it to decide this vital issue. 'Yesterday morning,' he wrote in his 'Experiences', 'being Saturday, Augt 5th 1758, I had it as I think manifested to me by a certain Sort of Indication (by a trial of tossing up a Joa.) that it is not expedient that I *denuo Uxorem ducere.*'[1] Grimshaw used a Latin expression to protect himself from any who might chance to see his words. Clearly the Joannes had indicated that remarriage would be inadvisable.

As if to check the veracity of the lot, Grimshaw tossed his Joannes once more, but this time on a matter over which he had no doubts at all – whether he was a child of God. As expected, this result proved positive, and so Grimshaw accepted the guidance of the first lot and never remarried. His financial worries too he decided to resolve in the same way that morning and so he tossed his coin for a third time to see if he would ever extricate himself from his pecuniary problems – for he was 'much involved in debitis'. Here again the lot proved positive.

On the following day, as if to ratify his decision not to remarry, Grimshaw renewed his covenant with God in a most earnest way:

I renew solemnly, devoutly and fully . . . from the very ground of my heart, I say this 6th day of August 1758, upon this paper the aforesaid solemn dedication; and purpose through grace to ratify and confirm the same this Day at the Holy Table. And I do earnestly implore and entirely rest upon the assistance of the Holy Ghost to perform the same to the sole glory of my All-glorious and All-gracious God, and my temporal, spiritual, and eternal comfort and happiness through Jesus Christ our Lord. So help me God. William Grimshaw.

Mrs Gallatin helped Grimshaw by a generous gift towards the

---

[1] Literally, 'lead a wife again', i.e., remarry.

building costs of his small preaching house which measured thirty-six feet in length by twenty-seven in width. In May 1759 he wrote to her once more: 'The building is nearly finished. Several friends have contributed cheerfully and handsomely to it; but it is still immers'd [in debt]. The Burden lies chiefly, I may say solely (which is considerable) upon myself; but I hope thro' the Blessing of God I shall ere long get extricated out of it, and see every penny paid.' A tablet let into the wall of Grimshaw's preaching house bore on it the words of the text which had become his life motto, and proclaimed the spiritual priorities of its first worshippers. It read: 'To us to live is Christ, to die is gain. A.D. 1758.'

The chapel, too small for the regular congregations which continued to meet each Sunday in Haworth, was seldom used in Grimshaw's lifetime. However, Charles Radcliffe, who became Methodist minister in Haworth early in the following century, informed Everett that Grimshaw would sometimes invite itinerant Methodist preachers, men like William Darney and Paul Greenwood, to join him for special services during the Haworth Wakes as a counter-attraction to the revelries of those festivals. On these occasions the preaching house would be used, Radcliffe maintained.[1]

The tension in Methodist circles appeared to have eased after the 1756 conference but there had been no real resolution of the problems and this period of calm could be only temporary. Early in 1760 the same issues flared up again. First was the question of licences both for the preachers and the buildings in which they ministered. In Rolvenden, near Tunbridge Wells in Kent, the local magistrates had tried to evoke the Conventicle Act of 1663 to prevent Methodist worship. The only way to circumvent such recourse to an old law would be to apply for a licence for both buildings and preachers in accordance with the Act of Toleration

---

[1]There is some difference of opinion about whether the preaching house was used in Grimshaw's lifetime. John Pawson, who was in Haworth in 1763 shortly after Grimshaw's death, maintains it was not, and that these preaching services were held in Grimshaw's kitchen. See Laycock, *Heroes*, p. 194.

of 1689. Few Methodist preaching houses had been licensed before this time and were therefore unprotected by the law. But to obtain a licence it was necessary for the preachers to declare themselves Dissenters. Most were unwilling to do this. Some merely evaded the question by calling themselves Protestant Christians, and this was often enough to satisfy the licensing courts. But in 1760, after the situation in Kent, John Wesley advised his preachers to buy licences for themselves and for their buildings if it should prove necessary. Full separation from the Church of England was moving one step closer.

Then in February 1760 three Methodist preachers stationed in Norwich, Paul Greenwood, Thomas Mitchell and John Murlin, took it upon themselves to administer the sacrament of the Lord's Supper. Grimshaw felt the event acutely because two of these three were his 'own men' – Paul Greenwood, his friend and associate since 1741, and Thomas Mitchell, who had been converted under his ministry and whom he had encouraged in his earliest venture into preaching.

Again it was Charles Wesley who took up his pen and began to write impassioned letters on the matter. He was apprehensive lest his brother John might weaken, faced by the mounting pressure from some of his preachers, and start to ordain them so that they might administer the sacrament. Alternatively, and more likely, Charles feared he might allow such a deviation to pass unchecked, so that separation would eventually become inevitable. To his brother he wrote in stinging terms:

We are come to the Rubicon. Shall we pass it or shall we not? . . . The case stands thus. Three preachers whom we thought we could have depended upon have taken it upon themselves to administer the sacrament without any ordination . . . Why may not all the preachers do the same? . . . Upon the whole I am fully persuaded almost all our preachers are corrupted already. More and more will give out the sacrament and set up for themselves, even before we die; and all, except the few that get orders, will turn Dissenters before or after our death. You must wink very hard not to see all this. You have connived at it too, too long.

Such language was unduly strong. As Tyerman comments, 'To say that "almost all the preachers were *corrupted*" because they wished to separate from a *corrupted* church . . . was to employ language either unmeaning or unauthorised; either extravagantly foolish or something worse."[1]

This was followed up by other burning letters to some of the most trusted preachers: to Christopher Hopper, Nicholas Gilbert, one of the oldest preachers, and to faithful John Nelson, to whom he concluded, 'John, I love thee from my heart; yet rather than see thee a Dissenting minister, I wish to see thee smiling from thy coffin.' Clearly distressed by the situation, such comments were not typical of Charles Wesley's spirit, but only illustrate the depth of his feeling and fear of Dissent. The same day, still burdened by the circumstances, he wrote to one who he felt sure would take his part, William Grimshaw:

Our preaching houses are mostly licensed, and so are proper meeting houses [Dissenting chapels]. Our preachers are mostly licensed, and so are Dissenting ministers. They took out their licenses as Protestant Dissenters. Three of our steadiest preachers give the sacrament in Norwich, with no other ordination or authority than a sixpenny licence. My brother approves of it. All the rest will probably follow their example. What then must be the consequence? Not only separation but general confusion, and the destruction of the work, so far as it depends on the Methodists . . . I cannot get leave of my conscience to do nothing in the meantime towards guarding our children against the approaching evil. They shall not be trepanned into a meeting house, if I can hinder it . . . [2]

When this letter arrived in Haworth, Grimshaw had just been settling down to write to Charles Wesley, and was wondering what to say. Now he knew. Doubly grieved because it was his 'own men' who had transgressed in Grimshaw's eyes, his reaction, in a letter dated 31 March 1760, was both over-stated and typically impetuous:

[1]Tyerman, *John Wesley,* vol. II, p. 382.
[2]Ibid., p. 384.

This licensing of preachers and preaching houses is a matter I never expected to have seen or heard of among the Methodists. If it had I dare say I had never entered into connexion with them. I am in connexion and desire to keep so, but how can I do it consistently with my relation to the Church of England? . . . I speak of my situation. Can I justify before my Consistorial Court my preaching in a meeting-house, or my connexion with a body of Dissenting ministers? Am I not liable to suspension? . . . Not many months ago it being reported that I was to preach at a fixed time in a licensed building, the minister and church wardens of the parish had determined to prevent me, but it turned out providentially that I preached in a barn near it.

I little thought your brother approved or connived at the Preachers' doings in Norwich. If it be so, 'to your tents, O Israel!' It is time for me to shift for myself, and disown all connexion with the Methodists; and stay at home and take care of my parish . . . I hereby, therefore, assure you that I disclaim all further or future connexion with the Methodists. I will quietly recede without noise or tumult. No one mindful to continue with them shall be either directly or indirectly hindered by me.

In general, as to licensing of preachers and places, I know no expedient to prevent it. The thing is gone too far . . . It has been gradually growing to this ever since erecting preaching houses was first encouraged in the land. So soon as you are dead, all the preachers will do as many have already done . . . Dissenters the Methodists will all shortly be; it cannot, I am fully satisfied, be prevented.

Nor is this spirit merely in the Preachers. It is in the people also. There are so many inconveniences attend the people, that in most places they all plead for a settled ministry. They cannot, they say, in conscience receive the sacraments as administered in our church. They cannot attend preaching at eight, twelve, and four o'clock on Lord's days, *and* go to church . . . For my part, though I do not approve of everything in our liturgy, yet I see nothing so materially amiss in it . . . No; where shall I go to mend myself? I believe the Church of England to be the soundest, purest, most apostolical, well-constituted national Christian Church in the world. Therefore, I can in good conscience, (as I am determined, God willing, to do) live and die in her. But my conscience is not another man's.[1]

[1]Complete letter in Laycock, *Heroes,* pp. 209–10.

Grimshaw feared the future course that Methodism would take. He realised the people could not be expected to attend both their own Methodist gatherings and the services at their parish churches. Charles Wesley, in Grimshaw's view, was trying ineffectually to reverse a trend which he himself had helped to set in motion. But for Grimshaw to 'resign' in so sensational a manner from a cause that had been at the heart of his ministry and thinking for the previous thirteen years was ill-considered. He too had helped to create the predicament and could not escape from the consequences in such a way.

When Charles Wesley received this letter he called together all the leaders of the London societies and read it aloud. The reaction was dramatic. It 'put them in a flame. All cried out against the licensed preachers' and the whole issue was shelved once more, not to surface again until long after Grimshaw's death. Other pressing issues soon took precedence in the thinking of the Methodist leaders. But the tensions remained still unresolved. Grimshaw wrote to Mrs Gallatin when the storm had abated, 'I follow my old calling and in the old way. I know of no better one'[1] – an apt description of his life during the few years that remained to him.

[1] Letter to Mrs Gallatin, 7 February 1761.

20

WHEN GOOD MEN DIFFER

ALTHOUGH WILLIAM GRIMSHAW HELD STRONG CONVICTIONS over the importance of retaining Methodism within the Established Church, he still maintained fellowship with those who differed from him on the issue. His friend Benjamin Ingham and his numerous societies had officially withdrawn from the Church of England and called themselves Dissenters in December 1755. Even though Grimshaw must have been grieved at the decision, he continued to accompany Ingham on preaching tours and to preach among the Inghamite societies. Batty records one such occasion in October 1758 when both Whitefield and Grimshaw preached at Winewall, centre of one of Ingham's largest societies.[1]

Invariably in the Christian Church good men will be found holding divergent positions over secondary doctrinal issues, and this has lead to controversy, discord and even enmity at times. Revival can accentuate such differences, and the eighteenth-century revival was no exception. But Grimshaw stood out to a marked degree against much of the contention which involved many of his contemporaries in sharp altercations. He had a genuine love for all true Christians, whatever their denominational label, declaring, 'I love them and will love them and none shall make me do otherwise, and my house shall always be open

[1] Batty, 'History', p. 78.

to them all.'[1] Like his friend, Whitefield, he could say, 'Do not tell me you are a Baptist, an Independent, a Presbyterian, a Dissenter; tell me you are a Christian, that is all I want; this is the religion of heaven, and must be ours upon earth.'[2]

Grimshaw was aware of the damage which can be wrought within a church or body of believers by an insistence on party labels above commonly held fundamental beliefs, and he wrote in his 'Experiences':

By these means Satan stirs up disputes, contentions, and controversies about opinions and doctrines; and then divides the church of Christ into sects and parties . . . They [would] have it believed that if men hold not so, they are not to be saved; as if the right and hope of salvation depended rather upon opinion or what we hold, than with what we are in CHRIST JESUS.

In 'The Believer's Golden Chain', Grimshaw expresses his ardent desire that Christians should be united, 'O dear brethren, Let me entreat you to live in love and to live in truth. You are all fellow-labourers, fellow-members, fellow-citizens, fellow-travellers, fellow-sufferers, fellow-servants, fellow-heirs, and should you not love one another?' Confronted by believers who refused to be reconciled to one another, Grimshaw had been known to fall on his knees and beg them with many tears to love each other in the bonds of the gospel. Going even further, Mrs Joseph Jones records that on one occasion, when he was trying to conciliate two querulous believers, she had heard him say, 'I beg you upon my knees: I will put my head under your feet, if you will but love one another.' His own passionate concern for unity between them had so great an effect both on them and others present at

---

[1]Mrs Joseph Jones, tribute to William Grimshaw, in Laycock, *Heroes*, p. 246.
[2]George Whitefield, *Sermons on Important Subjects* (London: 1825), p. 684, cited by Iain H. Murray, *Revival and Revivalism* (Edinburgh: Banner of Truth Trust, 1994), p. 26.

the time, that 'all in the house were melted down in tears and perfectly reconciled'.[1]

But such catholicity of spirit had not come easily to Grimshaw. He had faced circumstances in Haworth which tested his principles to the limit, particularly from the Baptists. At the close of his account of the work of God in Yorkshire to Dr John Gillies, he noted the problems that sprang from that source: 'The most material impediment met with and detriment received is, I fear, from the Anabaptists and Antinomians. These have, I am afraid, and still do make great rending in our Societies.'

John Newton recollected the occasion in 1760 when he and Grimshaw had stood together on the moors above Haworth – the second and last time the two men were to meet. Gazing round at the whole vista spread out before them, Grimshaw began to describe to his friend the development of the work of God in the area. He told him of the situation he had found when he arrived in 1742 when there were only a handful of communicants; but then he continued, 'And now, through the blessing of God upon the poor services of the most unworthy of his ministers, besides a considerable number whom I have seen and known to have departed this life, like Simeon, rejoicing in the Lord's salvation; and besides five dissenting churches or congregations,[2] of which the ministers and nearly every one of the members were first awakened under my ministry; I have still at my sacraments, according to the weather, from three to five hundred communicants.'[3]

Behind that brief reference to the five dissenting congregations which owed their existence to his own work lay many hard lessons learnt in the school of toleration. From it we discover the breadth of this man's sympathies and his acceptance of believers whose church principles differed from his, even when his own work suffered from their activities. Each of these five congregations, as he pointed out to Newton, were made up of pastors

---

[1]Laycock, *Heroes,* p. 245.

[2]All to be described subsequently except James Crossley, an Independent from Booth, near Luddenden.

[3]Newton, *Letters,* p. 86.

and members who had originally been amongst his own hearers. Rightly could Grimshaw be called 'the father of Yorkshire Dissent',[1] though he himself would not have liked the label. He might have preferred the description given him by William Crabtree, one of the five pastors to whom he referred: 'He [Grimshaw] may indeed be considered as the parent of nearly all the religion in that part of the country, which before he arose exhibited a sad scene of ignorance, barbarism and profaneness.'[2]

William Crabtree, who died in 1811 at the age of ninety-one, had memories of Grimshaw that stretched back to 1743. He could recollect the first time he had heard Grimshaw preach when he was twenty-three and he wrote in his memoirs. 'He was preaching on the Prodigal Son. He made this observation, "that one sin would damn a soul as well as a thousand". It struck me to the heart. Then I thought my case deplorable: I went after that to Haworth constantly to hear him.'[3] After his conversion Crabtree went on to embrace Baptist principles and became the first pastor of Westgate Baptist Chapel in Bradford, later extending his influence by founding three other Baptist causes in the area: Halifax, Farley and Leeds. Some of the believers in the societies founded by Grimshaw, Nelson and others in these places transferred their loyalties to Crabtree's churches.

Richard Smith, too, was one of Grimshaw's first converts. He is mentioned by William Batty in his account of Benjamin Ingham because he travelled round with Ingham for a time in 1747. But in 1748 he was baptised as a believer, and in 1750 gathered together some converts from his ministry and began Wainsgate Baptist Church in Hebden Bridge. No breach of fellowship occurred between either Crabtree or Smith and Grimshaw. Instead he rejoiced in their evident usefulness in Christ's kingdom. Smith's ministry bears eloquent testimony to the preaching under which he himself was converted:

[1]S. Baring-Gould, *Evangelical Revival* (1929), pp. 267–8.
[2]Isaac Mann, *Life of William Crabtree* (Shipley: Isaac Mann, 1815), p. 17, JEN.
[3]Ibid.

Mr Smith had a deep acquaintance with the depravity of human nature, the dreadful plague of the heart . . . And in his ministry he had a manner peculiar to himself of coming home to the conscience and touching all the springs and movements of the heart. To open the exceeding great and precious promises for the encouragement of the desponding soul was his peculiar delight.[1]

In the case of James Hartley, who built his Baptist chapel within the sound of the Haworth church bell, Grimshaw had more difficulty. Young Hartley was twenty when Grimshaw first went to Haworth, and he became one of his earliest converts. Though he was from a poor family background and had few educational advantages, he proved to have outstanding natural ability. This factor, coupled with a powerful work of God in his soul, soon marked James out as a young man of considerable spiritual promise. Grimshaw showed constant interest in his progress and a kindly concern for his welfare. But not many years later, Hartley came under Baptist influence, and no longer attended Grimshaw's ministry. Nevertheless, he continued to show understanding and kindness towards the young man. But even Grimshaw's patience was severely tried when Hartley drew many of his converts away and established a Baptist cause in Haworth in 1748.[2] This work flourished and in 1752 he and his congregation built a chapel in West Lane, scarcely more than two hundred yards from the parish church.

Despite these circumstances, Grimshaw maintained a good relationship with Hartley, helping him whenever he could, welcoming him to his home and officiating at his marriage, then conducting his first wife's funeral, and eventually officiating at his second marriage some years later. On meeting Hartley unexpectedly on one occasion, Grimshaw, with all the exuberance

---

[1]Cited by H. M. Pickles, *Benjamin Ingham* (published by author, 1995), p. 43, from Baptist register, ed. John Rippon (1801), p. 393.

[2]In Seymour's MS Life of Ingham, p. 267 (cited Pickles, *Ingham,* p. 42), Seymour confirms that a large number of Grimshaw's hearers left him at this time and attached themselves to Hartley.

of his generous nature, flung his arms around the young man, exclaiming, 'God bless thee, James; God bless thy undertaking! Perhaps God has given thee more light than he has given me – God bless thee!'[1]

Privately, however, and in his more reflective moments, Grimshaw found Hartley's behaviour hard to justify, and complained ruefully, 'They may go into my quarry and dig up as many stones there as they possibly can, but they shall not have the stones which I have dug up, and hewn and squared for the Lord's building if I can possibly help it.' Or, to change the metaphor, he joked, 'The worst of it is that so many of my chickens turn ducks.'[2] Commenting on this progress of Dissent as a by-product of Grimshaw's ministry, Newton wrote, 'The most that can be said against him (if it be indeed against him) is that he found them [his parishioners] little better than heathens, and left them evangelical dissenters.'[3]

Although he showed understandable reserve at James Hartley's activities, Grimshaw encouraged the setting up of Independent congregations in areas adjacent to Haworth where no other gospel witness had been established. One example of this can be found in the case of Titus Knight whose cause Grimshaw championed, despite the fact that Knight's views on church government differed from his own. Knight was an Independent, but, like Hartley, Crabtree and Smith, had been awakened and converted through Grimshaw's own ministry. Encouraged by Grimshaw, he began to preach, and went on to become a recognised Methodist lay preacher. But a change in his convictions concerning church government led him to leave the Methodists and to set up a Congregational church in Halifax. Blessed by God, his work prospered and soon his people wished to build their own place of worship. But they were a poor people and had few financial resources for such a venture. To whom

[1] JEN. [2] JEN. MS letter, William Leach to Everett.
[3] Newton, *Letters,* p. 91.

could Knight turn for help? Knowing Grimshaw's genuine concern for all true believers, it was with him he shared the need.

Grimshaw, whose personal generosity had become a byword, was often in straitened circumstances himself, but he knew of one person from whom he could confidently expect help for Titus Knight and his congregation – the Countess of Huntingdon. Undeterred by Knight's doctrinal divergence from his own position, he wrote a begging letter to 'Her Ladyship':

I have had two visits from Mr Knight. He professed great love and respect for your ladyship . . . He is actively labouring to rescue sin-slaved souls from the kingdom of darkness, and the Lord has put honour on his testimony, by giving him souls to his ministry. The people among whom he is sowing the seed of the kingdom are poor, their means are very limited, yet the Lord has put it in their heart to build a house for his word. Now I have come to the point – can your ladyship spare a mite to aid these worthy souls? The demands on your generosity I know to be great, and on that account I feel a repugnance at asking, because I am persuaded you would give even to the gown on your back if the case required it . . .[1]

As a consequence of this appeal, Lady Huntingdon sent timely aid to this hard-pressed cause, and a Congregational chapel was built in Halifax.[2]

Another young man whom Grimshaw influenced profoundly, and one destined to far greater prominence than any mentioned so far, was John Fawcett. Born in 1739, he was converted at the age of sixteen, and would walk across from Bradford each Sunday for two years in order to attend Grimshaw's ministry. A serious-minded youth with deep spiritual convictions, John Fawcett, too, espoused Baptist convictions and then began to attend James Hartley's ministry in preference to Grimshaw's. William Crabtree baptised him and in 1760 he became the illustrious successor to Richard Smith at Wainsgate. Fawcett's estimate of Grimshaw was

---

[1]Cited by Laycock, *Heroes*, p. 235.

[2]The chapel, now a theatre, became known as The Square, and was the church in which J. H. Jowett was brought up.

of the highest and he described him as a man whose 'whole soul was swallowed up upon the service of his divine Master'.[1] Later Fawcett was to establish an academy for the training of pastors for the Baptist ministry, and through his writings and hymns exercised a wide influence throughout the country.

William Grimshaw's love for all believers was sincere and deep. He deplored religious controversy, feeling it could bring nothing but harm to Christ's cause. 'Oh! the lamentable mischiefs occasioned by party zeal, bigotry and partial opinion of the body of Christ's people and in the breast of her private members,' he exclaimed in his 'Experiences', possibly after some unfortunate expression of such 'party zeal' had come to his attention.

But Grimshaw was not so concerned with accord among believers that he was willing to tolerate doctrinal error, particularly if such deviations were clearly detrimental to his own or to his people's spiritual progress. As we have seen, he was deeply concerned over the teaching which John Wesley favoured which suggested that Christians could live without known sin. Totally at one with Wesley in his desire for continual growth in sanctification among professing believers, he felt that this teaching, particularly as expressed in a far more extreme form by some of Wesley's followers than Wesley himself would sanction, could bring a sensitive believer into despair.

Mrs Gallatin was a case in point. Converted under Whitefield's preaching and a friend of both the Wesley brothers and Grimshaw, she often found herself uncertain and troubled because of the daily battle against the power of sin. From 1758 onwards the subject of Christian perfection occurred with increasing frequency in Grimshaw's letters to her, particularly because of some whose extravagant claims exceeded their attainments in daily life. On 30 November 1758 he wrote, 'Is it their pretending to perfection, or their not walking and behaving consistently with such pretence that troubles you?'

[1] *Life of John Fawcett, DD* (Halifax: 1818), p. 22.

The issue of Christian perfection burdened Grimshaw increasingly, especially after 1760 when some professing believers in Otley, well-known to him through his frequent visits to their society, made claims of sinless perfection which Grimshaw knew well were inconsistent with their manner of living. Writing to Charles Wesley, Grimshaw said:

The doctrine of perfection runs very high just now in these parts. About Otley and Leeds I am told not fewer than thirty profess sinless perfection; and thirty more will pretend thereto shortly. If it be of God, it is well. Time will prove it. I wish they knew their own hearts. My perfection is to see my imperfection; my comfort to feel I have the world, flesh and devil to overthrow through the Spirit and merits of my dear Saviour; and my desire and hope is to love God with all my heart, mind, soul and strength, to the last gasp of my life. This is my perfection. I know no other saving to lay down my life and my sword together.[1]

So troubled was Grimshaw about this matter that he felt it could constitute a further reason why he might not be able to continue in Methodism. Writing to John Wesley on 23 July 1761, he warned:

There are several things which have for some time been matters of so much uneasiness to me that I thought that I should be obliged to secede from the Connexion ... Sinless perfection is a grating term to many of our dear brethren; even to those who are desirous to be truly holy in heart and life. Should we not discountenance the use of it and exchange it for terms less offensive, but sufficiently expressive of true Christian holiness?

He then went on to demonstrate to Wesley his own understanding of Christian perfection after which all believers should aspire:

By this I mean (and why should I not tell you what I mean?) all that holiness of heart and life, which is literally, plainly, abundantly, taught us all over the Bible, and without which no man ... can ever expect

---

[1] Letter to Charles Wesley, 31 October 1760, cited by Laycock, *Heroes*, p. 204.

to see the Lord. This is that holiness, that Christian perfection, that sanctification, which without strange, offensive, unscriptural expressions . . . every sincere-hearted member of our societies strenuously labours to attain.[1]

With such a sentiment the two men were in complete harmony. But Grimshaw retained his basic dislike of the terminology frequently used in connection with the teaching until the end of his life. And in his *Creed* he could declare, 'I believe it is by the Spirit we are enabled, not to eradicate, as some affirm (for that is absurd) but to subjugate the ol*d man*; to suppress, not extirpate . . . our fleshly appetites . . . So that the best believer, if he knows what he says, and says the truth, is but a sinner at best.'[2]

The doctrine of the imputed righteousness of Christ formed a further area of divergence between Grimshaw and Wesley. This doctrine, set out by John Owen in his work on *Justification by Faith*, had been the bedrock of Grimshaw's thinking since it had finally delivered him from his futile efforts to please God by some measure of holy living and had given him an assurance of his acceptance before God on the grounds of the perfect righteousness of Christ. In his *Creed* he states his beliefs in these words:

I believe that this very righteousness . . . will be imputed to every penitent believing soul, and that to all intents and purposes, as if he, as indeed he should have done, had *himself* performed it. Glory be to God for *free grace* . . . I believe, in this righteousness every member of Christ stands, and will stand complete, irreprovable and acceptable in God's sight, both at death and judgment.

> *Jesus, thy blood and righteousness*
> *My beauty are, my glorious dress.*[3]

Writing to Mrs Gallatin he expresses the strength of his attachment to this doctrine:

---

[1]Cited by Everett, 'Curate of Haworth'.
[2]Grimshaw's *Creed*, XXII & XXIII. See Appendix 3.
[3]*Creed*, XVI & XVII. See Appendix 3.

'Tis for the sake of the righteousness of Christ that all I have or hope for in time or eternity are mine – remission of sins, acceptance with God, all the promises, all the grace and all the glory of God is mine for evermore. To whomsoever this righteousness is imputed through faith, all the blessing of the new covenant belong and are Yea and Amen. I can never say too much of it or for it.[1]

John Wesley, on the other hand, firmly rejected the doctrine of the imputed righteousness of Christ believing it led to antinomianism.[2] He argued that if the believer were to be clothed in the righteousness of Christ, he would then have no further incentive to grow in grace and produce fruits of holiness in his own life. In the Minutes of the first Methodist Conference held in June 1744, as the early preachers sought to clarify their doctrinal beliefs together, Wesley had asked, 'In what sense is the righteousness of Christ imputed to all believers?' And in answer he had replied, 'We do not find it expressly affirmed in Scripture that God imputes the righteousness of Christ to any: although we do find that faith is imputed to us for righteousness.'[3]

But, early in the 1760s, Wesley expressed his views in far stronger terms. This was in answer to some extremists in his London society, notably his former colleague Thomas Maxfield, whose claims to Christian perfection had led him and his followers to a rampant antinomianism. Failing to recognise that this was in fact the logical conclusion of his own teaching on perfection, and not the result of believing in Christ's imputed righteousness, Wesley made a stinging attack on this latter doctrine:

[1]Letter to Mrs Gallatin, 30 November 1758.

[2]Berkhof summarises Wesley's position in a short review of the historical misconceptions of this doctrine as follows: 'The Arminians limit the scope of justification, so as to include only the forgiveness of sins on the basis of the passive obedience of Christ, and to exclude the adoption of the sinner in favour by God on the basis of the righteousness of Jesus Christ.' L. Berkhof, *Systematic Theology* (London: Banner of Truth Trust, 1959), p. 513.

[3]Cited by Albert Outler, ed., *John Wesley* (New York: Oxford University Press, 1964), p. 136.

Christ's righteousness being imputed to us, we need none of *our own*; that seeing there is so much righteousness and holiness *in him*, there needs none more *in us* . . . This is indeed a 'blow at the root' – the root of all holiness and true religion. Hereby Christ is 'stabbed in the house of his friends', of those who make the largest professions of loving and honouring him, the whole design of his death – namely 'to destroy the works of the devil' – being overthrown at a stroke. For wherever this doctrine is cordially received, it leaves no place for holiness. It demolishes it from top to bottom . . . Here is a masterpiece of Satan. Men are holy without a grain of holiness in them – holy in Christ, however unholy in themselves.[1]

For nine years from 1757 to 1766 Wesley was also locked in literary conflict with James Hervey on this subject. Hervey, who had been an undergraduate at Lincoln College at the same time that Wesley was a Fellow, had maintained his friendship with Wesley over the years. But in 1755, following the publication of Hervey's work, *Theron and Aspasio* – a prolonged defence of imputed righteousness in dialogue form – the two were found on opposing sides on the issue. Not surprisingly, in the light of these things, Mrs Gallatin was thoroughly confused and wrote to Grimshaw complaining that Wesley was 'writing and preaching against imputed righteousness'. She even wondered whether Grimshaw himself might be misleading her. Grimshaw replied that he was 'surprised and sorry to hear' that Wesley was preaching against this truth and would give her a fuller answer on the question in his next letter. But other matters were engrossing his attention and he does not seem to have dealt with this matter fully in any subsequent letter.

However strenuously Grimshaw might try to avoid all discord among believers, it would have been impossible for him to remain neutral on that profound religious divide which had threatened to sever John and Charles Wesley from George

---

[1]John Wesley, *A Blow at the Root, or Christ Stabb'd in the House of his Friends*. Text based on 1773 edition of *Works*, vol. XX, pp. 265–75; Albert Outler, ed. *John Wesley*, p. 380.

Interior of Grimshaw's church

The Great Haworth Round and Beyond

NORTH SEA

Hartlepool 86m

to Newcastle 104m

Osmotherley

Helmsley

York

Hull 78m

Leeds

Otley

Keighley

Bradford

HAWORTH

Roughlee

Colne

Hebden

Halifax

Heptonstall

Todmorden

Luddenden

Sheffield 46m

Glossop

Manchester

Stockport

Kendal 58m

Ingleton

Preston

Blackburn

Brindle

Bolton

Liverpool

Chester 72m

IRISH

SEA

Whitefield in the early days of the revival and which was to split Methodism irrevocably after 1770 – the contention over Calvinism and Arminianism. But Grimshaw steadily refused to become embroiled in this controversy, feeling it could only be detrimental to the progress of the gospel. When Joseph Williams visited Haworth in 1746 he reported concerning two of Grimshaw's early assistants, 'In all this work he [Grimshaw] acknowledges he has had a great deal of assistance from two laymen . . . of these, one holds particular redemption [Darney], the other [Greenwood], universal redemption; his business is to hold the balance as evenly as he can.'

An obvious reason for his reserve on this matter was his love for both John and Charles Wesley and for George Whitefield. Speaking of this he had once exclaimed,

I love my God first and best, but not enough. Next to him, I love my dear brothers Wesley, with whom I am heartily joined, and hope never to be parted in time or eternity. Next to them I love my dear brother Whitefield, and next to him all the labourers, and all that love and desire to love the blessed Jesus. And I love mankind as well as them.[1]

Although, as he himself explained, his earlier acquaintance with John and Charles Wesley placed them paramount in his affections, Grimshaw was actually nearer to Whitefield in his theological position. His early nineteenth-century biographers, being of Arminian persuasion, were anxious to claim Grimshaw for the Arminian wing of the revival, but James Everett had to admit, though rather grudgingly, 'Much as he loved the Wesleys it is to be doubted whether Whitefield had not the pre-eminence, whatever a preceding biographer [William Myles] has advanced to the contrary.' Everett then concludes with this unexpected admission: 'Whenever Whitefield, therefore, appeared in the neighbourhood, he [Grimshaw] turned towards him like the sun-flower to its parent orb, and while basking in his beams,

[1]Laycock, *Heroes*, p. 244.

seemed to derive from his preaching and his conversation a degree of vigour not attainable from any other ministerial source.'[1]

John Newton, who understood Grimshaw's standpoint better than most, describes his friend's view of himself as 'a pensioner on mercy', and sums up his doctrinal position by saying:

He confesses man's depravity to be total, that he is not only dead in law as a transgressor, but dead in sin, destitute of all spiritual life, and incapable, as a dead body of any spiritual act, having in himself neither the will nor desire to turn to God. Consequently he ascribes the *whole* of his conversion to the distinguishable grace of God . . . He depends entirely on the influence of the Holy Spirit for his perseverance in grace. He owns his best services and warmest efforts were defective and defiled and needed forgiveness . . . He styles himself a child of God with an unwavering tongue, and maintains a sure persuasion of his final perseverance in grace . . . If the doctrine which ascribes the whole of a sinner's salvation, from the first dawn of light, the first motion of spiritual life in the heart, to its full accomplishment in victory over the last enemy, be Calvinism, I think Mr Grimshaw was a Calvinist. But I am not sure he thought himself so.[2]

The task to which God had called Grimshaw, together with the men who toiled with him in the eighteenth-century awakening, was not the task of formulating creeds or clarifying theological propositions.[3] His was the call to awaken the untaught masses to

[1]Everett, 'Curate of Haworth'.

[2]Newton, *Letters,* pp. 82–3.

[3]'The primitive [early] Methodists entertained not the remotest idea of reforming the doctrines of Christendom, nor of making their mark on the creed of the church future. They dealt with interests far more tangible and more speedily realised to their hearts – the spiritual renovation and rescue of millions of souls "dead in Adam" but "alive in Christ" from sin and hell. And from this mighty work they thought not to come down to break lances with theological combatants . . . These men were not fitted either by nature or by culture or experience for doctrinal reformers. And hence, we believe, that Methodism was never commissioned for this specific work.' *The British and Foreign Evangelical Review* vol. XI (London/Edinburgh: James Nisbet, 1862), p. 30.

their spiritual peril. Impelled by the enormity of this assignment, he went out with heart burdened for the needs of the people and a love for the souls of men. He believed that the gospel was for 'every creature' and must therefore be preached to all, whether they wished to hear or whether they did not. How the questions of election and the extent of the atonement tied up with this commission from God, he did not profess to know.

The explanation that he personally found most satisfying he wrote down in his 'Experiences', which as we have seen, he did not intend for publication. In it Grimshaw attempted to blend the two systems of thought held by his friends: God's sovereign electing grace, unconditionally bestowed on his chosen people, with what he called 'the universal scheme' – excluding none from the orbit of God's saving mercies:

It is clear from the holy Word of God, that both are true. Viz. that there are a select number of people chosen from all eternity, and predestinated to eternal life in Christ and given to CHRIST in the eternal purpose, decree and covenant of the Father with him, and that such are irresistibly called in time, convinced, converted, justified, sanctified and absolutely saved. Why may not the Lord in his infinite wisdom and goodness make the salvation of a certain number of persons absolute and irresistible as a gift to our Saviour as a reward for his toil and sufferings . . . and also the salvation of all the rest of mankind conditional, possible and attainable since the merits of our Saviour must be allowed to be as sufficient to save all men as a part.

Both parties may be thus at once united together. The advantages Satan has no doubt many a time taken by the two schemes to make rending, discord, bigotry, confusion and malice and strife in the church of Christ are utterly frustrated. The whole book of God is by the same means rendered consistent, easy, clear and intelligible. Burdened consciences are thus relieved entirely. And for my part, I must own, and I hope without the imputation of enthusiasm, that I feel great comfort and satisfaction in my own breast arising from such Scriptures as make for the consistency and verity of the two opinions. All bigotry in favour of the one dies, and a catholic affection glows in my heart towards all that are votaries of the other.

With his all-consuming concern for the salvation of his fellow men, Grimshaw felt that time spent in controversy was time ill-spent. Henry Venn declared of him, 'Seldom had the sun ever run half his daily course before this minister had once or oftener declared the testimony of the Lord which enlightens the eyes of the mind and rejoices the hearts of the poor.' John Newton in concluding his discussion of Grimshaw's doctrinal position, put the same thought in these words:

He kept nothing back from his people that he thought profitable; but he did not think it to their profit to insist upon subjects of controversy, which as they are usually managed, rather alienate the minds of religious professors from each other than promote love, peace or holiness. His zeal was too ardent, his time too precious . . . The sense he had of the evil of sin, the worth of souls, the nearness of eternity, and the love of the Saviour filled his heart and raised him far above a systematical accuracy.[1]

[1]Newton, *Letters*, p. 85.

21

FRIENDS AND FELLOW WORKERS

SOWDENS, GRIMSHAW'S HOME FOR TWENTY-ONE YEARS, is now a working farm tucked into the hillside above Haworth. A plaque on one of the walls, partially covered by overhanging bushes, reads:

> SOWDENS PARSONAGE
> WILLIAM GRIMSHAW
> 1742–1763
> HERE STAYED:
> JOHN AND CHARLES WESLEY,
> GEORGE WHITEFIELD,
> JOHN NEWTON,
> HENRY VENN

The significance of this notice becomes more apparent as we realise how remarkable it was that these five men, each outstanding in his own right, should find himself drawn time and again to this isolated spot high on the Pennines. The warmth of Christian friendship and love extended to them by William Grimshaw proved an attraction hard to resist.

The old farmhouse remains little changed over the years. J. W. Laycock, to whose work *Methodist Heroes in the Great Haworth Round* frequent reference has been made, visited Sowdens as a child and included a vivid description of it in his book:

My first visit to this house was paid when very young . . . It is a large farmhouse commanding the prospect of quiet fields, and the valley of the Worth. On the west a grove of stunted trees shield the house from the wild winds which very frequently sweep over the moorland immediately behind it. I remember how we stood in the kitchen, as the principal room would be called, where the Wesleys, Whitefield and many of the bravest of the first race of Methodist preachers sat at the hospitable board of the warm-hearted vicar of Haworth. We saw also the bedrooms and the study in which he poured out fervent prayers to God, and wrote burning words for his people.[1]

One notable feature of Sowdens recollected by Laycock and still to be seen today is the 'strong oaken door studded with nails guarding the porch'. Dr Frank Baker was also impressed with this substantial door, and included a description of the old house in his work:

The place has changed little. The dressed limestone walls, with courses of varying depth, the mullioned windows, the stone slates, blend perfectly with the bleak background, hewn as they were from the local quarry. At the end of a tunnel-like porch with stone seats is a massive door, built up of two thicknesses of timber clamped with a profusion of iron bolts.[2]

James Everett, who had a passion for buying up artefacts linked with the lives of his heroes, made an attempt to purchase Grimshaw's front door – but without success. Baker continues with a graphic description of Sowdens: the panelled seats, built into the two-feet thick walls, the great fireplace, eight feet in width, around which the household would have gathered, the cellars built into the hillside, and Grimshaw's tiny boxroom study over the porch.

Grimshaw's sturdy oak table, so large that it could only have been assembled *in situ*, has now disappeared without trace. Dating from 1688 and heavily carved, it was supported by six turned legs. It is evocative to imagine John Wesley and William

---

[1]Laycock, *Heroes*, p. 41.   [2]Baker, *Grimshaw*, p. 163.

Grimshaw seated at that table deep in conversation about the
state of the societies or the current problems facing Methodism. If
Grimshaw had become Wesley's successor, the principal duties
to have devolved upon him would have lain in the assignment of
the preachers to their varying spheres of service – appointments
which were changed annually – together with the final responsibility for the ministry in each Methodist preaching house.
During the 1750s five new buildings were erected, all with a trust
deed based on an original worded by Henry Thornton which
read:

John Wesley, late of Lincoln College, Oxford, clerk . . . and after his
decease . . . Charles Wesley, late of Christ Church College, Oxford,
clerk . . . and after his decease . . . William Grimshaw, clerk . . . And
after the decease of the said J. W., C. W., and W. G., then such persons
as shall be appointed at the yearly Conference of the people called
Methodists.

Grimshaw was to address seven letters to different Methodist
societies: those in Newcastle, Lincolnshire and London and two
letters which appear to be encyclical. Perhaps he intended Wesley
to carry them with him as he travelled around. One probable
reason why he wrote these collective letters was in case he should,
in fact, have to take over the Methodist leadership. Charles
Wesley suffered from indifferent health and often wondered how
long God would spare him; while in 1753 John Wesley himself
had been so seriously ill that his friends despaired of his recovery.
So by his letters Grimshaw would have become a trusted friend
and pastor even amongst societies where he was unknown in
person.

From 1755 onwards John Wesley records in his journal a visit
to the Haworth Round each alternate year. On 18 May 1757 he
was in Heptonstall where he discovered that not only was all
available ground space taken up by eager hearers, but even on
the roof tops of adjacent houses his congregation was awaiting
his message. Grimshaw was at his side, and the following day
after Wesley had preached at Ewood, he urged his friend to

preach once more to the people from a high mountainside nearby. Wesley records, 'Mr Grimshaw begged I would give them one sermon at Gawksham [Gawksholme, about a mile from Todmorden], after which we climbed up an enormous mountain, I think equal to any we saw in Germany.'

Two years later when Wesley returned to the north they were back together at the same spot. Wesley himself adds further details of the beauty of the area. 'Saturday 21st [July]: Mr Grimshaw led us to Gawksham, another lone house on the side of an enormous mountain. The congregation stood or sat, row upon row, in the sylvan theatre. I believe nothing on the post-diluvian earth can be more pleasant than the road from hence between huge steep mountains, clothed with wood to the top and washed at the bottom by a clear winding stream.' A small booth was erected for a pulpit, and Wesley preached with all his accustomed forcefulness and penetration. When the congregation joined to sing the doxology, set to Grimshaw's favourite tune, the *Old Hundredth,* the sound was unforgettable. As those thousands of voices blended together in the praise of God, the very hills seemed to reverberate with the anthem.

The next day the two men were in Haworth, and Wesley preached twice to crowded congregations from the scaffolding pulpit. 'Most of these were not curious hearers, but men fearing God. The communicants alone filled the church,' Wesley commented in his journal.[1]

Though they were far different in personality, an unusual quality of friendship existed between John Wesley and Grimshaw. Wesley continued to express an admiration and respect for Grimshaw throughout his life, though he was to outlive him by more than a quarter of a century. He had been the first to encourage Grimshaw to venture on that itinerant ministry which was to spread the influence of the gospel through Yorkshire, Lancashire and Cheshire, extending the revival throughout the north of England.

[1]John Wesley, *Journal*, vol. IV, p. 333.

Grimshaw too would often express his esteem for Wesley. On one occasion when he was preaching in Manchester, a friend hinted to Grimshaw that he should make his sermons a little shorter by pointing out that John Wesley's sermons seldom lasted more than an hour. 'Mr Wesley,' expostulated Grimshaw, 'God bless him! He can do more in one hour than I can in two!' And he preached for two hours.[1] Eighteen years after Grimshaw's death, John Wesley, now aged seventy-six himself, was still to refer to his friend with genuine affection, noting in his journal, 'I lodged at the Ewood, which I still love for dear Mr Grimshaw's sake.'[2]

William Grimshaw's close friendship with Charles Wesley has already been noticed. Apart from some preaching in Bristol and the south-west and his regular ministry in London, Charles ceased to itinerate after 1756, so we have no record that he and Grimshaw ever met again; but, as we have seen, they kept up a lively and regular correspondence. Only a handful of letters written to Grimshaw from any of his correspondents has survived, suggesting that he was in the habit of destroying most of his correspondence. Grimshaw's last letter to Charles Wesley, written only a month before he died, bears eloquent testimony to the warmth of friendship these two men enjoyed: 'God bless you and yours,' began Grimshaw, and then continues, 'Who wrote last I know not – you or I – judge as you please – this I know, I love you dearly.'

The dual friendship which Grimshaw enjoyed with both Whitefield and the Wesley brothers was an important factor in binding together the disparate wings of the evangelical revival. Occasionally he and Whitefield travelled together for several days in a preaching circuit: both were in Manchester in 1750, when they had hospitality with Major Gallatin and his wife; again Whitefield was with Grimshaw in Bolton in 1752 when they tried to heal the division in that society brought about by John

[1]A. Strachan, *Recollections of the Life and Times of George Lowe* (1841), p. 117.
[2]John Wesley, *Journal,* vol. VI, p. 229.

Bennet's departure from Methodism; and also they were together in Halifax and Ewood during 1755 as Grimshaw had noted in his diary.

As Whitefield's health fluctuated later in the 1750s his visits to Haworth became less frequent. Anxious for his friend's welfare, Grimshaw wrote to him in London during December 1761 where Whitefield usually spent the winter months. Forgetting how often Whitefield had expressed his dislike of northern winters, Grimshaw urged him to come to Yorkshire. Perhaps he imagined the bracing Pennine winds would have a restorative power: 'Do this as soon as possible, and rendezvous in Yorkshire,' he begged. 'You have hundreds of dear, decent, substantial, hearty friends in these parts. No one shall make you welcomer than myself . . . While I've a shilling you shall have sixpence.'[1] But Whitefield, understandably, declined to accept. However, both men were together once again on an extended preaching tour in the summer of 1762, in company with the Countess of Huntingdon, William Romaine, John Wesley and others. But Grimshaw wished to have his friend back at Sowdens and preaching from the scaffolding pulpit: 'I hope ere long to see my dear brother Whitefield in his own pulpit again,' he wrote wistfully to the Countess of Huntingdon in November 1762. But it was not to be. And they never met again for Grimshaw died the following spring.

John Newton, also named on the plaque outside Sowdens, did not meet William Grimshaw until 1758. Newton, who had not yet begun his ministry, travelled across to Haworth from Liverpool where he was employed as a tide-surveyor. Having heard reports of the work of God that had been taking place in West Yorkshire, he was anxious to meet Grimshaw and hear his first-hand account. He had 'an indifferent journey, the weather being rough', but was rewarded by finding Grimshaw at home, who afforded him 'a truly Christian welcome and entertainment'.

With his accustomed hospitality Grimshaw urged Newton to

[1]Letter to Whitefield, 20 December 1761, cited by Baker, *Grimshaw*, p. 239.

spend a few days with him, and during that time Newton would undoubtedly have told the older man of his past experiences as a hardened sailor and finally a slave trader. Converted to God, he now longed to redeem the wasted years and enter the ministry. But at thirty-three years of age, Newton had neither the educational requirements nor the correct social standing to gain a ready admittance to the Church of England ministry. Together the two men would have talked through the situation and perhaps it was on this occasion that Grimshaw confided to Newton many of the circumstances of his own early life which Newton in turn preserved for the Christian Church when he wrote his biographical sketch of Grimshaw forty years later. So delighted was Newton with his new-found friend, that he exclaimed later, 'Had it been the will of God, methought I could have renounced the world, to have lived in these mountains with such a minister and such a people.'[1]

But two years later a circumstance occurred which was to have an even more important impact in Newton's life. In addition to the setbacks he had already suffered in his desires to serve God, he had experienced considerable embarrassment in his early attempts to preach. If he tried to speak in an extempore manner without the aid of notes, he would falter and then be reduced to silence and confusion. But if he used a script he would become so slavishly bound to it that 'with my head hanging down (for I was near-sighted) and fixed like a statue, I conned over my lesson like a boy learning to read'.[2]

In this disheartened frame, he visited Haworth once more in 1760. Grimshaw often held services in his own home, and would occasionally invite a lay preacher to address those who gathered. To John Newton's astonishment, Grimshaw insisted that he should preach that day, refusing to listen to any excuses. Without time to become nervous, Newton found himself much helped in

---

[1] From Newton's unpublished diary, cited by Josiah Bull, *Life of Newton*, (London: Religious Tract Society, 1868), p. 96.
[2] Ibid., p. 106.

his delivery, and was able to preach without difficulty. Describing this occasion in a letter to John Wesley dated 14 November 1760, he wrote:

I forgot to tell you in my last that I had the honour to appear as a Methodist preacher. I was in Haworth; Mr Grimshaw was pressing, and prevailed. I spoke in his house to about one hundred and fifty persons; a difficult auditory in my circumstances, about half Methodists, and half Baptists. I was afraid of displeasing both sides; but my text, John 1:29, led me to dwell upon a point in which we were all agreed; and before I had leisure to meddle with doctrines (as they are called), the hour had expired. In short, it was a comfortable opportunity.

Newton continues in his letter to Wesley by explaining why he himself felt unable to take up an itinerant ministry. In short, he had 'not either strength of body or mind sufficient for an itinerant preacher'. His constitution had been broken by his experiences as a 'slave' in Africa.[1]

Writing long years after, Newton, who probably never visited Haworth again during Grimshaw's lifetime, freely acknowledged the debt he owed to Grimshaw:

I number it amongst the many great mercies of my life that I was favoured with his notice, edified (I hope), by his instruction, and encouraged and directed by his advice, at the critical time when my own mind was much engaged with a desire of entering the ministry. I saw in him, much more clearly than I could have learnt from books or lectures, what it was to be a faithful and exemplary minister of the gospel, and the remembrance of him has often both humbled and animated me.[2]

The biography he wrote of Grimshaw was Newton's attempt to repay the debt and to raise a 'monument to his memory'.

Henry Venn, the last named on the plaque outside Sowdens, also met Grimshaw when he was near the end of his ministry. Venn, who had come to Yorkshire in 1759 after two previous

---

[1]Newton to John Wesley, Tyerman, *John Wesley,* vol. II, p. 364.
[2]Newton, *Letters,* p. 132.

curacies in the south, became vicar of Huddersfield. Here he was to preach to men and women whom John Wesley had called the 'wildest congregation I have seen in Yorkshire',[1] when he had addressed them only a few weeks before Venn arrived. But during the twelve years he spent in the town, Venn witnessed a profound moral and spiritual transformation among the people.

Already a friend of George Whitefield, Lady Huntingdon and William Romaine, Henry Venn quickly came to know and value Grimshaw, describing him as 'that burning and most shining light, dear Mr Grimshaw'. A cordial friendship was soon established, and twenty years later Venn could still bear testimony to his friend's character, including him in his list of 'very dear friends, now high in glory'.[2] They met on many occasions, for Huddersfield was little more than twenty miles from Haworth, but notably when Lady Huntingdon, Whitefield or John Wesley were in the area. Then Venn and Grimshaw would join in conference or on preaching tours; or, alternatively, Grimshaw would call in at the vicarage in Huddersfield on one of his extensive preaching circuits.

The friendship with Grimshaw was to leave an indelible imprint on the ministry and thought of the younger man as Venn joined the small number of incumbents of parishes who were prepared to be 'irregular' for the gospel's sake. Some similarities may be noted between the methods they adopted. Both itinerated beyond their parish bounds, preaching in barns, private homes and wherever a congregation could be gathered together. Both placed strong emphasis on catechising, specially amongst the young, and both resolutely avoided sectarianism though remaining staunch churchmen. Like Grimshaw, Venn also encouraged the building of a preaching house before he left Huddersfield. Clearly in Venn, sixteen years his junior, Grimshaw found one of like spirit, a willing disciple, with similar convictions on certain important matters. A notable preacher himself, Venn drew people

[1]John Wesley, *Journal,* vol. IV, p. 210.
[2]*Letters of Henry Venn* (Edinburgh: Banner of Truth Trust), 1993, p. 277.

from many miles distant to Huddersfield, as Grimshaw had done in Haworth.

Through the friendship and esteem that were established between Grimshaw and Henry Venn, a yet more important benefit was imparted to the cause of true religion. For when Henry Venn left Huddersfield in 1771 for his final charge in Yelling, only twelve miles from Cambridge, he carried with him the life, ardour and principles he had admired so much in Grimshaw, and had practised to great effect in Yorkshire. These he communicated to Charles Simeon, vicar of Holy Trinity, Cambridge, and through him they were passed on to the students whom Simeon was to influence so profoundly. Venn's son, John Venn, was to become vicar of Clapham, and in that capacity won the respect of powerful Anglican laymen of the day: William Wilberforce, Henry Thornton, Zachary Macaulay, Charles Grant – men known as the Clapham Sect, whose influence for social change and the establishment of missionary endeavour was to become a byword in the land.

So, it may be argued, one lasting result of Henry Venn's labours was to pass on the torch of the evangelical revival to a new generation of preachers within the Established Church, bringing fresh life and vitality towards the end of the century.[1] This can in turn be traced back, at least in part, to the heritage bequeathed by the great evangelist of Yorkshire – William Grimshaw.

The list of names outside Sowdens Farm by no means exhausts the catalogue of men and women, some renowned in their own right, who enjoyed hospitality and mutual fellowship with Grimshaw. William Romaine, who held the Lectureship of St Dunstan's in London, was an occasional visitor after 1755, sometimes arriving with his wife without prior notice, as Grimshaw mentioned in a hasty postscript in one of his letters to Mrs Gallatin. Expected or unexpected, Romaine, whose bold

---

[1]This is illustrated by a comment made by William Romaine. He stated that in 1757 he knew only a dozen like-minded Anglican clergymen, but by the close of his ministry in 1795, he could number at least three hundred.

uncompromised evangelicalism had brought him persecution in London, would always be welcomed in Haworth. In September 1762 he joined Lady Huntingdon on one of her visits to the Inghams in Aberford. Grimshaw, hearing that the Countess had come, rode across from Haworth and finding Romaine also there engaged him to preach in Haworth. As usual the crowds gathered quickly and thronged the churchyard, but Romaine was unsure about preaching in the open air, and must have been a little startled when Grimshaw announced to his congregation that after the service in the church had concluded 'his brother Romaine would preach the glorious gospel from brother Whitefield's pulpit in the churchyard'.[1] It was hard to deny Grimshaw any-thing and Romaine complied with the request and preached with liberty to the waiting people.

Romaine's estimate of Grimshaw was of the highest order, and even though he knew that Grimshaw 'could never endure to have any commendation made to him about his usefulness', he was to say of him, 'For the good of souls he rejected all hope of affluent fortune, and for the love of Christ cheerfully underwent diffi-culties, dangers and tribulations. He preached Christ and Christ alone.'[2] Repeatedly Romaine had asked Grimshaw for some written statement of his beliefs, and at last on 8 December 1762 Grimshaw acceded to his request. 'As to my creed, so long looked for, and so long called for, such as it is, I here send it to you at last,' he wrote. Consisting of twenty-six points of belief, this *Creed* bears all the hallmarks of Grimshaw's own personality: racy, colourful and expressive, but above all, infused with a sense of the greatness and mercy of his God and the smallness and insignificance of man even at his best.

The names of many who toiled with Grimshaw on the Great Haworth Round have largely been forgotten. These men, whose only memorial lies in brief references in the circuit books of the period, were prepared to travel, preach and suffer with scant

[1]Seymour, *Countess of Huntingdon*, vol. 1, p. 274.
[2]Middleton, *Biographia*, vol. IV, p. 407.

financial returns, their reward the favour and presence of God and the joy of seeing lives transformed by the gospel they proclaimed. A few of Wesley's early itinerant preachers wrote accounts of their lives and experiences for Wesley's monthly magazine, *The Arminian Magazine,* which first appeared in 1778. Thirty-seven of these records were later gathered by Thomas Jackson and published in six small volumes in 1837. Subsequently they were edited and republished by John Telford under the title *Wesley's Veterans.*

We have already noted in passing the names of some of these veterans who were Grimshaw's fellow labourers, but several merit further mention. Prominent among these must be William Darney whose influence on Grimshaw at a critical time in his life earned him a permanent place in Grimshaw's affections. A rugged and unconventional person himself, Grimshaw was able to appreciate the fearless Scotsman, though John and Charles Wesley and even George Whitefield found Darney's eccentricities and tactlessness a trial hard to be borne. From 1747 onwards when Darney placed his societies under Wesley's care and sought a place himself among Wesley's preachers, he ran the constant risk of expulsion from Wesley's accredited list of itinerants, and each time he was in trouble he would resort again to Grimshaw to plead his cause. His main offence seems to have been his determination to preach his deeply-held Calvinistic beliefs among Wesley's societies – a thing which both Grimshaw and Whitefield were careful to avoid, for fear of stirring up needless controversy. Another 'offence' lay in his hymns, which were an undoubted trial to Charles Wesley's poetic sensitivities. Each time he was reinstated it would be with strict instructions that he must abstain from 'railing, begging and printing nonsense'.

But Darney was a stalwart pioneer, and not only did he open up Lancashire to the gospel, as Grimshaw acknowledged in his letter to Gillies, but he was also responsible for pioneering vast tracts of north Yorkshire and Cumbria. As we have seen, he and Grimshaw were together in Osmotherley in 1752. There are records of this powerful preacher penetrating as far south as

Shepshed in Leicestershire where he was 'plentifully bespattered with mud', no one inviting him into any house, or offering him refreshment; and as far north as Alnwick, near the Scottish border. In this latter place the work of God so prospered under Darney's ministry in 1755 that it aroused both hostility and insult. A local troupe of actors decided to put on a skit caricaturing Darney and the Methodists. Bills were distributed for the show, but before the play was performed, Darney rode past the actors as they relaxed near their makeshift theatre. 'Here is Scotch Will,' they cried gleefully, 'let us mob him!' But Darney, himself a man of impressive size, was riding a highly spirited horse, and on hearing the threat, he cantered up to them, caused his animal to rear up on its hind legs, and then with a crack of his whip roared, 'Come on, ye sons of Belial.' Over-awed, the actors asked his forgiveness and promised to mend their ways.

But many times Darney was ill-treated by the mob. Back in Grimshaw's circuit later in 1755, he was abused at Barrowford. On one occasion his coat was dipped into a vat of dye, and on another he was thrown into the river and tied by a rope to each bank so that he could not wade out. In Colne he was stripped of his clothing, daubed with mud and in this condition he was driven through the main street.

From 1758 it would seem that Darney was mainly in the Yorkshire Dales. Anxious that his friend Grimshaw should come north and visit his societies, he had pressed him to make the journey. Instead Grimshaw wrote to these northern societies on 18 October 1758:

I understand by brother Darney, the bearer thereof, that you entertained an expectation of my visiting your parts this summer, and indeed for some time I warmly purposed the same ... [but] it has fallen out that I could not conveniently come ... but I may see you, the Lord willing, next summer ... Brother Darney's labours have been useful in these parts: may they be blessed among you.

The following year, 1759, Grimshaw apparently managed to visit Barnard Castle, the main centre of the Dales circuit, as both local tradition and a letter to George Merryweather of Yarm, written on 22 June 1759, suggests.

After Grimshaw's death Darney had no-one to plead his cause when he acted injudiciously, and he appears to have been finally dismissed by the Wesleys late in the 1760s. Records exist of his preaching in the Newcastle area and in Derbyshire in 1767–8, often encountering vicious persecution. His best obituary is found in his own words:

I have known by happy experience, that when I have been in the greatest extremity of sufferings for my dear Lord and Master's sake . . . I have found always most of God's presence. There was one time in particular, when the persecutors had taken me and tumbled me head over ears in a nasty hole full of mire . . . Indeed I was infinitely more happy in that hole than all my enemies could have been if they had been lying on beds of down. I found such a manifestation of God's love [and] felt something of the heaven of heavens in my soul.[1]

Darney finally settled in Pendle Forest, because it resembled his own Scottish scenery, and there he died in 1779.

Paul Greenwood together with Jonathan Maskew shared the distinction of being known as 'Mr Grimshaw's men'. When Joseph Williams visited Haworth in 1746 he discovered this young man, remarkably converted with the rest of his family in 1741, already helping Grimshaw in the ever-increasing demands on his strength created by the revival. Described as 'an exhorter', his testimony had been owned by God so that Grimshaw could report to Williams that many had been converted through his exhortations.

Grimshaw must have recommended Greenwood to Wesley, either before the two men first met in May 1747 or on that occasion, for by October young Greenwood, then aged about twenty-three, was sent to Dublin. John Wesley himself had first ventured onto Irish soil in August of that year, followed by

---

[1]From Darney's treatise, *Fundamental Doctrines*, cited by Laycock, *Heroes*, p. 233.

Charles Wesley and Charles Perronet in September. Paul Greenwood left his Haworth home for the first time and arrived in Dublin in October 1747. A certain Samuel Handy was persuaded against his will to hear Greenwood preaching at Dolphin's Barn, though he was fearful of being pickpocketed by the 'poor mean-looking people' he discovered assembled there. C. H. Crookshank, historian of Methodism in Ireland, describes the scene:

Soon a tall thin man in plain black clothes with dark hair entered and took possession of the pulpit. He was Paul Greenwood, a native of Haworth, who had just entered the itinerancy; a man of great simplicity and uprightness of heart, and distinguished by deep seriousness, heavenly-mindedness and close communion with God. Mr Handy regarded him with surprise, being minus wig, gown and bands . . . He was still more astonished when the preacher, having given out a hymn, the congregation united singing it with heart and voice. 'Wonderful', thought he, 'that so despicable a people should sing so delightfully.' The extemporaneous prayer that followed, so full of sacred unction, thrilled his heart and prepared him to follow with no ordinary interest the preacher's discourse. This was accompanied with such light and power as produced a complete change in his views and feelings, and led him to resolve, 'This people shall be my people, and their God shall be my God.'[1]

The following year Greenwood was back in England and in 1750–51 he was with Grimshaw once more in the Haworth Round. Entries in the Todmorden circuit book record payments made to him for incidental expenses, 'December 4th, 1750, Paul Greenwood, for washing 1/-'. Perhaps his clothes had been soiled by mud slung by the vicious crowd. Certainly he met with remarkable providences protecting him from the mindless persecution so often the lot of these itinerant preachers. On one occasion in Middleton in the Dales circuit he was amazingly delivered from a mob intent on his death.

[1] C. H. Crookshank, *Days of Revival, History of Methodism in Ireland*, vol. I (First published 1885, republished, Clonmel: Tentmaker Publications, 1994), p. 30.

Greenwood laboured in Grimshaw's round once again in 1754-55, and his name is given as one of the trustees of the Methodist preaching house which Grimshaw built in 1758. In 1760 he was stationed in Norwich, and, as we have seen, was one of the two men who grieved Grimshaw by distributing the sacrament to the people. A fellow worker, however, described Greenwood as 'a man of truly excellent temper and exemplary behaviour. He was constantly serious, but not sad: he was always cheerful, but not light.'

Greenwood died four years after Grimshaw, in 1767, at the early age of forty-three after contracting a fever. His last night of life was remarkable. Semi-delirious though he was, his conversation throughout was on heavenly things. In the early morning as he was dying, he said, 'Another sun shall arise; Christ the Sun of Righteousness with healing in his wings.' His old mother, converted the same day as her son, also died that morning. John Wesley wrote of Greenwood, 'He could ill be spared; but he was ready for the Bridegroom; so it was fit he should go to him.'[1]

Jonathan Maskew, whom Grimshaw befriended at a young age and employed to farm the lands around Sowdens, was another who was prepared to labour and suffer, not counting the cost. Yeadon, near Leeds, had been notorious for its manhandling of Methodist preachers. Twice Maskew narrowly escaped death at the hands of the Yeadon mob. On the second occasion, the fury of the rabble was 'like the roaring sea'. Maskew was hauled from his pulpit, his outer garments torn from him and he was dragged along the gravel path until his back was lacerated. One lout then took hold of his neckerchief and was intending to strangle the injured man, until a merciful passer-by intervened and rescued him. But the crowd surged back with renewed fury. It was only the action of a brave woman, standing so close to Maskew that he could not be struck, which preserved him from further injury.

A warm friendship had sprung up between William Grimshaw and Thomas Colbeck, the young man who had introduced

[1] John Wesley's *Letters*, to Christopher Hopper, 18 June 1767.

Methodism to Keighley in 1742 and who was significantly used in the surrounding villages, as Grimshaw pointed out in his letter to Gillies. Far different from a man like Darney, Colbeck was a gentle personality, also lacking the robust physique of his friend Grimshaw. Grimshaw's reference to Colbeck's 'spindleshank' legs when the young man was being mercilessly kicked in the riot at Roughlee adds to that impression. On another occasion Grimshaw was across in Keighley at Thomas Colbeck's house when the latter was being shaved by one of the society leaders who undertook this task. As the barber was rubbing the lather on Colbeck's face, Grimshaw, who was standing watching, remarked in a droll tone, 'I tell thee what, Tommy, an ounce of grace on thy face will shine as much as a pound on mine.' Grimshaw clearly had no great looks, his face rugged and plain in keeping with his character.

Although Colbeck did not itinerate widely, he was held in high esteem by the Wesley brothers, attending several of the most significant conferences by personal invitation. His business commitments usually kept him in the Keighley area, but also provided him with the means to help the work by generous financial support. More than this he was a constant travelling companion for Grimshaw, providing welcome fellowship for him as their horses picked their way along the moorland tracks between one appointment and the next.

Thomas Colbeck died in 1779 when he was not quite sixty; like Greenwood he had caught an infection from one whom he was visiting. A Methodist preacher wrote of him twenty years later, 'For many years he was a faithful and indefatigable local preacher, and it pleased God to crown his labours with great success. His memory is still precious to many who speak of him with the greatest respect and bless God that ever they heard the truth of the gospel from his lips.'[1]

These early fellow-workers who toiled with William Grimshaw on the Great Haworth Round, though now mostly forgotten,

[1]Laycock, *Heroes,* p. 140.

were men of spiritual stature and zeal whose heroism deserves a permanent record in the annals of the Christian Church. Many more names could be mentioned, but these must stand as typical of the larger number, whose tireless help in evangelising the north of England and far beyond may never receive any earthly recognition, but whose labours are known by God and will not be forgotten by him.

22

'What Has God Wrought!'

'WHAT HAS GOD WROUGHT in the midst of those rough mountains!' exclaimed John Wesley as he concluded his journal entry for 12 July 1761 after spending the day in Haworth. He had been visiting Methodist societies in Yorkshire and had just ridden across from the east of the county where he had preached to attentive congregations in Hull, Beverley, Pocklington and York. Glad to be back again in his friend William Grimshaw's round, he had called at Otley, Bingley and Keighley before arriving at last in Haworth. Here he was due to preach at one of the vast communion services which had become a characteristic of Grimshaw's ministry. Each time he visited this rugged Pennine town it was the same: 'I had appointed to be at Haworth, but the church would not near contain the people who came from all sides: However, Mr Grimshaw had provided for this by fixing a scaffold on the outside of one of the windows through which I went after prayers . . . The afternoon congregation was larger still.'[1]

The early 1760s were days of marked spiritual quickening throughout Methodism. Conscious of this new movement of God's Spirit, Wesley had called his preachers together from the northern rounds to Leeds in March 1761 in order to discover from them the state of their societies. The story was the same

---

[1]John Wesley's *Journal*, vol. IV, p. 469.

everywhere. 'I find the work of God increases on every side,' he recorded as he wrote up his journal that night. As the year progressed the renewed quickening became yet more widespread. The authority and fresh vitality that accompanied the preachers as they held forth the words of life to the people were so significant that it reminded John Wesley of the earliest days of the revival: 'It seems,' he wrote after he had met his preachers at their annual conference in Bristol during October 1761, 'God was pleased to pour out his Spirit this year on every part both of England and Ireland, perhaps in a manner we have never seen before, certainly not for twenty years.'[1] And this blessing was to continue, extending over the next few years.

References to these days of God's manifest blessing can be gleaned from Grimshaw's letters, both to individuals and particularly in his later letters to the society in Newcastle. He had begun to notice an added measure of blessing in Haworth during 1758, and so in a letter written in May of that year he had reported, 'I hope the gospel spreads in your parts ... Since Christmas, blessed be the Lord, fifty new members have been added to ours.' The following year John Berridge, vicar of Everton, near Bedford, newly converted to God, had begun to preach the gospel with astonishing power. A revival broke out accompanied by unusual physical phenomena as an awareness of their lost condition swept over the people.

When Grimshaw wrote once more to the society in Newcastle in January 1761, he could report, 'To the everlasting praise of our dear Jesus be it known to you, that his work of grace prospers in these parts. Our congregations are generally large: new members are added to our societies, and our old ones go on in full assurance; and some of them in the triumph of faith to heaven.'[2] By the beginning of the following year this stream of God's grace had become a river: 'We have lately had many members added to our societies. There is just now such a stirring among the people

[1]Ibid., vol. IV, p. 477.

[2]Grimshaw, letter to Newcastle Society. Whole letter in Hardy, *Incumbent*, pp. 207–8.

in my parish as has not been for twelve years past. I mention this for the glory of God and for your joy.'[1]

One of the notable features of this new work of God had been an emphasis on holiness, causing many in the Methodist societies to seek a deeper experience of the grace of God than they had known before. Wesley's teaching on Christian perfection, which he had emphasised consistently, with occasional modifications, now became increasingly popular. The essential elements in his views, as he had summarised them as early as 1740, were these:

1. That Christian perfection is that love of God and our neighbour which implies deliverance from *all sin*.
2. That this is received merely by faith.
3. That it is given *instantaneously* in one moment.[2]

This teaching, rejected, as we have seen, by William Grimshaw, George Whitefield, Henry Venn, William Romaine, Benjamin Ingham and many other leaders of the eighteenth-century revival, now brought its own harvest of misunderstanding and division.

As mentioned earlier, in 1760 thirty members of the society in Otley, only fifteen miles from Haworth, had begun to affirm that they had received this gift of 'perfect love' (as Wesley preferred to call it). Grimshaw himself, who knew the society well, was disturbed by the extravagant claims made by some whose veracity he doubted. But Wesley, who was less familiar with the society, had included Otley in his itinerary of Yorkshire that July and was not displeased with what he found: 'Here', he wrote, 'began that glorious work of sanctification which had been nearly at a stand for twenty years; but which now from time to time spread through Yorkshire, and afterwards in London . . . and wherever the work of sanctification increased, the whole work of God increased in all its branches.'[3] Grimshaw's comment on the situation contained in a letter to Charles Wesley was far different, as we have noted.[4]

---

[1]Letter to Newcastle, 12 January 1762. Myles, *Life and Writings*, p. 188.
[2]John Wesley, *Plain Account of Christian Perfection* (London: 1960), p. 16.
[3]Tyerman, *John Wesley*, vol. II, pp. 416–7.
[4]See Chapter 20, *When Good Men Differ*, p. 237.

Without a doubt after Wesley had preached in Haworth on 12 July he and Grimshaw would have spent the evening together at Sowdens. One of the topics under discussion would certainly have been this teaching of Wesley's and the situation which was developing in Grimshaw's round as more members began claiming instantaneous deliverance from any known sin. The following morning at the five o'clock service in Haworth Wesley preached on the subject in order to clarify his views to his friend. 'At five I preached on the manner of waiting for 'perfect love', the rather to satisfy Mr Grimshaw, whom many had laboured to puzzle and perplex about it,' he reported in his journal for that day.

But Wesley's problems were soon to increase. Among the London societies two of his preachers, Thomas Maxfield, who had worked with him since 1739, and George Bell began to make yet more extravagant claims. Maxfield, one of the few lay preachers who had received ordination, together with the society for whom Wesley had given him responsibility, were not only claiming entire sanctification but were pressing Wesley's teaching to its logical conclusion, maintaining they could never fall and were spiritually superior to other believers.

Wesley wrote an urgent letter to Maxfield, trying to reclaim him:

I like your doctrine of Perfection, of pure love; love excluding sin, your insisting that it is merely by faith; that consequently it is instantaneous (though preceded and followed by a gradual work), and that it may be now, at this instant . . . But I dislike your supposing man may be as perfect as an angel; and that he can be absolutely perfect; that he can be infallible, or above being tempted. But what I most of all dislike is your littleness of love to your brethren, your counting every man your enemy that reproves or admonishes you in love: in a word, your divisive spirit.[1]

But it was too late for by that time the society had split with many following Maxfield, and censuring all who disagreed with them. George Bell was yet more extreme in his fanaticism. His claims of

---

[1] Wesley's *Letters*, vol. IV, pp. 192ff.

possessing miraculous powers, coupled with his wild predictions about the end of the world, which was supposed to happen on 28 February 1763, brought much discredit upon the work of God. At last Wesley had to expel Bell from the society, but the damage to Methodism was considerable; especially when the secular press chose to make capital out of the situation.

Writing to Charles Wesley in a semi-humorous vein, Grimshaw referred to some of these things: 'Last Monday should have been the Day of Judgment. Therefore to have answered your letter sooner would have been waste of labour, time and paper . . . Besides, the day itself would have revealed the verity or vanity of those perfectionists. But who was mistaken, God or Bell? Just as much truth I suspect in all their other reveries. Scriptural or Christian Perfection I allow and avow. Sinless perfection I disclaim. Sinless is not only an unscriptural expression, but I fear, though I will not certainly affirm, has given birth and being to all those extravagant, presumptuous, scandalous and irreligious vagaries among our London brethren.'[1]

Problems relating to John Wesley's brand of Christian perfection were not the only stratagem of Satan to disrupt the work of God. In the north of England serious difficulties also arose among Benjamin Ingham's societies during the early 1760s. As we have seen, from December 1755 these societies had seceded from the Established Church and had become Dissenters. Ingham had been recognised as 'General Overseer' with William Batty and James Allen ordained as 'general elders' to assist him in the administration and preaching among these groups of believers who were widely scattered among the Fells of Cumbria, the Yorkshire Dales and as far south as Leeds and Bradford.

When William Romaine had preached in Ingham's societies during the late 1750s he was warm in his admiration of their faith and order: 'If ever there was a church of Christ upon earth, that was one. I paid them a visit, and had a great mind to join them. That was a blessed work of God among that people.' But all soon

---

[1]Grimshaw to Charles Wesley, 5 March 1763, in Laycock, *Heroes*, p. 238.

changed, and as Romaine recollected those days twenty years later,[1] he had to add that this promising work had been devastated when 'that horrid blast from the north came upon them and destroyed all'.[2]

The 'horrid blast from the north' was a reference to the influence which John Glas and his son-in-law, Robert Sandeman, had upon Ingham's work. Glas, a minister of the Church of Scotland, had been expelled by the Assembly of 1728 from his church near Dundee for his unorthodox views. He had then established a number of independent churches which claimed to be organised after the pattern laid down in the New Testament and his son-in-law became an elder in one of these churches. Glas's main theological aberration, which Sandeman also embraced and expounded, lay in his teaching on the nature of saving faith. Salvation, he insisted, required nothing more of a man but a notional assent to the truths of Scripture. Commending what he called 'naked faith', he rejected any teaching which 'would have us to be conscious of something else than the bare truth of the gospel . . . in order to our acceptance with God'. That a man should feel himself a sinner, should repent and cast himself on Christ in a warm, believing acceptance of his work and merits on his behalf, was to Sandeman and Glas a return to justification by works. Sandeman's teaching struck at the heart of the evangelical gospel as preached by Wesley, Whitefield, Grimshaw and, of course, Benjamin Ingham himself.[3]

[1]Romaine was in the home of D. Parker in the Kings Mews, London, in 1780 when he made this remark in the hearing of George Burder who later recorded it in the *Evangelical Magazine,* 1814 of which he was then editor. Cited, Pickles, *Ingham,* p. 111.

[2]Tyerman, *Oxford Methodists,* p. 140.

[3]'Those holding Sandemanian views are always opposed to warm emotional preaching . . . Sandemanianism leads to coldness of spirit, lack of prayer; it affects profoundly also one's assurance of salvation . . . It does away with the spirit of brokenness, and a spirit of humility. Is this not the most serious thing about us modern Christians? When did you last see someone weeping because of sinfulness? Can what we have today be truly called piety? It appears rather to be an intellectual acceptance of certain propositions,

Unfortunately Ingham, who had been reading the work by his Oxford friend James Hervey, *Theron and Aspasio,* now picked up an answer to Hervey's book entitled *Letters to the Author of Theron and Aspasio,*[1] which propagated this erroneous teaching. He also read *The Testimony of the King of Martyrs,* in which John Glas expounded his views of church government. So attracted was Ingham by all he read that he sent his two elders, Batty and Allen, to Scotland to find out at first hand more of the life and organisation of the Glasite churches.[2] In Edinburgh they met Robert Sandeman and in Dundee were introduced to John Glas. All they saw and heard of their order and practices made a favourable impression on the two men and they returned full of enthusiasm and anxious to implement the same system of church government among the Inghamite societies. The results were disastrous.

Attempts were made to introduce aspects of church life which were pressed with rigour in the Glasite churches – customs such as feet-washing, the holy kiss and the community of goods. The insistence on a plurality of elders undermined the peaceable arrangements which had hitherto proved beneficial. But most divisive of all was the mandate of total unanimity on every issue. A recipe for disunity, this became the chief stumbling block which destroyed the Inghamite churches. James Allen, complaining that Ingham wielded too much authority, withdrew peremptorily and set up a Glasite church. 'Disputes without end arose, excommunication upon excommunication followed, they condemned one another for hair-breadth differences, and were thus split like a wrecked ship, into a thousand pieces,' wrote the Countess of

---

accompanied by hardness, an absence of feeling . . .' D. M. Lloyd-Jones, *Sandemanianism* (Puritan Conference Papers, 1967).

[1]Written under the pseudonym 'Palaemon', this was thought to be the work of Robert Sandeman rather than his father-in-law. Published 1757.

[2]Probably Ingham was attracted to Sandeman's teaching by an over-reaction to the hyper-subjective emphasis of the Moravians which had damaged his earlier societies after 1742.

Huntingdon's biographer, Aaron Seymour.[1] William Batty commented sadly in his 'Church History': 'Thus were the people squandered and thrown into confusion and many turned back to the Church of England, and some into the world again.'[2] Ingham's eighty flourishing societies were reduced to a mere thirteen.

But Batty's dismal account was not altogether true for many former members of Inghamite churches joined their local Methodist societies. William Grimshaw confirms this in a letter to Whitefield written on 4 April 1762. 'The work of God prospers in these parts,' he wrote, and adds, 'We have taken above a hundred of Mr Ingham's scattered members into society, who behave well and are very solicitous for the life and power of godliness.'

The effect of the break-up of his life work on Ingham was grievous. Romaine, Whitefield and the Countess of Huntingdon did all in their power to bring about some degree of reconciliation between the dissenting parties, but to no avail. A deep depression settled on Ingham's spirit: 'I am lost! I am lost!' he would cry out in despair. The Countess wrote letters seeking to lift him from the depths of his gloom and he was grateful. 'A thousand and a thousand times do I bless and praise my God for the words of comfort and consolation your Ladyship's letters conveyed to my mournful heart, dismayed and overwhelmed as it was with the pressure of my calamities. Righteous art thou, O Lord, and just are thy judgments.'[3]

But despite all these setbacks the tide of blessing continued to flow particularly among the Yorkshire Methodist societies. In August 1762 the Countess of Huntingdon, accompanied by Whitefield, Venn, Romaine and others visited Yorkshire. Grimshaw and John Wesley joined them as they gathered in conference together at Leeds, and then toured around the area preaching to vast crowds. Later Grimshaw was able to write

[1]Seymour, *Countess of Huntingdon*, p. 275.
[2]Batty, 'History', p. 119.
[3]Tyerman, *Oxford Methodists*, p. 153.

to the Countess in glowing terms as he recollected those days: 'What blessings did the Lord shower upon us the last time you were here!'

In that same letter, written in November 1762, he reported a continuation of this movement of God among his people. 'I know you will excuse what may appear neglect [he had not answered her last letter] when informed I have been about my Master's business. Indeed, I have the pleasure of assuring you that the Lord's work prospers amazingly among us. My exhortations are visibly blessed, and I bless God daily and hourly for it. The Lord is adding many seekers of the blessed Jesus – many lively souls who have come to a sense of the pardoning love of God, and are eagerly hungering and thirsting after your inestimable Redeemer and mine.'[1]

Grimshaw, too, had called on his friend Benjamin Ingham in his need, and, despite all that had taken place, could report in this letter to the Countess that he had found him 'preaching Christ crucified with wonderful success and inexpressible benefit to the souls of many'. Not only had Grimshaw visited Ingham on that journey, he had also called on Henry Venn in Huddersfield and then travelled north to see Dr Richard Conyers in Helmsley in the Yorkshire Dales. Both of these men, he reported, were preaching the gospel with good effect though Conyers had only recently been brought into spiritual understanding himself. Others too were visited as Grimshaw passed by. Such an itinerary would have meant riding at least one hundred and forty miles, and would have included many preaching appointments *en route*.

But Grimshaw's ceaseless endeavours for the kingdom of God were beginning to take an exacting toll on his strength. Often he urged himself onwards in spite of weakness or even pain. Expressing his determination to use his powers to the utmost in Christ's service, he had written robustly to Mrs Gallatin in 1756, 'Lord, grant that I may never faint . . . till weakness, old age or

[1]Letter to Countess of Huntingdon, 20 November 1762, cited by Seymour, *Countess of Huntingdon,* vol. 1, pp. 283–4.

death invalidate me. By the grace of God, I'm resolved never to flag while I can ride, walk, creep or crawl.'[1] And now, five years later, faced with pain and increasing weakness, his determination remained unchanged and all admonition from his friends fell on deaf ears. Susanna Wright, an elderly parishioner who retained clear childhood memories of Grimshaw, recollected a Sunday in 1760 when he had collapsed in the pulpit at the close of a service. It was the fourth time he had preached that day, starting with the five o'clock service in Keighley, and probably all without adequate sustenance.

Nor was Grimshaw content that he alone should labour night and day in the interests of his Saviour. Any young preacher who came under his influence was urged to display the same unflagging endeavour. Writing in 1757 to Thomas Lee, one of Wesley's preachers who came from Keighley and whom Grimshaw had influenced and encouraged in his early days as an itinerant, he could say:

I hope your bow abides in strength and that you can preach twenty times a week. If you can preach oftener, do. Preaching is health, food and physic to me, and why not to thee, my brother. Besides, Tommy, there is very great need of preaching now, for iniquity aboundeth, the love of many grows cold and God's judgments are out in the earth. Tommy, let us preach four times a day or thirty times a week, whichever you please or can better bear. Our Master well deserves it. Yea, and infinitely more. O that we may spend and be spent in preaching HIS everlasting gospel, in converting sinners and confirming believers.[2]

Tommy Lee would not have felt that Grimshaw was asking too high a standard for he had already shown steadfast courage in the face of mob violence. Under a hail of stones and other missiles the young preacher had once admitted, 'I did indeed reel to and fro, and my head was broken with a stone. But I never found my soul more happy . . .'[3] But if Tommy Lee wondered how he could

[1]Letter to Mrs Gallatin, 3 June 1756, cited by Baker, *Grimshaw,* p. 259.
[2]Myles, *Life and Writings,* pp. 174–5.
[3]*Lives of Early Methodist Preachers,* ed. Jackson, p. 157.

maintain such unwearied diligence as Grimshaw recommended, he had a ready example in Grimshaw himself.

A typical Haworth Sunday in 1761, recalled by one who remembered Grimshaw from those days, will suffice to illustrate the point. Starting out from Sowdens at about 4 o'clock in the morning, Grimshaw walked across to Keighley, a distance of four miles – clearly without the assistance of his horse on this particular Sunday. Arriving in time to preach at an early morning service at 5 o'clock, he afterwards walked home to Haworth and preached at the morning and early afternoon services in his own church. After the second service in Haworth he set off across the moors to visit a sick parishioner who lived three miles away. Hurrying back once more, he found he had insufficient time to cross the River Worth by the bridge, but he knew a short cut where he might ford the river – a place known as The Great Stride – where there were stepping-stones. But to his dismay, when he arrived he discovered the river in full spate, with swirling waters covering the stones. No option remained but to wade through, and so he arrived for his final service that day in dripping wet clothes. Nothing daunted, he conducted it just as he was, and at last arrived home, having walked fifteen miles and preached four times.

Yet William Grimshaw did not derive satisfaction merely from the effect of his labours among 'those rough mountains' of Yorkshire; his ultimate desire and joy was to love and serve his God. When his friends urged him to take a little rest he would answer, 'Let me labour now; I shall have rest enough bye and bye. I cannot do enough for Christ who has done so much for me.' And in those words lies the explanation of that tireless zeal, which caused John Wesley to write in a letter to his friend Ebenezer Blackwell in July 1761 when he visited Haworth for the last time during Grimshaw's life: 'I have been for some days with Mr Grimshaw, an Israelite indeed! A few such as him would make a nation tremble. He carries fire wherever he goes.'[1]

[1]Wesley's *Letters*, vol. IV, p. 160.

23

'FOR TO ME TO LIVE IS CHRIST'

LITTLE REMAINS OF WILLIAM GRIMSHAW'S personal possessions apart from a pint-sized black teapot and a handsomely carved chair.[1] The small teapot subsequently passed into the keeping of the Brontë family and is now in the Brontë Museum in Haworth. Not surprisingly, in addition to the name of its original owner, it bears on its side, lettered within gilt scrolls, Grimshaw's avowed purpose for living: 'WM. Grimshaw A. B., To me / To live is Christ / To die is Gain.' As we have seen, he took these words as his life's motto. Not only did he have them inscribed on his Haworth pulpit, but he also had them placed on the walls of the church and on the candlestick used to provide light in the building.

Lines found in one of Grimshaw's letters to Mrs Gallatin, in all likelihood his own composition, reveal the same aspiration:

> Christ is my Meat; Christ is my Drink;
> My Christ, on whom I call;
> Christ is my Prophet, Priest and King,
> My Christ is all in all.[2]

It was love for Christ which made his physical sufferings and privations seem of little consequence; and love for Christ which brought a dimension of spiritual enjoyment into the long hours

[1] A plate and jug, also said to have belonged to Grimshaw, are on display in Epworth Rectory.
[2] Letter to Mrs Gallatin, 31 March 1761.

spent journeying across the barren Pennine moors to some isolated village. An example of this can be found in his diary entry for 9 October 1755. After riding over thirty miles on horseback and preaching five times at various places as he travelled, Grimshaw could record: 'It was a day of hard labour – But how true I find it is, He that waiteth on the LORD shall renew his Strength.'

'For to me to live is Christ,' the apostle Paul had written, and Grimshaw strove after this same ideal. How far he succeeded may be judged from a tribute paid by Mrs Jones:

I was taken ill at Mr Grimshaw's house and confined there for six months, during which time he was more than a father to me. I then had the happiness of seeing the glorious life he lived, showing forth the power and goodness of his Saviour and Master as he was wont to call him, whom he loved, honoured and obeyed ... He would often say, 'I love my God and Saviour, but how shall I love him enough?' He was so filled with love that at only mentioning the name of God he has stood still, ten minutes together. At last he said, 'What shall I do, what can I do to love and serve my God better?' I have seen him so overpowered with love, that he seemed as though he would have taken wing and fled ... to the throne of God.[1]

Erasmus Middleton also drew attention to this aspect of Grimshaw's spiritual experience when he wrote of him, 'He had drank deep into the love of God.'[2] But perhaps one of the finest descriptions of this quality of love for God after which Grimshaw aspired comes from his own pen in his last letter to the societies in Newcastle:

And now, what doth the Lord require of you between this day and death: this new January and the New Jerusalem? Only love and the fruits of love. Love six things, and happy will you be for ever. 1. Love the Lord. 2. Love his word. 3. Love his people. 4. Love his ways. 5. Love his works. 6. Love his cross; and be sure your love be sole, whole and pure, and perfect love; as constant and immutable as his love to

---

[1]Mrs Joseph Jones, in Laycock, *Heroes,* pp. 243–4.
[2]Middleton, *Biographia,* vol. IV, p. 406.

you; for truly, what is genuine Christian love, but love to God resulting from his love first to you, and shed abroad in your hearts by the Holy Spirit which is given to you?.[1]

Middleton noted the practical results of this love of God in Grimshaw's life, for, he added, it had produced in him 'the most disinterested love towards men'. This selfless compassion and generosity towards those in need was a characteristic that several of the elderly residents of Haworth recalled long after Grimshaw's death. With clear memories of Grimshaw from her childhood days, Susanna Wright, seventy-seven at the time, recollected how Grimshaw would give away his last penny to the poor, until he himself had 'not a crust of bread in his house . . . nothing to live on but a few onions'. When reduced to such penury himself, he would sometimes be obliged to borrow a little money from some well-placed parishioner if he had some pressing financial commitment. In sincere gratitude for such assistance, he would repay the kindness by his earnest prayers for God's blessing to rest upon his benefactor. Susanna Wright could remember an occasion when she was playing in the road near her house and Grimshaw walked past. Oblivious of the child's presence, he was praying aloud: 'The Lord bless him, the Lord bless him in his basket, the Lord bless him in his store,' was his petition.[2] Arrested by hearing such unexpected words from the lips of the curate, the child hurried inside and told her mother, 'Mother, Mr Grimshaw was talking to himself as he was passing by. He was saying, 'God bless him in his basket and in his store.' 'Oh, no,' assured her mother, 'he was praying for your father.'

Another old couple recalled the day that Grimshaw arrived to collect the rent due to him for the cottage which they occupied. The cottage belonged to the church – being built on church property – and therefore the rent formed part of his salary. Confessing that they were too poor to pay and needed the money

---

[1] Letter to Newcastle Society, 12 January 1762. For whole letter, see Myles, *Life and Writings*, p. 188.

[2] Quoting Deuteronomy 28:5.

to buy food, the couple begged to be pardoned the debt. But Grimshaw replied that he too was in financial difficulties: 'You must try at all events to pay the rent. I myself have borrowed money, and need this rent in order to repay the loan. I cannot do without it.' To their astonishment, however, the curate arrived again the next day, not to insist upon his dues, but this time he had a sack of flour for them slung across the back of his white horse.

William Grimshaw's generosity was a trait of his personality which even caused John Newton some astonishment, and remained as an abiding memory of his friend. Unashamed of begging on behalf of his neediest parishioners, Grimshaw would gather together old boots and shoes which his wealthier parishioners had discarded, and after having had them repaired, he would give them away to those in need. More than this, he would part with his own clothes too, if he discovered someone whose need he considered to be greater than his own. Much to the despair of Molly, his housekeeper, he would give away all except the clothes he was wearing and be left without any change when he came in drenched to the skin.

Never did he collect any money to which he was entitled in a rigorous fashion; rather he would say, 'I will not deserve your curses when I am dead, for what I have received for my poor labours among you: I want no more of you than your souls for my God, and a bare maintenance for myself.'[1] His friends feared Grimshaw would die penniless, or even in debt, particularly as he used to say, 'If I should die today, I have not a penny to leave behind me.' But this was not the case for he died solvent, and even left Molly £5 and his feather bed, bolster, blankets and a rug. As Middleton commented, 'He had prudence as well as grace, a justice as well as generosity of soul. His accounts were easily kept for he lived from day to day upon his Master.'[2]

As we have seen, Grimshaw's friends were impressed by his cheerful spirit which sprang from inner contentment of heart. 'He

[1]Middleton, *Biographia,* vol. IV, p. 404.   [2]Ibid., p. 405.

was always happy in Christ', Mrs Joseph Jones reported after she had stayed at Sowdens, 'and never lost sight of him from the first day of his conversion.' 'His very countenance proclaimed that the joy of the Lord was his strength,'[1] added Henry Venn. And in Grimshaw's own words: 'The true Christian . . . is well-provided for both worlds. He is sure of peace here and glory above and therefore enjoys a light heart and a cheerful face.'[2]

But it was in the grace of humility that Grimshaw's love for Christ found its brightest expression. On this his contemporaries were unanimous. William Romaine declared, 'He was the most humble walker with Christ I ever met with; insomuch that he could never endure to hear any commendations made to him upon his usefulness, or anything which belonged to him.'[3] A friend of John Newton's, in all probability Dr John Fawcett, whom Newton describes as 'a judicious respectable dissenting minister who still lives in the neighbourhood of Haworth', speaks of Grimshaw in these terms:

I have often heard Mr Grimshaw with great astonishment, and I hope with profit. In prayer before his sermon, he excelled most men I have ever heard. His soul was carried out in that exercise with such earnestness, affection and fervour, as indicated most intimate communion with God. His love and compassion for the souls of poor sinners, and his concern for their salvation, were manifested in the strongest manner in all his proceedings. Yet though his talents were great, his labours abundant, and his success wonderful, he had the meanest and most degrading thoughts about himself and of all he did. Humility was a shining feature in his character.[4]

Despite his own outstanding gifts as a preacher, he appears to have entertained an unduly low estimate of his abilities, comparing himself unfavourably with other preachers. Those who

[1]Venn, Funeral sermon, p. 11.
[2]Grimshaw, 'Nature, State and Conduct of a Christian'.
[3]Romaine, cited by Middleton, *Biographia*, p. 407.
[4]Newton, *Letters*, p. 123.

remembered Grimshaw recalled one memorable example of this spirit when young Benjamin Beanland, one of his own converts, first began to preach. Regardless of the fact that a congregation had gathered to hear him preach, Grimshaw insisted that Benjamin should address the eager listeners instead. After he had preached, Grimshaw flung his arms around the young man, declaring, 'The Lord bless thee, Ben! This is worth a hundred of my sermons!' On another occasion, when Grimshaw arrived in Leeds where he was due to preach, he declared to the waiting congregation: 'Now many of you are come here today because you have heard the minister of Haworth was to be here, and you think I can preach better than the rest of my brethren: but you are quite mistaken; many of them preach full as well as I do. But in truth we are all alike; there is not a chip to choose; in good faith, there is not.'[1]

On one occasion a young Methodist preacher, William Thompson, was on his way to Scotland where John Wesley had designated he should begin his ministry. Anxious to meet Grimshaw and hear him preach, he called in to Haworth on his way north. Enquiring from an old man where he might find the curate, he spoke in a way which betrayed the fact that he had not yet met Grimshaw. 'What!' exclaimed the elderly parishioner, 'not know old Grimshaw? Why, I thought the whole world knew old Grimshaw!' As the visitor approached down the lane leading to Sowdens, Grimshaw caught a glimpse of him, and quickly summoned his housekeeper, Molly. 'Mol, Mol,' he said urgently, 'go out and tell me what he is like.' Molly went outside to obtain a clearer view and then came in with her report, 'He is a Methodist preacher, sir.' This was commendation enough for Grimshaw. 'Go, tell him directly to come in,' was her master's next injunction. As the unsuspecting young preacher entered the house, Grimshaw boomed out, 'You must preach today, Sir, in my church.' 'But I have come to hear you,' replied the hapless man.

[1]John Pawson's Letter, *Methodist Magazine*, 1803, p. 451, cited by Hardy, *Incumbent*.

Argument was useless, for Grimshaw insisted he was not prepared to do another stroke of work until his visitor had agreed to preach to his people. As Thompson concluded his sermon, Grimshaw exclaimed, 'There is preaching for you! There is preaching for you!' The visitor was obliged to extend his visit by many days, as his admiring host conducted him on a preaching tour through parts of the Haworth Round.[1]

In John Newton's opinion, this low estimate of his own abilities, coupled with an exaggerated evaluation of the abilities of others, was not necessarily a good thing. He seemed unaware of his God-given gifts and potential, and this occasionally led him to extremes in his judgments. If a totally uneducated man were to preach the same truths with zeal and earnestness, Grimshaw would regard those sermons as better than his own. As Newton pointedly remarked, 'If a man possesses a large estate, humility will not require him to think he is poor, but it will teach him moderation and thankfulness.'[2]

Nor was Grimshaw's humility of mind confined to his estimate of himself as a preacher. In the ordinary details of his life the same attitude prevailed. John Newton records that when one of his friends was staying at Sowdens the house was so full of guests that without any indication of a problem Grimshaw himself went to sleep in the hayloft, giving up his own bed for a visitor. Even more surprising to this friend, who must have been an early riser himself, was the discovery in the morning of Grimshaw busy cleaning his muddy boots for him, at an hour when he had expected his friend would still be asleep. Summing up this unpretentious and humble spirit which he had observed so markedly in Grimshaw, John Newton wrote, 'A stranger might be in company with Mr Grimshaw from morning till night, without observing anything which would lead him to suppose he was a minister; he would only think he saw and heard a pious, intelligent, plain man.'[3]

The mainspring of his spiritual life was no closely guarded secret. He himself spells it out clearly in that same final letter to

[1] JEN.   [2] Newton, *Letters,* p. 121.   [3] Ibid., p. 119.

the Newcastle Societies: 'O that you may be always filled with this love, this heaven, this Christ, this God! In order to this blessed end, pray keep close to every means of grace, and every ordinance of God. Read, meditate, examine, watch, pray and communicate cheerfully'. Since his first searching after God he had given time and priority to secret prayer. 'Praying Christians are growing Christians', he maintained, 'for they are not blessed *for* praying, yet I find they are blessed *in* praying.'[1] Even when prayer seemed unavailing and the heart disinclined to make the necessary spiritual effort, Grimshaw urged believers to pray on. Clearly drawing on his own experience, he writes, 'The anxious desire after liberty to pray is indeed the best of prayer. Stick fast to it, hold you there, and all will be well.'[2]

Henry Venn's description of Grimshaw's communion with God speaks eloquently of both the cause and the results of that life of prayer which Grimshaw recommended to others and diligently tried to follow himself: 'His soul at various times enjoyed very large manifestations of God's love . . . and at some seasons, his faith was so strong and hope so abundant, that higher degrees of spiritual delight would have overpowered his mortal frame.'[3]

Such manifestations of God's love had made of Grimshaw an eminently loving and humble man. And his people loved him in return. He was 'happy in being beloved,' wrote Henry Venn, 'for several of the last years of his life, by everyone in his parish, who, whether they would be persuaded by him to forsake the evil of their ways or no, had no doubt that Mr Grimshaw was their cordial friend.' And the tangible results of such a ministry and life were also evident in Haworth:

He saw an effectual change take place in many of his flock; a sense of evil and good, and a restraint from the commission of sin, brought upon the parish in general. He saw the name of Jesus exalted and many souls

[1]'Experiences'.
[2]Grimshaw, *Answer to White,* Myles, *Life and Writings,* p. 87.
[3]Venn, *Sketch,* p. 35.

happy in the knowledge of him, and walking as becomes the gospel of Christ.[1]

As the 1760s progressed, however, William Grimshaw recognised that his health was continuing to deteriorate. On several occasions he had visited the Methodist societies in Newcastle at the beginning of a year, but in 1761 he felt unable to make the arduous journey north in the winter. Perhaps he might be able to go in the summer, he thought, but even that was uncertain. So he enclosed in his New Year letter to the society a little note, probably addressed to the itinerant preacher who had the responsibility for the area. It had these words: 'My love to all enquirers – Who knows, but next summer I may see you. I could be glad to visit my Newcastle brethren once more before I die.'

But this was not to be. By early 1762 it became evident that Grimshaw was an ill man even though he was only fifty-three. Never having allowed himself any recreation, he now admitted to Mrs Gallatin, 'As to my health, I cannot say it is the best, or by much so good as it was when I last saw you. Since then it is much impaired – and no wonder. I may say, as we do of a drunkard, "I live too fast to live long." I am a wonder to myself that I am not worse than I am; or even that I am alive ... I am seldom free from pain in my limbs and in my bowels. I write even now in pain.' Clearly meditating upon death, he added, 'I often think these shall be my dying words, "Lord Jesus, receive an unprofitable servant."'[2]

Despite his increasing debility Grimshaw was now witnessing greater blessings in his own parish than he had seen for twelve years. And then, as we have already noted, in August 1762 – the last summer of his life – he had been able to join all his friends in an extended period of conference and preaching when the Countess of Huntingdon came to Yorkshire. These were the people Grimshaw loved best in the world: John Wesley, George

---

[1] Ibid.

[2] Letter to Mrs Gallatin, 10 January 1762, cited by Baker, *Grimshaw,* pp. 259–261.

Whitefield, Henry Venn, William Romaine and others, together with the Countess. A unique gathering, it was one which Grimshaw looked back on with delight as together they proclaimed the gospel of God's grace to the people. 'How did our hearts burn within us to proclaim his love and grace to perishing sinners!' he recollected as he wrote to the Countess begging her to come back to Yorkshire again

Much as he enjoyed the company of like-minded Christians, it still seemed strange to Grimshaw that dying believers should take leave of each other as if they were to be parted for a long time. Instead, he suggested, 'a Christian's dying words should be, "I am going to heaven, to God, to glory, a bit before you . . . " If a man and his wife are invited to dine with a friend, and he sets out an hour before her, would he bid her farewell at his setting out, when both are to dine together at noon?'[1] A Christian, he explained in another manuscript, 'makes no more of dying, than when he is weary, to fall asleep. Whether he lives, he lives to the Lord: or whether he dies, he dies to the Lord. For whether living or dying, he is the Lord's. *For to him to live is Christ, to die is gain.*'[2]

[1] 'Experiences'.
[2] Grimshaw, 'Nature, State and Conduct of a Christian'.

24

'. . . AND TO DIE IS GAIN'

'I EXPECT MY STAY ON EARTH WILL BE BUT SHORT and will endeavour
to make the best of a short life, and so devote my soul to God as
not to go creeping to heaven at last.'[1] Such was William Grimshaw's
often-repeated prediction and aspiration. Despite a hardy
physique and years of excellent general health, his expectation of
a short life proved true. Unlike John Wesley, whose eighty-eight
years spanned the greater part of the century, Grimshaw died
before he had attained his fifty-fifth birthday. Conscious of a
steady deterioration in his health, he referred in some of his
letters written between 1759 and 1762 to increasing pain in his
limbs and stomach and also to debilitating headaches. Whether
he was suffering from cancer, we are not now in a position to say,
but clearly he was not a man to complain without good cause.

As we have seen, the fresh wave of revival since 1759 had
brought Grimshaw's ministry to a climax of fruitfulness and joy.
'The Lord's work prospers amazingly among us,' he had written
to the Countess of Huntingdon in November 1762. But even
as his heart rejoiced over this further evident work of God, he
sensed that his own remaining time on earth would not be long.
Expressing his gratitude to God for giving the Church such a
woman as the Countess, he could say in this letter, 'God has
raised you up for the accomplishment of a mighty work in the

[1]Mrs Joseph Jones, in Laycock, *Heroes,* p. 246.

land; I may not live to witness it, but I shall assuredly see some of the triumphs of the cross, the blood-bought slaves, the ransomed captives, rescued from the tyranny and slavery of the great enemy of souls in the chapels of your Ladyship, all arrayed in dazzling white . . . praising and blessing the Lamb for ever.' Then in a note almost anticipating coming events, he continued, 'Yes, when I am before the throne – then I shall see and hear and know what you have been made the instrument of accomplishing upon earth.' But lest even the Countess should begin to glory in her own achievements, he adds, 'and at last we shall meet as *two poor worthless sinners,* stripped of every fancied good, to bless and praise him through eternity!'[1] Within six months of writing those words, William Grimshaw was indeed before the throne of the Lamb.

Death held no fears for Grimshaw. 'He spoke of death with pleasure, as letting him into a better world, and bringing him into the arms of his Saviour,' reported Mrs Jones.[2] Foretastes of the love of God which he described as 'heaven in the soul' had been his privilege over many years, and these had sharpened his expectation of heaven itself, robbing death of its power to cast its frightening shadow across his path. Like Richard Baxter, whose works he had studied, Grimshaw encouraged his people to meditate often on the joys awaiting believers.

Death was an ever-present reality to the people of Haworth, where average life expectancy was low, and epidemics frequently swept through the community, leaving few homes untouched, as Grimshaw himself knew well. So, in order to face death whenever it should strike, he wrote: 'When you put off your clothes, think of putting off your earthly tabernacle. Go to your beds as you would to your graves. When creeping within the sheets, think of your winding sheet; and close your eyes in this world, as you would open them in another. Today is your living day: tomorrow may be your dying day. Meditation on death will prepare you for death.'[3]

[1]Grimshaw to Countess of Huntingdon, Laycock, p. 236.
[2]Mrs Joseph Jones, in Laycock, *Heroes,* p. 246.
[3]Grimshaw, 'The Believer's Golden Chain'.

But not only had Grimshaw prepared himself for death by confronting its reality in his thought, he also maintained that constant reflection on the world to come would bring heaven into the heart of a believer even in this life. 'When our contemplation and conversations are in heaven, we then enjoy heaven on earth,' he noted down in his record of his own spiritual experiences.[1] And to Mrs Gallatin he wrote, urging her to lift her thoughts above the sorrows and uncertainties of her present circumstances to the immovable heritage of the children of God, 'Again, dear sister, let me desire you to be mindful of your heavenly origin, your new birth, that you are born from above, and that your native home is the New Jerusalem, the City of God; that your glory is his face, and your company himself and all the glorified host of heaven.'[2]

Throughout the last months of William Grimshaw's life, as he battled against ill-health, he had adamantly refused to slacken his pace, riding tirelessly around his vast 'parish'. Greatly loved by his people, he was welcomed in their homes. But there was one home in which he knew a special welcome awaited him. One of Grimshaw's earliest converts had been a farmer's wife who, it may be recalled, had been forced to hear Grimshaw preach, being driven like an animal to Haworth by her well-intentioned husband. Cursing and swearing all the way, she had nevertheless been remarkably converted and became one of Grimshaw's most receptive hearers. Often on a Sunday afternoon he would ride the six miles across to the farm to preach and many conversions had taken place in that neighbourhood. Sometimes he would spend the night with the farmer and his wife, and an anecdote has survived, recorded by one who knew Grimshaw personally, describing his final visit to this farmstead:

Mr Grimshaw's custom was to go to bed about nine and rise at four; but the last time he lodged in this house he rose about three in the morning. This woman waked her husband at five, and said, 'Mr Grimshaw must

[1]'Experiences'.
[2]Letter to Mrs Gallatin, 10 May 1754, cited by Laycock, *Heroes,* p. 145.

have something particular to do this day; rise and feed his horse.' Accordingly he rose but as he attempted to go out of the door, Mr Grimshaw prevented him by saying, 'There shall no foot cross this threshold until thee and thy wife and I have joined in prayer together'; for, says Mr Grimshaw, 'I have been wrestling with God two hours for you, and I believe he will bless you.' They told me they never heard him pray in such a manner, or take so solemn a leave of them before. This was but a few days before his death.[1]

As Grimshaw's punishing schedule of travelling and preaching was beginning to exact its heavy toll, a virulent epidemic of typhus fever broke out in Haworth early in 1763. It found him in a weakened condition and in no state to sustain an attack of such an infection.

Such epidemics were common in Haworth where cramped and insanitary living conditions intensified the risk and an outbreak of this nature would occur almost every five years. But an exceptionally hard winter in 1763, followed by sudden mild weather with severe flooding as the snows melted, made the people more vulnerable than usual to infection. As the first villagers fell victim, those able to do so fled their homes until it was safe to return. But never would such a consideration have occurred to Grimshaw. His duty lay with his sick and dying parishioners, and to minister effectively to them he had to expose himself to considerable risk. From the outset of this epidemic, Grimshaw was convinced that at least one member of his household or family would succumb to the disease and die. So he warned each of them repeatedly to prepare themselves in spirit against such an eventuality.

Mounting his pulpit on 20 March 1763, Grimshaw preached with all his accustomed fervour. But by the next day he knew which of his household it was who would be taken. Realising he had contracted the infection after visiting a sick parishioner, he prepared detailed instructions for his funeral. He wished 'a poor man's burial suit and a poor man's coffin'. He then stipulated that

---

[1]*Christian's Magazine,* November 1792, p. 435.

only about twenty of his 'spiritual brethren and nearest relatives' should attend a simple meal following the interment – a request that stood in marked contrast to the drunken 'arvills' [feasts] that were the common custom after funerals. He would have told those around him that he still wished to be buried beside Sarah in Luddenden, in spite of the fact that Elizabeth had died subsequently. On the Thursday of that week, 24 March, Grimshaw made his will and named his executors as an increasing fever with its attendant weakness drove him to his bed. His faithful housekeeper, Molly Shackleton, cared for her master as best as she was able, and on her fell a double burden, for Martha Whitehead, one of Grimshaw's maids, was also taken ill at the same time.

Although the typhus fever was by no means fatal in all cases, Grimshaw seemed to entertain no doubts as to the final outcome of his condition. Giving further instructions for his funeral, he asked that a Methodist should preach the sermon and should base his message on Philippians 1:21. Grimshaw also stipulated that his coffin itself should bear the words of that text on its lid as a testimony to all who should follow it to its final resting place – so declaring that not only in his living, but also in his dying, Christ was the mainspring of his being, both for time and eternity.

Communications were slow in the mid-eighteenth century and few of Grimshaw's fellow Methodist leaders knew of his illness. John Wesley was busy overseeing affairs in Lewisham before leaving for Bristol; and Charles was at home with his wife Sally and their family in London; George Whitefield, an ill man himself, was journeying to Scotland, from where he hoped to sail for America once more. But at Aberford Benjamin Ingham was much closer and as soon as he heard of his friend's serious condition, he rode the twenty-five miles to Haworth, and made his way down the uneven track to Sowdens.

As Ingham entered the room where he lay, Grimshaw greeted him with the words, 'My last enemy is come! The signs of death are on me, but I am not afraid – No! no! blessed be God, my hope is sure, and I am in his hands.' Ingham realised that Grimshaw's condition was indeed life-threatening, and he spoke with him for a few moments before praying earnestly that if it should be God's will he would spare his servant for further effective labours in the kingdom of Christ. Rallying his failing strength, Grimshaw responded wistfully, 'My dear brother Ingham, if the Lord should raise me up, I think I could do more for his glory than I have hitherto done. Alas! What have my wretched services been? And I have now need to cry at the close of my unprofitable course, God be merciful to me a sinner!' Such words must remind us of his prediction to Romaine, that his last words would be, 'Here goes an unprofitable servant.'

In his heart Grimshaw knew that it was not the will of God that he should recover. Molly summoned the local apothecary – eighteenth-century equivalent to the village doctor – but all to no avail: his condition steadily worsened. By the time Ingham returned to Haworth a few days later, on 2 April, he could see that his friend was sinking rapidly and could no longer indulge the hope he might be spared. But Ingham, brought with him a message from 'her Ladyship', the Countess of Huntingdon, which must have lifted the suffering man's spirits. Touched by her concern, he replied in words simple but moving: 'Tell her Ladyship, that dear elect woman, that I thank her from the bottom of my heart for all her kindnesses to me during the years that I have known her. With my dying breath I implore every blessing, temporal and spiritual, to rest upon her. May the God of Abraham, Isaac and Jacob bless her — bless her in body, soul and spirit. I can never repay the spiritual good I have reaped at her hands. O may she be eminently useful in her day and generation!'

But the effort had exhausted him. Falling back in his bed he lay still and silent for a long time. Perhaps in those moments God in pity and grace revealed himself to his dying servant in an unusual manner. For when he spoke again, his words, like those of many dying Christians, reflected a renewed confidence in that solid foundation of his spiritual hope – the redeeming sacrifice of the Lord Jesus Christ: 'I am quite exhausted,' he began, 'but I shall soon be home, for ever with the Lord – a poor miserable sinner redeemed by his blood.' After Ingham had once more commended his friend to the mercies of God, Grimshaw spoke again, 'I harbour no desire of life, my time is come and I am entirely resigned to God.' Then raising his hands and eyes to God, he said, 'Thy will be done.'

As Benjamin Ingham rose to go, knowing that he and Grimshaw would never meet again on earth, footsteps could be heard approaching the house. Henry Venn had just heard of Grimshaw's condition and was anxious to visit him, though he too recognised that the infection was highly contagious. With a high fever, Grimshaw was evidently in much pain when Venn entered the room but he said to Venn, 'I am as happy as I can be on earth, and as sure of glory as if I were in it.' And clearly referring to some recent disclosure of God's love, he confided, 'Never had I such a visit from God, since I knew him.' Venn did not stay long for Grimshaw could sustain little more, but before he left, Grimshaw asked him to undertake the responsibility for his funeral. Leaving the sick man's bedside, Venn wrote sadly to a correspondent: 'He lies ill of a dangerous fever, and how the good Lord of the Harvest designs to dispose of him, I know not. But whenever he enters into rest one of the great ornaments of the gospel will be taken from us.'[1]

News spread around the locality that the beloved curate of Haworth was seriously ill, and many came to visit Grimshaw as he lay evidently dying. Knowing how infectious was his condition, Grimshaw begged his friends to stay away, but regardless of the risk involved, they still wished to catch some last words of encouragement or challenge before he was taken from them. 'Our people die well,' John Wesley had once declared, and in days when faith and hope burned brightly and few palliatives were available to drug the senses, many were the sayings of dying Christians long treasured in the memories of those who heard them spoken.

Jerry Robertshaw was there. Looking at the young preacher in

---

[1]Unpublished letter, cited by G. C. Cragg, *Grimshaw of Haworth* (London: Canterbury Press, 1947), p. 90.

his first flush of youthful enthusiasm, Grimshaw said, 'The Lord bless you, Jerry; I will pray for you as long as I live; and if there be such a thing as praying in heaven, I will pray for you there also.' To another he gave 'strict charge to adhere close to his much loved Master, and to the Methodists'. Thomas Colbeck from Keighley could not stay away. Fifteen years had passed since the mob riots at Roughlee, when he had lain on the ground, mercilessly kicked by the mob until the burly Grimshaw came to his rescue. To him we owe the fullest account of Grimshaw's death, for he wrote down all that he could remember, and passed it on in a letter to Charles Wesley.

But there was another who came to Grimshaw's bedside: it was John Grimshaw, now twenty-seven years of age. A waster and a drunkard, John had brought untold distress to his father. What passed between them as John watched by his dying father we do not know. Perhaps little was said. But there John saw enacted a sermon without words which affected him more deeply than any of the rebukes and exhortations administered to reclaim him from his careless ways over the years. He went away burdened by a realisation of his own sinfulness.

As Sunday 3 April 1763 dawned, Grimshaw was desperately ill and was drifting in and out of consciousness. But in his lucid moments the burden of his thoughts was for his people, now meeting in worship. He knew how sad they would be, how they had hung upon his ministry, and how they would miss him. As he lay there, he prayed earnestly for them, that they might be blessed in their worship that day. He sent messages to console them for many of them were his own children in the faith and they loved him dearly. 'Tell them I am happy,' he said, and continued, 'Be not discouraged. We shall all be in heaven soon.'

Molly watched helplessly over her master as he sank rapidly during the following three days. As his condition worsened, his physical distress became more acute. After a sleepless night when the fever raged so fiercely that Colbeck, who was with him, said 'His flesh burnt as if it had been in an oven', Grimshaw admitted to the younger man, 'I have been entreating the Lord, if it pleased him, to mitigate my affliction,' adding, 'It is only ask, and have; I lie in my Saviour's arms.'

Martha Whitehead died on the Wednesday of that week, and Molly must have realised that Grimshaw would soon follow. So intense had his fever become by that Wednesday night, that when she spoke to him in the morning, he replied, 'Oh Mary, I have suffered last night what the blessed martyrs did! My flesh has been as it were roasting before a hot fire. But I have nothing to do but to step out of bed into heaven. I have my foot upon the threshold already.' Indeed he had. And later that same day William Grimshaw crossed over that threshold, and into the light and blessedness he had anticipated so long.

In his account to Charles Wesley of all that he had heard and witnessed, Colbeck added these words:

Our dear and much regretted friend was divinely persuaded that, as life had not, so neither could the ghastly tyrant [death] separate him from the love of God which is in Christ Jesus our Lord. His consolations from almost the moment the fever seized him, were neither few nor small. He frequently expressed himself as if he was as happy as it was possible to be while clothed with mortality, and as fully satisfied that when the silver cord of life should be loosed, an abundant entrance would be ministered to his joyous soul, into the holiest, through the blood of atonement, as if he had already been an inhabitant of the heavenly Jerusalem.[1]

Grief swept across Haworth and throughout the neighbourhood as news of William Grimshaw's death spread rapidly from town to town, from village to lonely farmstead – and all alike mourned, for he had become their friend and guide. All his wishes, so clearly stated, were carried out, and 'what of him [that] could die' was 'wrapped in a plain poor man's burial suit and laid in a plain poor man's coffin'.

The day after his death vast crowds followed the alder-wood coffin, engraved with the text that had been his beacon in life and death, from his home in Haworth to Ewood, twelve miles away,

[1]Colbeck to Charles Wesley, cited by Laycock, *Heroes*, p. 241.

where his son John and his wife were living. Two horses carried the litter containing the coffin slung between them as they walked in single file – along the very path which he had so often travelled in his preaching tours. But now he was followed by all his grieving people, sometimes weeping, sometimes singing, as they went.

The following day the funeral procession continued on its way from Ewood, along the narrow mountain track for over a mile, down the steep hillside, and across a rushing stream which ran close to the parish church of Luddenden. Here it halted as the vast concourse of people, singing Psalms 23, 39 and 91 in accordance with their pastor's request, gathered in and around the churchyard. Standing there in the open air, Henry Venn conducted the service, his voice clear as a bell, as those who heard him recalled, ringing out across the wooded valley:

Do you then ask what proof real believers give that to them 'to live is Christ'? Who in our time was more deeply affected with this self-abasing doctrine than your late minister? It was engraved on his heart; and not all his diligence in doing the work of his ministry, nor his great success in it, not all his joys in God, though abundant, nor his unblameable conversation . . . ever led him to obscure the glory of the cross of Christ. Still upon his atoning blood and justifying righteousness alone, did every hope of his soul's acceptance with God depend.

And so they buried him: next to Sarah, as he had requested. This was not in the graveyard, but in the church itself near the pulpit – an appropriate spot for one whose meat and drink had been to preach Christ. The original stone engraved with his name and dates has now disappeared, but a small plaque in Grimshaw's memory remains on the wall near where he was buried: his very name a silent preacher for those who have ears to hear.

The following day was Sunday, and Henry Venn repeated his sermon in Haworth for the benefit of all those many parishioners and friends who had not been able to follow their pastor's coffin to its last resting place. Ten days later, as the news of Grimshaw's death spread far and wide across the country, William Romaine preached another sermon, also on Philippians 1:21, at St Dunstan's, in London. Part of the sermon survives, recorded by Erasmus Middleton, and concluding his remarks, Romaine quoted words that were often on Grimshaw's lips, words which hold the secret to Grimshaw's ceaseless labours and which might form a fitting epitaph to his life: 'I cannot do enough for Christ, who has done so much for me.'[1]

Urged by many who had known and loved William Grimshaw, Venn managed to publish the sermon he had preached by the end of the month, calling it *Christ the Joy of the Christian's Life and Death his Gain.* To this sermon he added an eight-page account of his friend's life, from which we have quoted extensively.[2]

When Charles Wesley learnt of Grimshaw's death, he felt the loss keenly and made a careful attempt to collect together all the material he could respecting his friend's character and his last days. Not many weeks after, Charles gave a two-hour lecture on the life and influence of 'blessed Mr Grimshaw' to a crowded congregation. Regrettably, it was never printed, but later he marked the event by two elegies in Grimshaw's memory, one of which contained these words:

> *My father, my guide (our Israel may say),*
> *Is torn from our side, is ravished away!*
> *A prophet's translation we justly deplore*
> *With calm lamentation and weeping, adore.*
> *Devotion in tears expresses its love,*
> *Till Jesus appears our souls to remove:*
> *The loss of a Stephen we greatly bewail:*
> *He triumphs in heaven, we mourn in the vale.*[3]

[1]Middleton, *Biographia*, vol. IV, p. 407.

[2]Published Leeds, 1763. Nehemiah Curnock included much of this material in John Wesley's *Journal*, supposing it had been written by Wesley. A number of others who have written on Grimshaw have also used the material in this pamphlet almost verbatim, but with no acknowledgement.

[3]Charles Wesley's *Journal*, vol. 2, p. 365.

Dan Taylor, who was to found the New Connexion of General Baptists, had also enjoyed a warm personal friendship with Grimshaw and he too felt the loss deeply. Taylor wrote a glowing ninety-five line elegy commemorating his life and ministry. Entitled, *A Thought on the Death of the Late Reverend Mr Grimshaw*, he described Grimshaw as:

> *The brother and the friend of human race*
> *The Son of Learning and the Child of Grace.*
> *The unwearied servant of his dear-lov'd Lord,*
> *The powerful preacher of thy sacred Word.*

Slowly life began to return to normal in Haworth, though William Grimshaw left behind a void which none could fill. But for one young man nothing could ever be the same again. Memories of his father filled John Grimshaw with regrets – regrets over his prodigal ways, and regrets over the grief he had caused. John inherited little from his father apart from his papers, for his father had little to leave; but one thing to which he laid claim was the sturdy white horse that had carried the evangelist of Yorkshire on his ceaseless travels, preaching wherever he went. Every time John rode the horse, he thought of his father. Addressing it he would say, 'Once you carried a saint but now you carry a devil.'

Gradually the burden of his sinfulness became intolerable and John began to seek his father's God in true penitence of heart. Three years later John himself was taken seriously ill, and though only thirty years of age, it was soon apparent that he too was dying. One who came in to pray with him reported that John had indeed found the mercy and forgiveness of God, and John himself exclaimed just before he died, 'What will my father say when he sees me in heaven!'

We are reminded of Grimshaw's words in his 'Admonition of a Sinner', written in faith and hope that he might see his own son in heaven: 'What inconceivable, incomprehensible, eternally durable pleasure it will afford us to meet and dwell for ever with those in heaven (whether they have gone thither before us or shall follow after us), whom we have been instrumental in converting to God and bringing thither. O what exquisite pleasure to see their faces ... There is also, as I think, equal probability that parents departed hence in the Lord, [will] rejoice over the conversion of their children, whom they left behind in their sins.' And how must William Grimshaw have rejoiced over the conversion of his son, John!

Concluding that treatise, Grimshaw quoted words from the book of Daniel: 'They that be wise shall shine as the brightness of the firmament and they also that turn many to righteousness shall shine as the stars for ever and ever.' These words can surely be applied most aptly to this man of God, who in life and in death turned many from their sins to a life which was life indeed. And through such changed lives the face of eighteenth-century Yorkshire was transformed.

APPENDICES

Appendix 1

William Grimshaw's Letters

To Mr Wesley

Ewood, August 20, 1747

Rev. and Very Dear Brother,

 Wherever these lines find you, may they find you full of the spirit of power, and of love and of a sound mind, fighting, in the strength of our Lord, the good fight of faith, pulling down strongholds of Satan, and industriously labouring to deliver multitudes of poor sin-slaved souls out of the kingdom of darkness, into the glorious light and liberty of the sons of God! Such success let us daily and heartily beseech our dear Redeemer to bless all his faithful ministers with, wherever he sends them. You will desire to know how I do. O, dear Sir, hearty and happy in the Lord; and how my ministry, or rather the present state of my parish. Blessed be God, flourishing still more and more; our societies are, in general, very lively in the Lord, and several others, though not as yet joined in society, are nevertheless come to a sense of the pardoning love of God; others are under deep concern, or eagerly hungering and thirsting after our Redeemer. Two under my own roof are just now under true conviction; one a girl about eighteen years old, and the other a boy about fourteen; and, I hope, my own little girl, between ten and eleven years old. It is near six months since she first began to show a serious concern for her sinful state.

The method which I, the least and most unworthy of my Lord's ministers, take in my parish is this: I preach the gospel, glad tidings of salvation to penitent sinners, through faith in Christ's blood only, twice every Lord's day the year round, (save when I expound the Church Catechism, and thirty-nine Articles or read the Homilies, which, in substance, I think my duty to do in some part of the year annually on the Lord's-day mornings.) I have found this practice, I bless God, of inexpressible benefit to my congregation, which consists, especially in the summer season, of perhaps ten or twelve hundred; or, as some think, of many more souls. We have also prayers and a chapter expounded every Lord's-day evening. I visit my parish in twelve several places monthly, convening six, eight or ten families, in each place, allowing any people of the neighbouring parishes that please to attend that exhortation. This I call my monthly visitation. I am now entering into the fifth year of it, and wonderfully, dear Sir, has the Lord blessed it. The only thing more are our funeral expositions or exhortations, and visiting our societies in one or other of the three last days of every month. This I purposed, through the grace of God, to make my constant business in my parish, so long as I live.

But, O dear Sir, I know not what to say; I know not what to do. Sometimes I have made more excursions into neighbouring parishes, to exhort, but always with a Nicodemical fear, and to the great offence of the clergy, which, till lately almost made me ready to sally out no more, but to content myself in my own bounds: till lately, I say; for on Wednesday was six weeks, from about five o'clock in the afternoon, to about twelve at night, and again for some hours together, I may say, the day following, my mind was deeply affected with strong impressions to preach the gospel abroad; the event I left to the Lord, fearing to be disobedient to what, I trust, was the heavenly call. The first thing suggested to me was to visit William Darney's societies: I accordingly met one of them about a month ago. Last week I struck out into Lancashire and Cheshire, Mr Bennet bearing me company. We visited the societies in Rochdale, Manchester and Holme, in Lancashire, and Booth-bank in Cheshire. At the same time we made a visit to Mr Carmichael, a clergyman at Tarvin, near Chester. He says he received remission of sins last September; and, I believe, preaches the same truth to his people.

From thence we came back by Booth-bank to Manchester, visited the society a second time and there we parted. I called and spent part of two days with William Darney's societies, particularly those in Todmorden, Shore, Mellor-barn, Rossendale, Bacup, Crosstone, Stoneshawfate, Crimsworth-Dean; everywhere the Lord was manifestly with us: great blessings were scattered and much zeal and love, with great humility and simplicity, appeared in most people everywhere. The whole visit found me employment for near five days. O it was a blessed journey to my soul! I now, in some measure, begin to see into the import of our Lord's design, by that deep impression on my mind above-mentioned. I am determined, therefore, to add, by the divine assistance, to the care of my own parish, that of so frequent a visitation of Mr Bennet's, William Darney's, the Leeds and Birstall societies, as my own convenience will permit and their circumstances may respectively seem to require, all along eyeing the Lord's will and purposes for me. If I find the Lord's pleasure be that I must still launch out further, I will obey; for he daily convinces me more and more what he has graciously done and will do for my soul. O! I can never do enough in gratitude and love to him, for the least mite, if I may reverently so speak, of what his blessings are to me. O, dear Sir, that I may prove faithful and indefatigable in his vineyard! that I may persevere to the last gasp steadfast, immovable, and always abounding in his work! Do you pray – the same shall be mine for you, your dear brother, and all our fellow-labourers.

What I purpose concerning surveying the above said societies, as I have great cause to believe it is the Lord's will, from the freedom I feel thereto in my heart, so I question not it will be agreeable to your conception of it. I desire to do nothing but in perfect harmony and concert with you, and beg therefore you will be entirely free, open and communicative to me. I bless God I can discover no other at present, but every way a perfect agreement between your sentiments, principles, &c. of religion, and my own, and therefore desire you will (as I do to you) from time to time lay before me such rules, places, proposals, &c., as you conceive mostly conducive to the welfare of the church, the private benefit of her members, and, in the whole, to the glory of the Lord. My pulpit, I hope, shall be always at yours and your brother's service; and my house, so long as I have one, your welcome home. The same I'll make it to all our fellow-labourers, through the grace of God.

Please wink at the faults you meet with in this long incoherent ramble; and assure yourself,

I am ,

Your affectionate, but very unworthy

Brother, in the Lord,

WILLIAM GRIMSHAW

To Mr Wesley

Ewood, Nov. 27, 1747

Rev. and Very Dear Brother,

Yours bearing date the 20th of this month, I yesterday received. I answer again, and by the length of my letter it will appear, I answer not in haste; though I must assure you, I have as little leisure for writing as anything I do. The want of preachers here at present is very great. That the harvest in these parts is really large, and the labourers but very few, is very manifest: why it is so, perhaps the Lord of it only knows. Indeed, you, in some sort, assign a reason for it. But dear Sir, are there such plenty of helpers in Cornwall? Send us one or two of them without further entreaty.

You desire a particular account of the progress of the Lord's work here. Indeed, I have the pleasure of assuring you, that I think it never went better, from its first appearance amongst us, than it has done within these two months. I may say, at Leeds, Birstall, Keighley, Todmorden, Rossendale, Heptonstall, Pendleforest, and in my own parish, the societies are very hearty; souls are daily added to the church; and, I may say, multitudes on all sides, (many of whom have been enemies to us and our MASTER'S cause), are convinced of the truth, run eagerly to hear the gospel, and, (as I told you in my last) are continually crying out for more preachers. New and numerous classes have been lately joined. Were not matters thus with us, you may easily suppose I should not be so urgent with you for assistance. I think my public exhortations (alias what I call my monthly visitations) were never so visibly blessed, I praise God, for these four years past, as they have been within these last two months. Such a mighty presence of God has been in those visitations, and also in many of our weekly class meetings, as I have rarely seen before. This evening I am venturing , by the divine assistance, upon a public exhortation in a wild unchristian place called Midgeley, four miles west from Halifax, where of late I have a great part of my residence; and I hope my attempt will have the Lord on my side.

I hope brother Bennet fails not to inform you how well the work of grace flourishes in Derbyshire, Cheshire and the south of Lancashire, particularly around Bolton, Chowbent, &c. Mr. Lunelle (whose wife has lately experienced the pardoning love of God) wrote me a delightful account of the state of the church at Leeds. Thus much of my incoherent relation of our Lord's work in these parts.

Brother Bennet, Nelson and I, not only, I hope, love as brethren, but are cordially united in carrying on the Lord's work. I hope we believe and profess and preach one thing – JESUS and HIM crucified. If you know them, you know me. About three weeks since brothers Nelson and Colbeck were all night with me. Before then I accidentally met with Brother Bennet at Bank, near Heptonstall, where I went to meet all the Heptonstall parish classes. Last week I met brother Colbeck, and all the Keighley parish classes: and about six weeks ago I visited those of Leeds and Birstall: about a month since, those of Todmorden, Shore and some of Rossendale.

Dear Sir, I beg you will present my hearty respects to all your societies, classes, &c. in London or elsewhere . . . (then there follows a pastoral letter to these societies).

WILLIAM GRIMSHAW

Best known of Grimshaw's pastoral letters is one addressed 'To the Society in London,' and dated 9 January 1760 – a letter reproduced in John Wesley's Journal *for April 1762.*[1]

TO THE SOCIETY IN LONDON

Haworth, January 9, 1760

My Dear Brethren,

Grace, mercy and peace be to you from God our Father and from our Lord Jesus. It is well with four sorts of people that you have had, or now have to do with. It is well with those of you in Christ who are gone to God: it is well with those of you in Christ *who are not gone to God*: it is well with those who earnestly *long to be in Christ*, that they may go to God: it is well with those who *neither desire to be in Christ nor to go to God*. And it is only bad with such who, being out of Christ, are gone to the devil. These it is best to let alone and say no more about them.

But to be sure, it is well with these other four. It is well with those of you, who, being in Christ, are gone to God. You ministers and members of Christ have no more doubt or pain about them. They are now, and for ever, out of the reach of the world, flesh and devil: they are gone, 'where the wicked cease from troubling, and where the weary are at rest'. They are sweetly reposed in Abraham's bosom. They dwell in his presence, who

[1] John Wesley's *Journal*, vol. IV, p. 496. Curnock has inserted material concerning Grimshaw at this point in the *Journal*, supposing his death was in April 1762 rather than April 1763.

hath redeemed them, where 'there is fulness of joy and pleasures for evermore.' They are waiting the joyful morning of the resurrection, when their vile bodies shall be made like unto his glorious body, shall be re-united to their souls, shall receive the joyful sentence, and 'inherit the kingdom prepared for them from the foundation of the world'.

It is well also with those of you who are in Christ, though not gone to God. You live next door to them. Heaven is begun with you too. The kingdom of God is within you: you feel it. This is a kingdom of righteousness, and peace, and joy in the Holy Ghost. It is begun in grace and shall terminate in glory. Yea, it is Christ within you, the hope of glory. Christ, the rock, the foundation, laid in your hearts, hope in the middle, and glory at the top. Christ, hope, glory; Christ, hope, glory. You are washed in the blood of the Lamb, justified, sanctified, and shall shortly be glorified. Yea, your lives are already hid with Christ in God. You have your conversation already in heaven. Already you sit in heavenly places in Christ Jesus. What heavenly sentences are these! What can come nearer paradise! Bless the Lord, O ye happy souls, and let all that is within you bless his holy name. Sing unto the Lord, so long as you live, and praise your God while you have your being. And how long will that be? Through the endless ages of a glorious eternity.

O my dear brothers and sisters! this is my hope, and this is my purpose. But to whom and to what are we indebted for all this, and infinitely more than all tongues and hearts of men and angels can tell or conceive? Christ within us is Jesus to us. We were poor, lost, helpless sinners, aliens from the commonwealth of Israel, and children of wrath. But Jesus lived, and Jesus died, the just for the unjust, to bring us to the enjoyment of it.

And what does all this require at our hands? Why infinitely more than we can render him to all eternity. However, let us praise and glorify God in the best manner, and with the best member that we have. Let us do it constantly, cordially, cheerfully, so long as we live; and then, no doubt, we shall do it in heaven for ever.

Keep close, I beseech you to every means of grace. Strive to walk in all the ordinances and commandments of God blameless, 'giving all diligence to make your calling and election sure: add to your faith virtue; to virtue knowledge; to knowledge temperance; to temperance patience; to patience godliness; to godliness, brotherly kindness; to brotherly kindness charity. For if these things', says St. Peter, 'be in you and abound, they make you that you shall neither be barren nor unfruitful in the knowledge of our Lord Jesus Christ.' Thus you will give the best token of your thankfulness to him for what he hath done for your souls; and you shall, not long hence, in heaven sing his praise with your happy brethren, gone thither before you.

It is well with all those of you who do truly desire *to be in Christ,* that you may go to God. Surely he owns you. Your desires are from him: you shall enjoy his favour. By and by you shall have peace with him through our Lord Jesus Christ. Go forth by the footsteps of the flock; and feed ye by the shepherd's tents. Be constant in every means of grace. He will be found of them that diligently seek him. 'Blessed are they that mourn for they shall be comforted.' Though your sins be never so many, never so monstrous, all shall be forgiven. He will have mercy upon you and will abundantly pardon. For where sin hath abounded, grace doth much more abound. He who hath begun this good work in you, will accomplish it to your eternal good, and his eternal glory. Therefore doubt not, fear not; a broken and contrite heart God will not despise. The deeper is your sorrow, the nearer is your joy. Your extremity is God's opportunity. It is usually darkest before day-break. You shall shortly find pardon, peace and plenteous redemption, and at last rejoice in the common and glorious salvation of his saints.

And, lastly: it is well for you who *neither truly desire to be in Christ* nor to go to God. For it is well for you that you are out of hell; it is well your day of grace is not utterly past. Behold now is your accepted time! Behold, now is your day of salvation! O that you may employ the remainder of it in working out your salvation with fear and trembling. Now is faith to be had, saving faith. Now you may be washed from all sins in the Redeemer's blood, justified, sanctified, and prepared for heaven. Take, I beseech you, the time while the time is. You have now the means of grace to use; the ordinances of God to enjoy; his word to read and hear; his ministers to instruct you, and his members to converse with. You know not what a day may bring forth. You may die suddenly. As death leaves you, judgment will find you. If you should die as you are, *out of Christ*, void of true faith, unregenerate, unsanctified, snares, fire and brimstone, storm and tempest, God will rain upon you, (Psalm XI. 6) as your eternal, intolerable portion to drink.

Suffer me, therefore, thus far, one and all of you. God's glory and your everlasting welfare is all I aim at. What I look for in return from you, is, I confess, much more than I deserve – your prayers. Pray for me, and I will pray for you, who am, your affectionate brother,

WILLIAM GRIMSHAW

APPENDIX 2

WILLIAM GRIMSHAW'S COVENANT WITH GOD

ETERNAL AND UNCHANGEABLE JEHOVAH! Thou great Creator of heaven and earth, and adorable Lord of angels and men! I desire with deepest humiliation and abasement of soul, to fall down at this time in thine awful presence, and earnestly pray that thou wilt penetrate my heart with a suitable sense of thine unutterable and inconceivable glories! Trembling may justly take hold upon me, when I, a sinful worm, presume to lift up my head to thee, presume to appear in thy majestic presence on such an occasion as this! What is my nature or descent, my character or desert, that I should mention or desire to be one party in a covenant, where thou, the King of kings, art the other? I blush even to mention it before thee. But, O Lord, great as is thy majesty, so also is thy mercy. If thou hold converse with any of thy creatures, thy superlatively exalted nature must stoop infinitely low.

I know that through Jesus the Son of thy love, thou condescendest to visit sinful mortals, and to allow their approach to thee, and their covenant communion with thee; nay, I know the scheme and plan are entirely thine *own,* and that *thou* hast graciously sent to propose it unto *us*; as none, untaught by thee, could have been able to form it, or inclined to embrace it, even when actually proposed.

To THEE, therefore, do I now come, invited by thy Son, and trusting in his righteousness and grace; laying myself at thy feet with shame and confusion of face, and smiting upon my breast saying, with the humble publican, God, be merciful to me a sinner! I acknowledge, O Lord, that I have been a great transgressor. My sins have reached unto heaven, and mine iniquities have been lifted up unto the skies. My base corruptions and lusts have, numberless ways, wrought to bring forth fruit unto death; and if thou wert extreme to mark what I have done amiss, I could never abide it. But thou hast graciously called me to return to thee, though I am a prodigal son, and a backsliding child.

Behold, therefore, I solemnly come before thee. O my Lord, I come convinced of my sin and folly. Thou knowest, O Lord, I solemnly covenanted with thee, in the year 1738; and before that wonderful manifestation of thyself unto me, at church, and in the clerk's house, between the hours of ten and two o'clock on Sunday, September 2, 1744, I had again solemnly devoted myself to thee on August 8, 1744. And now once more and for ever, I most solemnly give up, devote and resign all I am, spirit, soul and body, to thee, and to thy pleasure and command, in Christ Jesus, my Saviour, this 4th of December, 1752; sensible, O Lord, of my vileness and unworthiness, but yet that I am thy pardoned, justified, and regenerated child, in the spirit and blood of my dear and precious Saviour, Jesus Christ, by clear experience.

Glory be to thee, O my Triune God! Permit me to repeat and renew my covenant with thee. I resolve and desire to be wholly and for ever thine, in thy spirit. Blessed God! I most solemnly surrender myself unto thee. Hear, O heaven, and give ear, O earth! I avouch this day, the Lord to be my God, Father, Saviour, Portion, for ever! I am one of his covenant children for ever! Record, O eternal Lord, in thy book of remembrance, that henceforth I am thine for ever! From this day I solemnly renounce all former lords, world, flesh, and devil, in thy name. No more, directly or indirectly, will I obey them. I renounced them many years ago, and I renounce them for ever. This day I give myself up to thee, a living sacrifice, holy and acceptable unto thee, and which I know is my reasonable service. To thee I consecrate all my worldly possessions.

In thy service I desire and purpose to spend all my time,

desiring thee to teach me to spend every moment of it to thy glory, and the setting forth of thy praise, in every station and relation of life I am now, or may hereafter be in; and earnestly pray, that whatever influence thou mayest in any wise give me over others, thou wouldest give me strength and courage to exert it to the utmost to thy glory, resolving not only myself to do it, but that all others, as far as I can rationally and properly influence them, shall serve the Lord.

In that course would I, O Lord, steadfastly persevere to my last breath, steadfastly praying that every day of my life may supply the defects, and correct the irregularities of the former, and that by divine grace I may be enabled, not only in that happy way to hold on, but to grow more daily active in it. Nor do I only consecrate all I have to thy service, but I also most humbly resign and submit to thy holy and sovereign will all that I have. I leave, O Lord, to thy management and direction, all that I possess, and all I wish, and set every enjoyment and interest before thee to be disposed of as thou pleasest. Continue or remove what thou hast given me; bestow or refuse what I imagine I want, as thou seest good; and though I dare not say I will never repine, yet I hope I may say, I will labour not only to submit, but to acquiesce; not only to bear thy heaviest afflictions on me, but to consent to them, and praise thee for them, contentedly resolving, in all thy appointments, my will into *thine;* esteeming myself as nothing, and thee, O God, as the great Eternal All, whose word should determine, and whose power should order, all things in the world.

Use me, O Lord, I beseech thee, as the instrument of thy glory; and honour me so far as, either by doing or suffering thy appointments, I may bring praise to thy name, and benefit to the world in which I live. And may it please thee, from this day forward, to number me amongst thy peculiar people, that I may no more be a stranger or foreigner, but a fellow-citizen with the saints, and of the household of God. Receive, O heavenly Father, being already washed in thy blood, and clothed with thy righteousness, me thy child, and sanctify me throughout by the power of thy Holy

Spirit. Destroy, I beseech thee, more the power of sin in my heart; transform me more into thine image, and fashion me into the resemblance of Jesus, whom I would henceforth ever acknowledge as my Teacher and Sacrifice; my Intercessor and my Lord. Communicate unto me, I beseech thee, all needful influences of thy purifying, cheering and comforting Spirit; and lift up that light of thy countenance upon me, which will put the sublimest joy and gladness into my heart.

Dispose of my affairs, O God, in a manner which may be wholly subservient to thy glory, and my own true happiness; and when I have done, borne and endured thy will upon earth, call me hence at what time, and in what manner thou pleasest; only grant that in my dying moments, and the near approach of eternity, I may remember these my engagements to thee, and may employ my latest breath in thy service: and do thou, when thou seest me in the agonies of death, remember this covenant too, though I should be incapable of recollecting it.

Look down upon me, O Lord, thy languishing dying child; place thine everlasting arms underneath my head; put strength and confidence into my departing spirit, and receive it to the embraces of thine everlasting love! Welcome it to the abodes of those who sleep in Jesus, who are with him above, to wait with them that glorious day, when the last of thy promises to thy people shall be fulfilled in their triumphant resurrection, and that abundant entrance which shall be administered unto them, into that everlasting kingdom of which thou hast assured them by thy covenant; in the hope of which I now lay hold of it, desiring to live and die with my hand upon that hope.

And when I am thus numbered with the dead, and all the interests of mortality are over with me for ever, if this solemn memorial should fall into the hands of any surviving friends or relatives, may it be the means of making serious impressions upon their minds, and may they read it not only as my language but as *their* own, and learn to fear the Lord my God, and with me, to put their trust under the shadow of his wings, for time and for eternity: and may they also learn to adore with me, that grace which inclines our hearts to enter into the covenant, and condescends to admit us into it when so inclined; ascribing with me, and with all the nations of the redeemed, to the Father, Son and Holy Ghost, that glory and honour and praise, which is so justly due to each divine person, for the part he bears in this illustrious work. Amen.

I solemnly subscribe this dedication of myself to the for ever blessed Triune God, in the presence of angels, and all the invisible spectators, this fourth day of December, 1752.

WILLIAM GRIMSHAW
Minister of Haworth.

I renewed this solemn dedication in a most awful [awesome] manner, 5th of June, 1760. O that I may carefully remember and keep it!

I purpose to renew this dedication with a quarterly fast, the first Friday in January, April, July and October, during life.

Appendix 3

William Grimshaw's Creed[1]

The Reverend Mr *Grimshaw* to the Reverend Mr. *Romaine,*

Haworth, December 8, 1762

Reverend and dear Sir,

Yesterday I received your kind letter, and must assure you, I reap as much benefit and comfort, and, I dare say, much more from your letters, than you can do from mine ...

As to my CREED, so long promised, so long looked for, and so often called for, such as it is, I here send you at last.

I.   I BELIEVE that GOD made man, like all other animals created out of the earth, perfect; endued him with a reasonable and immortal soul, and united his soul to HIS SPIRIT. Thus created and thus related to HIMSELF, He laid man under a covenant of works. This covenant he was competent of keeping, not by virtue of his created abilities, as the old, particularly the Puritan divines feign, (for I think there is no clear proof from the Scripture for it,) but by the power of the HOLY SPIRIT to WHOM he was united. And,

II.   I BELIEVE so long as his soul kept an eye to the dictates of the SPIRIT, excited HIS power, and in so doing, fulfilled his

[1]Retaining Grimshaw's original capitals, italics and punctuation.

condition of the said covenant, and kept his natural appetites within bounds; so long he continued innocent and happy within Paradise. – But,

III.   I BELIEVE that the moment he was prevailed upon by the serpent, at second hand, (viz. by means of his wife) to eat the forbidden fruit, he died, (that is, he was divested of his relation to GOD;) he that instant lost his life, light, power, innocence and happiness. He became a mere *Ichabod,* a dead, dark, helpless, guilty, miserable mortal.

IV.   I BELIEVE the way the old serpent went to effect man's fall, was the very same he uses at this day. First he assailed the animal part, and then the rational part, if I may so speak of the man; and by other way would not answer. The soul was too near the SPIRIT to operate, or attack first. Reasoning with him first will not do. Alluring the senses must be the first step. The eye was first allured with the beauty, and then the taste with the sweetness of the apple. By this means Satan crept nearer to the soul, diverted the eye of his mind from GOD, and got the desired opportunity to reason deceitfully with him, in the manner recorded in *Genesis,* chap. 3, and gained his point.

V.   I BELIEVE that *Adam,* by this means reduced into the above said miserable condition, begot a son in his fallen image, and thence all his posterity in the same, a dead, dark, helpless, guilty and miserable brood.

VI.   I BELIEVE there was in *Adam,* and is in every man, an innate principle which I call DESIRE of HAPPINESS. It may seem that Satan, in reasoning with him, chiefly wrought upon this principle to bring about his downfall; and upon this principle, in every child of man, he chiefly acts to bend them to a sensual gratification of all fleshly and earthly enjoyments. This is what I think is chiefly meant by *natural depravity.* And,

VII.   I BELIEVE that while man is seeking happiness in a thousand preposterous ways, his mind is filled by the devil with an utter enmity against GOD, his will and his law; and also with self-sufficiency and pride, and every evil and diabolical temper. And by all these means, he is inevitably and condignly [deservedly] exposed to the wrath of GOD and eternal death and damnation.

VIII.   I BELIEVE also, that notwithstanding the fall and all its baleful effects, and though man has utterly lost all power thereby to obey, or perform the condition of the old covenant, yet the LORD did not lose his right and power to command the same obedience: Nor could his justice and holiness, as such, in the least degree dispense with it. HE could in no wise, consistently with these attributes, commute or relax the condition on man's part. – And yet,

IX.   I BELIEVE, nay I experience, and have done ever since I was awakened, to my great grief, and self-abhorrence, that though man has lost all power to obey, yet he still loves the scent of the old cask – *quo semel est imbuta recens, &c.*[1] He is still [a] silly caitiff, [despicable fellow] proud elf, filthy devil, for DO and LIVE. – And thus he became, and naturally ever will be, averse to all the compassionate, kind intentions and provisions of Divine wisdom, grace and mercy for his redemption and salvation.

X.   I BELIEVE further, that every actual sin, suppose ever so small a sinful thought, will expose the soul, yea and the body too, from the last judgement forward, to the eternal, intolerable wrath of GOD: And that the transgressor's whole life, though inwardly and outwardly, and every way as pure and holy as that of an archangel, will not, cannot, prevent it.

XI.   I BELIEVE further still that GOD would be just were HE to send any infant immediately from the womb to hell: Seeing the NATURE is polluted, and the seeds of evil are in them: not only *born*, but *conceived* in sin.

[1]Perhaps a well-known quotation meaning approximately, 'With what [a cask] is once saturated [that smell will remain] fresh [linger on]'.

XII.   I BELIEVE that the blessed TRINITY, foreseeing all this rebellious and wretched fall of man, before his creation, yea, before the foundation of the world, did, out of HIS infinite wisdom, goodness compassion and power, and yet consistently with HIS inexorable and inflexible justice, devise an effectual way of rescuing him from wrath and hell, and restoring him to favour and glory; I call *this* the NEW COVENANT: – This, REDEMPTION. In this scheme harmonises every attribute of the Deity; yea, justice itself, that knows not to remit the least mite, is become so placable and propitious, as to forgive the confessing penitent all his sins, and to cleanse him from all unrighteousness.

XIII.   I BELIEVE, that GOD the FATHER required that, in the new covenant, the old covenant should be fulfilled, the breach repaired – His violated law made honourable – the curse thereof removed, HIS justice satisfied – HIS wrath appeased and HIS holiness revered. And this too (though no one in heaven or earth, save HIS only begotten, GOD-coequal, SON, was competent of) by the very nature strange to tell! that had transgressed. – And this, glory be to GOD, was regular, lawful, right and just.

XIV.   I BELIEVE therefore that GOD, the SON, *engaged* to assume our nature, and place HIMSELF in our law-place; and became GOD-Man, or GOD *manifest in the flesh*. – And this I plainly see was absolutely needful: Because there was that to be done for us, in order to redeem and save us; which as GOD, HE could; but as man, HE could not: And which as man, HE could; but as GOD, HE could not, do. – For

XV.   I BELIEVE, as GOD only HE could DO; as man only, he could SUFFER. – As GOD-Man, HE could and did *fulfil the law so* as to *deserve eternal* glory: As Man-GOD, (if I may so speak) HE could and did so suffer, as that HIS sufferings full atoned and satisfied divine justice for sin, and effectually delivered us from eternal wrath and misery. – But, if, as man, we must say, HE did both do and suffer; be it so; yet as being in union with GOD, the divinity so deified and divinely impregnated all HIS obedience, both active and passive, as rendered it completely competent of the important ends abovesaid. This is that *righteousness of GOD;* so called, because GOD the FATHER must *require* it, and GOD the SON *only* could *perform* it, for our justification, redemption and salvation.

XVI.   I BELIEVE, that *this* very righteousness is sufficient to redeem all mankind; but it only is, and will be, *imputed* to every penitent, believing so, and that to all intents and purposes, as if *He*, as indeed He should have done, *had Himself performed it.* – Glory be to GOD for *free Grace* – No reason can be assigned for this; only, *HE would have mercy; BECAUSE HE would have mercy.*

XVII.   I BELIEVE, in this righteousness, every member of CHRIST stands, and will stand complete, irreproachable and acceptable in GOD'S sight, both at death and judgement – "JESU, THY Blood and Righteousness, &c."

XVIII. I BELIEVE also, that JESUS came to restore to us *Adam's* losing, the HOLY SPIRIT. – Without this we are none of HIS – Without GOD, CHRIST, hope in the world – Dead and void of all interest in HIS merits – To receive and enjoy this, is that NEW BIRTH; – So expedient , that without it we cannot enter into the kingdom of GOD – A state of grace here, and a state of glory above. – By it, we are sons of GOD and heirs of that inheritance, which CHRIST, by his righteousness, hath purchased for us.

XIX.   I BELIEVE, through this blessed SPIRIT, therefore, the soul is not only enlivened but enlightened to see and feel her guilty, helpless, and miserable estate, through original, carnal, actual and self-godly sinning. – And

XX.   I BELIEVE, that though it is faith to believe the gospel-report; for *faith comes by hearing; Yet* to be fully convinced in conscience, that we are such guilty, helpless wretched sinners, and obnoxious to the Divine wrath, is eminently that faith which is said to be THE GIFT OF GOD. By this faith we are cordially enabled to hear, embrace, and lay hold of, the righteousness of CHRIST, to justification and are conscious thereof.

XXI. I BELIEVE that the HOLY SPIRIT is not only a vital, but an instructive and active principle in us also. HE witnesseth to our hearts that we are GOD'S children, and reports to our conscience that we are at peace with GOD. For though we may have peace with GOD, yet conscience, I am persuaded, till informed by the SPIRIT, is a stranger to it.

XXII. I BELIEVE it is by the SPIRIT we are enabled, not to *eradicate*, as some affirm (for that is absurd) but to *subjugate*, the old man: To *suppress*, not *extirpate*, the exorbitancies of our fleshly appetites: To resist and overcome the world and the devil; to grow in grace, *gradually,* not *repentively, [i.e. suddenly*, or *all at once*] unto the perfect and eternal day. – This is all I know, or acknowledge to be Christian Perfection, or Sanctification.

XXIII. I BELIEVE, that all true believers, will be daily tempted by the flesh, as well as the world and the devil, even to their lives end; and that they shall feel an inclination, more or less, to comply, yea, and do comply therewith. So that THE BEST BELIEVER, if he knows what he says and says the truth, IS BUT A SINNER AT BEST. And

XXIV. I BELIEVE that their minds are incessantly subject to a thousand impertinent, unprofitable thoughts, even amidst their readings, meditations and prayers; – that all their religious exercises are deficient; – that all their graces, how eminent soever, are imperfect; that GOD sees iniquity in all their holy things; and, though it be granted that they love GOD with all their hearts, yet they must continually pray with the Psalmist, *enter not into judgement with thy servant, &c.* But with all

XXV. I BELIEVE that JESUS is a full, as well as a free SAVIOUR: *The same yesterday, to day, and for ever.* HE alone is not only the believer's wisdom and righteousness, but his sanctification and redemption: And in HIM is the fountain ever open for sin and uncleanness unto the last breath of his life. Here is my daily, necessary privilege, my relief and my comfort.

XXVI. I BELIEVE, lastly, that GOD is faithful and unchangeable: That all HIS promises are YEA and AMEN: that HE will never, never, as the apostle's words are, leave me, will never, never, never, forsake me. But that I, and, all that believe, love and fear HIM, shall *receive the end of our faith, the salvation of our souls.*

Here is the sum and substance of my CREED. – It is at least what I presume to call, my FORM of sound Words – In it, I can truly say, I have no respect to men or books, ancient or modern; but to the holy scriptures, reason and experience. – According to the CREED, hitherto I have, and I hope, hereafter, so far as I apprehend, to proceed in all my preaching; *debasing man, and exalting my dear LORD* in all HIS offices. If we materially differ; be it so – let brotherly love continue. – I am fixed, being resolved not to have my religion, like some dear men among us of late, to seek, after more than twenty years experience and profession. – All that I know of you hitherto, is by your conversation and books which I cordially love and approve.

I think, we are both agreed to pull down man, and when we have the proud chit down, to keep him down. For this is the main. – And never let him recover so much as his knees, till with a broken heart and a contrite spirit, the dear REDEEMER raise him. He ought to be convinced that a good life will no more conduce, than a wicked life, to his justification. – That all that is not *of* faith, and consequently *before* faith, is sin. Nor will I allow that it is anymore by good works after grace received, than before, that a believer is saved, – For however our LORD may graciously consider them at the last day – *Eternal life* is certainly *the gift of GOD through our LORD JESUS CHRIST* – CHRIST alone has purchased for us what grace in heart and life makes us meet for –

what have We to boast of? – or *what have We that We have not received?* Surely, *By grace We are saved.* When I die, I shall then have my greatest grief and my greatest joy – My greatest grief that I have done so little for JESUS; and my greatest joy that JESUS has done so much for me. My last words shall be; "here goes – *An unprofitable Servant!*"

Pray for me, and I'll pray for you
being your &c: W. G.

SELECT BIBLIOGRAPHY

PRIMARY SOURCES

William Grimshaw's Unpublished Writings[1]

'The Admonition of a Sinner'.

'The Believer's Golden Chain'.

'Experiences gather'd by Conversation with my own & the Souls of others'.

'The Nature, State and Conduct of a Christian'.

Letters – about 30 mostly to Mrs Gallatin.

William Grimshaw's Published Writings

'A Diary of my Life begun Sepr. 14th, 1755: on which Day I enter'd into ye. 48th of my age.' Published in *The Proceedings of the Wesley Historical Society, XXIV*, 1933.

An Answer to a Sermon Lately Published against the Methodists by the Rev. George White, A.M. Published in William Myles, *The Life and Writings of the late Reverend William Grimshaw, A.B.* London: 1813, pp. 75–160.

[1]All Grimshaw's writings, and manuscript material on next page, are held in the John Rylands University Library of Manchester.

Published letters, in Myles, *Grimshaw;* Laycock, *Methodist Heroes*; Hardy, *Incumbent of Haworth* and Baker, *Grimshaw 1708–63*.

Manuscript Material

John Bennet's 'Diary'.

'Church History, Collected from the Memoirs and Journals of the Revd. Mr Ingham and the labourers in connection with him. 1779'. By William Batty (transcribed by M. Rattenbury).

Everett, James. Manuscript Biography, 'The Curate of Haworth', c.1825.

Early Biographical Material on William Grimshaw

Jones, Mrs Joseph. *Account of the Rev. Mr. Grimshaw.* Copied by Charles Wesley, 1763, Methodist Archives, London, printed Laycock, *Heroes.*

Middleton, Erasmus. *Biographia Evangelica.* Vol. IV. London: 1786. (Largely following Venn but including original additions).

Myles, William. *Life and Writings of the Late Reverend William Grimshaw, A.B.* First published 1808. London: 1813.

Newton, John. *Memoirs of the Life of the Late Rev. William Grimshaw, A.B. in Six Letters to the Rev. Mr Henry Foster.* First printed 1799. Edinburgh: Hamilton, 1814.

Venn, Henry. *Christ the Joy of the Christian's Life and Death his Gain.* Leeds: 1763.

Williams, Joseph. Accounts of visit to Grimshaw in Haworth in 1746, first copy from *Williams' Diary,* ed. B. Hanbury, 1815, pp. 225–9. (There are at least four versions of this episode extant, but fullest account found in a letter from an anonymous writer in July 1746 in which he copies out a letter written by Williams on 5 March 1746. Reprinted by Laycock in *Heroes*).

SECONDARY SOURCES

Biographies and Biographical Sketches of William Grimshaw

Baker, Frank. *William Grimshaw 1708-63*. London: Epworth Press, 1963.

Cragg, George C. *Grimshaw of Haworth. A Study in Eighteenth Century Evangelicalism*. London: Canterbury Press, 1947.

Hardy, R. Spence. *William Grimshaw, Incumbent of Haworth*. London: 1861.

Laycock, J. W. *Methodist Heroes in the Great Haworth Round*. Keighley: Wadsworth and Co., 1909.

Loane, Sir Marcus L. *Cambridge and the Evangelical Succession*. London: Lutterworth Press, 1952, pp. 15–64.

Ryle, J. C. *Christian Leaders of the 18th Century*. Pages 106–148. Edinburgh: Banner of Truth Trust, 1978.

Wood, Dr A. Skevington. *William Grimshaw*. Annual Lecture, Evangelical Library, 1963.

Background Material

Abbey, C. J. and Overton, J. H. *The English Church in the Eighteenth Century*. Vols. I & II. London: Longmans, Green & Co., 1878.

Babbage, B. H. *Report to the General Board of Health on a Preliminary Inquiry into the Sewage, Drainage and Supply of water and the Sanitary Condition of the Inhabitants of the Hamlet of Haworth in the West Riding of the County of York*. London: 1850.

Balleine, G. R. *A History of the Evangelical Party*. London: Longmans, 1909.

Barker, Juliet. *The Brontës*. London: Weidenfeld and Nicolson, 1994.

Baumber, M. L. *A Pennine Community on the Eve of the Industrial Revolution*. Keighley: 1977. Unpublished manuscript, 'From Revival to Regency, A History of Keighley and Haworth, 1740–1820'.

Bayne-Powell, Rosamond. *Travellers in Eighteenth Century England*. London: John Murray, 1951.

Bready, J. Wesley. *England: Before and After Wesley*. London: Hodder and Stoughton, 1938.

Brown-Lawson, A. *John Wesley and the Anglican Evangelicals of the Eighteenth Century*. Edinburgh: Pentland Press, 1994.

Chew, R. *James Everett*. London: Hodder and Stoughton, 1875.

Cragg, G. R. *The Church and the Age of Reason, 1648–1789*. London: Hodder and Stoughton, 1962.

Crowther, Jonathan. *The Methodist Manual*. Halifax: 1810, largely following Venn, but with original material.

Curnock, Nehemiah. *Methodist Recorder,* 1899: Lengthy illustrated articles entitled 'The Yorkshire Storm-Centre of the Evangelical Revival, by H.K. & H.D.W'.

Dallimore, Arnold A. *George Whitefield: The life and times of the great evangelist of the 18th century revival*. Vols. 1 & 2. London & Edinburgh: Banner of Truth Trust, 1970 & 1980.

Defoe, Daniel. *A Tour through the Whole Island of Great Britain*. Reprinted, Exeter: Webb and Bower: 1989.

Elliott-Binns, L. E. *The Early Evangelicals: A Religious and Social Study*. London: Lutterworth Press, 1955.

Everett, James. *Methodism in Sheffield*. Sheffield: 1823.

Fawcett, John. *Life of John Fawcett, D.D.* Halifax: 1822.

Gaskell, Elizabeth. *Life of Charlotte Brontë.* Reprinted, London: Dent, Everyman's Library, 1966.

Gillies, John. *Historical Collections of Accounts of Revival.* Edinburgh: Banner of Truth Trust, 1981.

Gillies, John. *Memoirs of the Life of the Reverend George Whitefield.* London: 1772.

Harrison, G. E. *Haworth Parsonage, A Study of Wesley and the Brontës.* London: Epworth Press, 1937.

Heitzenrater, R.P. *Diary of an Oxford Methodist.* Durham, US: Duke University Press. 1985.

Hutton, James. *History of the Moravian Church.* London: Moravian Publications Office, 1909.

Jackson, Thomas. ed. *Lives of Early Methodist Preachers.* Vols. I–VI. London: Epworth Press, 1873.

Jackson, Thomas. *The Life of the Rev. Charles Wesley M.A..* Vols. I & II. London: Mason, 1841.

Jones, Tudur R. *Congregationalism in England, 1662–1962.* London: Independent Press, 1962.

Knight, Helen C. *Lady Huntingdon and her Friends.* Grand Rapids, Michigan: Baker Book House, 1979.

Knox, Ronald. *Enthusiasm.* Oxford: Clarendon Press, 1950.

Myles, William. *The Chronological History of the People Called Methodists.* London: 1803.

Nelson, John. *The Journal of Mr John Nelson, The Lives of Early Methodist Preachers.* Vol. I. London: 1875.

New, A.H. *The Coronet and the Cross. Memorials of Selina, Countess of Huntingdon.* London: Partridge & Co. 1857.

Outler, Albert C. ed. *John Wesley.* New York: Oxford University Press, 1980.

Pawson, John. *Arminian Magazine.* London: 1803, largely following Venn, but with original material.

Pickles, H. M. *Benjamin Ingham, Preacher amongst the Dales, Forests and Fells.* Published by author: 117, Dane Road, Coventry, 1995.

Seymour, A. C. H. *The Life and Times of Selina, Countess of Huntingdon.* Vols. I & II. London: W.E. Painter, 1840.

Southey, Robert. *Life of John Wesley.* Vols. 1 & 2. London: Longmans, 1846.

Stevens, Abel. *History of Methodism.* London: 1861.

Turner, J. Horsfall. *Haworth – Past and Present.* Brighouse: 1879.

Tuttle, R. G. *John Wesley – His Life and Theology.* Grand Rapids, Michigan: Zondervan, 1978.

Tyerman, Luke. *The Life and Times of John Wesley.* Vols. 1–3. London: Hodder and Stoughton, 1880.

Tyerman, Luke. *The Life of George Whitefield.* Vols. I & II. London: Hodder and Stoughton, 1876.

Tyerman, Luke. *The Oxford Methodists.* London: Hodder and Stoughton, 1873.

Venn, Henry. *Letters of Henry Venn.* Edinburgh: Banner of Truth Trust, 1993.

Viney, Richard. 'Diary'. 1744. *Wesley Historical Society,* Vols. XIII–XV.

Watts, Michael. *The Dissenters.* Oxford: Oxford University Press, 1978.

Wesley, Charles. *The Journal of.* London: Mason, 1849, reprinted Grand Rapids, Michigan: Baker Book House, 1980.

Wesley, John. *The Journal of.* Standard edition, ed. Nehemiah Curnock, Vols. I–VIII. London: Kelly, 1909–16.

Wesley, John. *Works.* Letters. ed. J. Telford, Vols. XII & XIII. London: Epworth Press, 1931.

Wesley, John. *Works.* Sermons. Vols. I & II. London: 1872.

Whitefield, George. *Works.* Letters. Vols. II & III. London: 1771.

Whiteley, J. H. *Wesley's England.* London: Epworth Press, 1945.

INDEX

Aberford 39, 85, 132–3, 149, 194, 255, 288
Act of Uniformity 12, 47
Act of Toleration 126, 224
Adams, Thomas 86n
Addingham 81, 168
'Admonition of a Sinner, The' (Grimshaw's unpublished MS) 94, 107, 204–9, 295–6
Allen, James 267, 269
Alnwick 257
Alpraham 166
Ambrose 27
Answer to White, against Methodists 5, 87, 97, 134–6, 281
Antinomianism 239
Arminian Magazine 256
Arminianism 241–3
Ashworth, J. 70n
Astbury 166

Babbage, B. H. 54–5
Bacup 87, 162, 169
Baildon 81, 168
Baker, Dr Frank 2–3, 6, 15, 24, 72, 90, 93, 103–4, 113, 147, 190, 196, 246, 272, 282

Balleine, G. R., *History of Evangelical Party* 14n
Baptists 231–3
Baptist Church, Haworth 233–4
Baring-Gould, S., *Evangelical Revival* 232n
Barker, J., *The Brontës* 51n, 141–2
Barnard Castle 257
Barrowford 129–30, 257
Batty, William 34–5, 38–9, 63, 111, 123–4, 127–8 133, 229, 267, 269–70
Baumber, Michael 51, 53n
Baxter, Richard 205, 213, 285
Bayne-Powell, Rosamond, *Travellers in 18th Century* 7
Beanland, Benjamin 279
Bell, George 266–7
'Believer's Golden Chain, The' (Grimshaw's unpublished MS) 90, 203, 209–11, 230, 285
Berkhof, L. *Systematic Theology* 239n
Bennet, John 95, 119n, 121, 131n, 157, 161, 164–5, 171, 216

Berridge, John 264
Beverley, East Yorkshire 263
Bingley 38, 81, 92, 263
Birstall 41–3, 64, 81, 119, 121, 166, 217
Black Bartholomew's Day 12, 33
Blackburn 3
Blackburn Grammar School 4, 6, 52
Blackwell, Ebenezer 273
Blake, Malachi 9, 100
Boggart House, Leeds 126n
Bolton 171, 219, 249
Borthwick Institute for Historical Research, York 48, 51
Boston, USA 32
Bradford 2, 33, 48, 98, 102, 167–8, 174, 235, 267
  Vicar of, see Kennet
Brighouse 38
Brindle 3–4, 10–11, 13, 52
British and Foreign Review 242n
Bristol, Kingswood School 132, 156–8
Brontë family 56, 140
Brontë Museum, 153, 274
Brooks, Thomas *Precious Remedies* 14, 24–5
Bull, Josiah, *Life of Newton* 251
Bunyan, John, *Grace Abounding* 59
Burdsall, Dicky 92–3

Caius College, Cambridge 7
Cambridge 6–7
  Caius 7
  Christ's College 6–7, 9, 52
  Peterhouse 7
  Holy Trinity Church 254
  Magdalene 7

Westminster College 123n
Calder Valley 21
Canon Law 150
Cambuslang 69
Carlisle, Bishop of 13
Carmichael, Rev. 161
Cartwright, Thomas 8
Cennick, John 82
Charles II 12
Cheshire and Cheshire Round 119n (see also John Bennet)
Chester 136, 161, 166, 171, 189
Chester, Bishop of (S. Peploe) 11
Christian History 113
Christian's Magazine 26, 28, 61, 86, 286–7
Christian Miscellany 64n
Chorley 3
Chrysostom 27
Clapham Sect 141, 254
Clegg 112
Cleckheaton 38
Clifford, William 47
Cockcroft, Mary and Elizabeth 31 (see Grimshaw's family).
Cockermouth 166
Colbeck, Thomas 82, 110, 113, 129–30, 217, 260–1, 291–2
Coley 33, 46
Colne 63, 111–13, 123, 126, 128, 139, 145, 155
Confirmation 51
Conventicles 113
Conventicle Act 224
Conyers, Dr Richard 172, 271
Cook, Paul E. G., *Westminster Conference Papers*, 1995 209n

Cornwall 165

Covenants with God 73-4, 177-80, 186-7

Crabtree, William 174, 232

Cragg, G.C, *Grimshaw of Haworth* 290

Creed, Grimshaw's 97, 238, 255, (see also Appendix 3)

Crimsworth-Dean 162, 301

Crookshank, C. H., *Days of Revival in Ireland* 259

Crosse, Rev. John 2

Crossley, James 231n

Cross Stone 31, 162

Cumbria 256, 267, 310

Cullingworth 167

Curate, perpetual 53

Curnock, Nehemiah 294n

Darney, William 68-73, 78, 83, 87, 89, 111, 116-7, 119, 128, 155, 159, 164, 166, 172, 201, 224, 241, 256-8

Dean Head 112

Dean, John 139, 190

Dedham 32

Deism 12-13, 24

Defoe, Daniel 15-16, 54

Denholme (Denham) 167, 182

Dewsbury 38

Dissenters 66, 115, 126, 218, 225ff., 267

Doddridge, Dr Philip 76n, 178-80

Douai, France 126

Dracup, Nathaniel 88-9

Dublin 116n, 189, 259

Duke Chapel 171

Dunster, Samuel 10-11, 14

Earwaker, *Local Gleanings* 6

Edwards, John 219

Eldwick 92

Emmott Hall 53, 64, 115

Everett, James 2, 5n, 16, 20, 48, 60, 90n, 96, 142-6, 173, 214, 234, 241, 246, 280

Methodism in Sheffield 2n, 171

Everton, Bedford 264

Ewood Court, Ewood Hall 152, 159, 167, 182, 201, 247, 292-3

'Experiences' (Grimshaw's unpublished MS) 21, 29, 60, 72-3, 79, 102, 184-6, 214, 230, 236, 238, 243, 281, 283, 286

Fawcett, Dr John 235-6, 278

Fetter Lane 36, 39

Firth, Ann, (see Grimshaw's mother)

Fletcher, John of Madeley 98, 214

Foster, Jonas 46

Fulwood, see Sheffield

Gallatin, Col. Bartholomew 152, 190, 199, 296-8;

Gallatin, Lady 24, 84, 152-3, 158, 169, 171, 188, 190, 199, 216-9, 222-4, 228, 238-40, 254, 271-2, 274, 282, 286

State Lottery 221-2

Gardiner, Col. J. 76n

Gaskell, Mrs, *Life of Charlotte Brontë* 140-1

Gateshead 115

Gentleman's Magazine 147n

George I 3

Georgia 35

Gilbert, John, Archbishop of York
    197–8
Gilbert, Thomas 226
Gillies, Dr John 37–8, 43, 57, 61,
    79–81, 111, 133, 133n,
    188, 231, 256
'Gin age' 21
Glanville, William 131
Glas, John 268–9
    Testimony of King of Martyrs
    269
Glasgow 37, 69
Glasite churches 268–9
Glossop 172
Gomersal 38, 43
Goodwin, Thomas 32
Grant, Charles 254
Green, J. R., *History of English
    People* 12
Greenwood, Esther 108
Greenwood, Paul 29–30, 58,
    81, 83–4, 89, 116n, 155,
    164–5, 224–5, 241, 258–
    60

Grimshaw:
    Ann (*mother*) ?–1767, 4–5, 6
    Henry (*father*) 1674–1754, 4–
        5, 6
    Sarah (*first wife*) 1710–1739,
        20–3, 288
    Sarah's parents – Lockwood,
        John & Mary 21–2, 131–2
    Elizabeth (*second wife*) ?–1746
        31, 45, 71, 105, 114–5,
        222, 288
    John (*son*) 1736–1766, 22, 31,
        105, 131–2, 156–8, 167,
        207–8, 291, 294–6
    Jane (*daughter*) 1737–1750,
        22, 31, 105, 131–2,
        156–8, 208
    Grace (*daughter-in-law*)
        c.1731–1811, 2
    John (*brother*) 1711–1777, 31
    Mary Cockcroft (*brother's wife*)
        31

*GRIMSHAW, WILLIAM (1708–
1763)*
LIFE:
    birth 3
    childhood 3–6
    education 4–10
    ordination 11
    first curacy (see Littleborough)
    second curacy (see
        Todmorden)
    marriage to Sarah Sutcliffe 20
    birth of John and Jane 22
    death of Sarah 22
    conviction of sin 19–20, 24–6
    conversion 24–8
        attempts to please God
            20, 22
        depression 22–5
        reads Brooks, *Precious
            Remedies* 24
        reads Owen on *Justification*
            26–8
    marriage to Elizabeth Cockcroft
        31
    moves to Haworth 52–3, 55
    early preaching 58–61
    lack of assurance 72
    trance experience 73–7, 79
    becomes 'irregular' 85–6
    eloquent preacher 88–94
    death of Elizabeth 115
    first visit of John Wesley 116
    begins to work fully with
        Methodists 118–21

delivered from fear 118–9
itineracy (beginning 1747 and thereafter) 118–20
first persecution 124
discipline in Haworth anecdotes 95–6, 102–6
horsewhip anecdote 140–1, other anecdotes 142–8, Grimshaw's cow 147
death of Jane 156–8, 208
as Haworth schoolmaster 157
idle week and busy week 167–9
possible remarriage 222–3
financial worries 221–5, 276–7
failing health 271–2, 282–4, 286
readiness for death 283, 285–6
dying words 288–92
death 292
funeral 292–4
tributes 293–5

MINISTRY:
Answer to White against Methodists 5, 87, 97, 134–7, 281
appointed as Wesley's successsor 1, 172, 247
before Archbishop Gilbert 197–8
Calvinist or Arminian 240–44
care for individuals 96,
communion services 149–51, 153–4, 160, 195–6, 248, 263
conversion of John 291, 295–6
covenants 73, 202–6, 223 (see also Appendix 2)
Creed 97, 238, 255 (see also Appendix 3)
Diary 3, 5, 150, 167–9,181–

3,191–2, 275
early blessing in Haworth 60–2, 66–7
examples of rebuking sin 202–3 (see also 'Admonition of a Sinner')
favourite hymn 202
favourite text 58, 224, 274–5, 288, 292–3
favourite tune 248
first visit of Charles Wesley 113–4
first visit from Whitefield 132
form of burial 23
friendship with Darney 71, 78,
further blessings in Haworth 264–5, 271, 273, 282–3
floodtide of blessing in Haworth 79–81, 86–7
Great Haworth Round 82, 164–72, 219, 247, 255, 259–62, 280
Haworth preaching house 221–4
his table 246–7
Ingham's first visit 63–4
letters to Charles Wesley 126n, 226–8, 249, 265, 267
letters to John Wesley 65, 117–21, 165 (see also Appendix 1)
love for all believers 100, 122, 229–36
pastoral letters 247, 264–5
physical appearance 92n, 212–3, 261
prayer and communion with God 95, 123–4, 281
problems with Wesley's Christian perfection 185, 236–8

Grimshaw: Ministry *(continued)*
  problems with Wesley's views
    of imputed righteousness
    238–40
  separation from Methodism
    115, 121, 215–20, 225–8
  stipend 51
  Sunday evenings at Sowdens 63
  traits of Christian character
    274–80
    generosity 277
    joy 212–3, 275
    humility 278–80
    zeal 271–3
  sensitivity to sin 183–4
  use of tracts 84
  visitation of parish 65
  wills 23, 277, 288
Guisley 155

Hainsworthshaw 181
Halifax 15–16, 33, 37, 43, 55,
    101, 110, 127, 169, 184,
    234–5, 250
Handy, Samuel 259
Hardy, R. Spence, *Incumbent of
    Haworth* 19, 23, 48, 49,
    64n, 90n, 140, 146, 212–
    3, 264, 279
Hargrave, James 129–31
Harris, Howell 19
Harrison, G. E., *A Study of Wesley
    and the Brontës* 56
Harte, Bret 191
Hartlepool 172
Hartley, James 233–4
Haslingden 111
Hastings, Theophilus 39
Hastings, Ladies Ann, Frances,
    Catherine, Margaret 39 (see
    also Lady Margaret Ingham)

Haworth:
  Black Bull 53, 64, 75, 83
  Brontë Museum 153
  cottage industry 54–5, 174–5
  ducking pond 53
  effects of revival 45, 60–2, 78–
    81, 86, 281
  Emmott Hall 53, 115
  Haworth Baptist Church, built
    1752 233–4
  Haworth Methodist Church
    196
  Haworth Round (see
    Grimshaw)
  Haworth Wakes 146, 224
  King's Arms 53
  Main Street 53, 83
  school 66
  social conditions 3, 45, 54–6,
    333
  White Lion 53
Haworth church (St Michael and
    All Angels) xiv, 47
  churchwardens 62,
  communicants 51, 66
  communion services 66, 149–
    51, 153–4, 196, 248
  communion flagons 153–4
  enlargement 62, 189–91
  graveyard 87, 151, 154, 196–
    7
  pews 190–1
  preaching platform 192–3,
    195–7, 255, 306
  pulpit 58, 97, 190
  registers 52, 62
  trustees 50–1

Heaton 38
Heitzenrater, R. P., *Diary of an
    Oxford Methodist* 34n

Hebden Bridge 281
Helmsley 172, 271
Heptonstall 111, 121, 168, 184, 247
Herring, Thomas, Archbishop of York 51, 65–6, 125, 150
Herrnhut 40
Hervey, James, *Theron and Aspasio* 240, 269
Heskin Free School 5–6, 8, 52
Heywood, Oliver 33
  Diary 46–7
High Binns 182
Holdworth 182
Holy Club, Oxford 9, 34
Hopper, Christopher 226, 261n
Horbury 38
Horton 43
Horneck, Dr Anthony 163
Huddersfield 253–4, 271
Hull 16, 32, 166, 263
Huntingdon, Countess of 40, 64, 85, 132, 149, 152, 160, 190, 193–5, 203, 250, 253, 255, 270–1, 282–5, 289
Huntingdon, Lord 39, 85
Huntingdon, Earl 202–3
Hutton, James, *History of Moravian Church* 41n
Hutton, Matthew, Archbishop of York 57, 125–6n, 150, 197

Illingworth 169
Industrial Revolution 55
Ingham, Benjamin 26, 33–4, 63–4, 68, 77, 85, 111, 113, 123–4,132, 149, 181, 194–5, 218, 223, 229, 265, 267–71, 288–90;
Ingham, Lady Margaret 39, 64, 68, 85

Inghamite societies 194, 229, 267–70
Ingleton 172
Ireland 116n, 188, 258–9

Jacobite Rebellion 1715, 3
  1745, 125
Jackson, Thomas
  Life of Charles Wesley 126n, 219
  Lives of Early Methodist Preachers 84, 155–6 272
John Rylands University Library of Manchester 3, 5, 20–1, 95, 104, 107, 160
Johnson, Thomas 52
Jones, Mrs Joseph 109, 151, 174–6, 183, 201, 275, 278, 284–5
Jones, Joseph 217

Keighley 45, 81, 99, 110, 121, 128, 154, 168, 183, 261, 263, 272–3, 291
Kendal 172
Kennet, Benjamin 48, 50–3, 126
Kidderminster 58, 74, 99
Kilsyth 69
Kingswood School, Bristol 132, 156–8, 208
Knight, Titus 234–5

Laycock, J.W, *Methodist Heroes* 9–10, 24, 28, 44, 58, 79, 84, 87, 100, 109, 151, 174–6, 183, 192, 199, 201, 218, 224n, 230, 235, 241, 245–6, 258, 261, 267, 275, 284, 286, 292

Ledstone Hall 39, 64, 85
Ledsham Church 39
Lee, Thomas 272–3
Leeds 37, 43, 70, 81, 119, 121,
    172, 189, 194, 217, 221,
    237, 263, 267, 270, 279
  Pudsey 69n, 70
Leeds Mercury 48–9
Lewisham 288
Littleborough 11, 14, 33
Liverpool 250
Lloyd-Jones, Dr D. M., *Puritan
    Conference Papers,* 1967,
    Sandemanianism 269n
Locke, John, *Reasonableness of
    Christianity* 13
Lockwood, John and Mary 21,
    131–2
London Society 266–7, 304
Lot, decision by 223
Lottery, State 221–2
Luddenden 21–2, 208, 280, 293

Macaulay, Zachary 254
Mackford, William 127–30
Magdalene, Cambridge 7
Manchester 111, 117, 161, 171,
    189, 249
Madin, John 87
Mann, Isaac, *Life of Wm.
    Crabtree* 232
Manningham 83
Marsh Lane 5
Martyr, Justin 27
Maskew, Jonathan 81, 83,105,
    112n, 155, 217, 258, 260
Maxfield, Thomas 82, 239, 266
Menston(e) 81, 168
Merryweather, George 258
Methodism:
  administration 163–6

annual conferences 119n, 172,
    189, 216–21, 239, 264
band meetings 164
circuit books 166
class leaders or stewards 164
class meetings 164
class tickets 165–6, 173
defence of (see *Answer to
    White*)
Methodist Magazine 94, 164,
    279
Methodist Recorder 50
preachers (see under names)
preaching houses 164, 172,
    221–8
quarterly meetings 184, 190,
    198
rounds 165
separation from Church of
    England 215–28
United Societies 163
Meyrick, Thomas 165
Middleton, Erasmus *Biographia
    Evangelica* 17, 95, 105,
    187, 255, 275–8, 294
Middleton, Yorkshire Dales 259
Midgeley 20
Midgley, Joseph 221
Milton, John 6
Mirfield 38
Mitchell, Thomas 155–6, 225
Mixenden 182
Mob attacks 124, 128–31, 257,
    259–60, 272
Molther, Philip 39–40
Moorfields 41
Moravians 35–6, 39–43, 63–
    4, 68, 111, 218
Murlin, John 225
Murray, Mrs Grace 127, 171
Murray, Iain H. 133n, 230n

Musselburgh 153
Myles, William, *Grimshaw* 5,
    70, 78, 97, 112, 117, 133–
    6, 151, 202, 241, 272,
    276

'Nature, State and Conduct of a
    Christian' (Grimshaw's
    unpublished MS) 91, 186,
    211–3, 283
Nelson, John 41–4, 64, 68–9, 81,
    110, 116, 121, 192, 217,
    226, 232
  his journal in *Lives of Early
    Methodists* 42
Newcastle 110–11, 115, 172,
    258, 282
  pastoral letters from Grimshaw
    to societies 182–3, 264–5,
    275–6, 281
Newton, John 1, 17, 25, 45–6,
    56–8, 75, 92, 98, 101,
    106, 137, 140, 142, 146,
    170, 178, 222n, 231, 234,
    242, 244, 250–2, 277–8,
    280
Newsholme (Newsham) 168
New World 32
Nicolson, Bishop of Carlisle 13–
    14
Northowram 33
Northallerton 172
Norwich 225, 260

Osmotherley 172, 256
Ordination, see Grimshaw.
Otley 168, 237, 263, 265
Outler, A, *John Wesley* 239
Overton, J. H., *Evangelical
    Revival of 18th Century*
    138–9

Ossett 33–5, 37–8
Owen Dr John, *On Justification
    by Faith* 26–7, 238
Oxenhope 52, 65
Oxford 7, 9
  Christ Church College 247,
  Holy Club 9, 34
  Lincoln College 247
  Queen's College 34

Palaemon – pseudonym 269n
Parish clerk, see Whitehead
Pawson, John 93–4, 224n, 279
Pendle Forest 121, 272, 258
Penistone Flats 145
Peploe, Samuel (Bishop of
    Chester) 11, 14
Perfection, Christian 40, 77,
    185, 236–8, 265–7
Perpetual curacy 53
Perronet, Charles and Edward
    217, 220, 259, 290
Peterhouse, Cambridge 7
Pickles, H.M, *Benjamin Ingham*
    233, 268n
Piggot, Henry 4, 11, 13
Pocklington 166, 263
Preston, Battle of 3

Radcliffe, C., letter to Everett 90,
    104, 224
Religious Societies 163
Reproof, duty of 200–4
Revival phenomena 80–1
Ribble Valley 3
Roads, condition of 44, 111, 169
Robe, James 69
Robinson, Edmund 47
Robertshaw, Jerry 290–1
Rochdale 4, 14–15, 33, 111, 161,
    177

Rogers, Ezekiel 32–3
Rogers, John, of Dedham 32
Rolvenden, Kent 224
Romaine, William 89, 97, 176,
    187, 214, 250, 254–5,
    265, 267–8, 270, 278, 283,
    289, 293
Rossendale 69, 111, 117, 121,
    162
Rotherham 166
Roughlee 128–31, 133,154, 189,
    261, 291
Rowley 32–3
Ryle, J.C 1–2, 198n

Sandeman, Robert 268–9
Sandemanianism 268–70
Scaitcliffe Hall 90n
Scholfield, James and Susan 19
Schools
    Blackburn 4, 6, 52
    Haworth 66
    Heskin, 5–6, 8, 52
    Kingswood, (Bristol) 132, 156–
    8, 208
Scotch Will, see William Darney.
Seacroft, Leeds 194
Seagrave, Robert
    Hymns 30
    Letter to People of England 30
    on *Justification* 29–30, 84
Seven Years War 199, 204
Seymour, A.C. H.
    Countess of Huntingdon 40,
    85, 123–4, 193–4,
    255, 270–1
    'Life of Ingham' 233, 312
Shackleton, Mary (Molly) 161,
    277, 279, 288, 291–2
Sheffield 166, 170–1
Shepshed 257

Shirley, Lady Fanny 152
Silsden 81, 168, 193
Simeon, Charles 141, 254
Smith, Isaac 47–50, 63, 75, 102,
    201
Smith, George 4
Smith, Richard 232–3
Smith Thornley 64n
Smith, W. W. *Methodism in
    Bradford* 180
Societies, United see Methodism.
Southey, Robert, *Life of John
    Wesley* 37, 138
Sowdens 49–50, 53, 55, 64, 75n,
    83, 100, 115, 120, 161,
    184, 245–7, 266, 273, 278–
    80, 288
SPCK 163
St Dunstans 254, 294
Stanbury 51, 58, 65
Stockport 166, 172
Stoneshawfate 162
Strachen, A. *George Lowe* 198,
    249
Sunderland 16n
Sutton 81, 168
Syms, John 84

Tadcaster 192
Taylor, Dan 295
Telford, John, ed., *Letters of John
    Wesley* 1n, 309
    Wesley's Veterans 256.
Theron and Aspasio 240, 269.
Thompson, William 279–80
Thornton, Henry 221, 247, 254
Todmorden 15–16, 44–5, 52, 55,
    58, 90n, 111, 117, 121,
    166, 169, 188, 248, 259
Toeltschig, John 41
Towers, William 7

Towne, Robert 47

Townsend, W.J., *New History of Methodism* 119n

Tracts, distribution of 84

Trinity College, Cambridge 10

Turner, J. Horsfall, *Haworth – Past and Present* xiv, 47, 191

Tyerman, Luke 2, 214, 220n
  Life of John Wesley 136, 173, 215, 226, 152, 265
  Oxford Methodists 9, 40, 132, 267–8, 270
  Wesley's Designated Successor 98

Uffenbach, von 7

Vazeille, Molly (Mrs John Wesley) 171n

Venn, Henry 252–4, 283, 290, 293–4
  Letters of 253, 294
  Sketch of Grimshaw 10n, 11, 24, 28, 58, 60, 63, 65, 78, 109, 112, 150–1, 161, 173, 244, 265, 281, 293–4

Venn, John 254

Viney, Richard *Diary* 68–9, 72, 116

Wainsgate Baptist Church, Hebden Bridge 231, 283

Wakefield 37, 125

Waldensians 178

Walker, Samuel of Truro 220

Wesley, Charles 1, 25, 34–5, 64, 68, 80, 82, 113–6, 121, 158–9, 188, 195–6, 215, 219, 247, 249, 288, 291–2

and Darney 68, 116, 256

elegy on Grimshaw 294

hymns 114,174

Journal 113–4, 158–9, 189, 194–6, 294

letters to Grimshaw 226–7

Sally, his wife 158, 219, 288

separation from Church of England 44, 219–20, 225–8

visits Haworth 113–15

Wesley Historical Society 3n, 69n, 116

Wesley, John 1, 7, 9, 18–19, 25, 35–6, 38, 41, 43, 56, 64–5, 68, 77, 80, 82, 86, 110–1, 116, 121, 128–31, 150, 159, 162, 170, 185, 188–9, 200, 214–5, 217, 247–9, 253, 256, 258, 268, 270, 273, 283, 288

assurance of salvation 36

at Roughlee 128–31, 189

Christian Library 213

Duty of Reproving Neighbour 200

education of Grimshaw's children 131–2, 156–7

his preaching 248–9

Imputed Righteousness *Blow at the Root* 240

Journal 19, 20, 36, 110–1, 116, 129, 156, 219, 221, 248, 253, 263–4, 266, 294n

last visit to Grimshaw; 263, 273

Letters 86, 131n, 185, 260, 273, letters from Grimshaw 65, 117, 144 (see also Appendix 1)

Minutes of Conferences 165, 219, 239

Wesley, John *(continued)*
nominates Grimshaw his successor 1, 172, 247, 294
Plain Account of Christian Perfection 265 (for Wesley's teaching on, see Perfection)
relationship with Darney 116–7, 256, 258
rift with Ingham 40, 42, 111
separation from Church of England 215ff.
visits Haworth 116, 128, 189, 247–8, 263–6, 273
Wesley, Mrs John 171n
Wesley, Susanna 156
Westgate Baptist Chapel, Bradford 232
West Lane Baptist Church 233–4
Westminster, Queen Square Chapel 11
Westminster College, Cambridge 123n
Westminster Conference Papers 209n
White, George 124, 126–30, 133–7, 155
Sermon vs. Methodists 127, 133–6, 200
Whitefield, George 1, 18, 25, 36, 82, 84, 132–4, 149, 168, 183, 188–9, 195–7, 214, 229–30, 249–50, 253–6, 265, 270, 283, 288
and Gallatins 152–3
anecdotes 154, 193–4, 196–7
crowded communion services 149–54, 160, 195
first visit to Haworth 132
Grimshaw's preaching tours

with Whitefield 249, 270
his special pulpit 192–6, 250, 255
Journals 18, 133n
letters to Grimshaw 133–4
subsequent visits to Haworth 149–55, 160, 168, 193–6
unpublished journal 133
Works 152, 192–3
Whitaker, John 164n
Whitaker, Samuel 195
Whitehaven 188
Whitehead, Jonathan (parish clerk) 63, 75n
Whitehead, Martha, 288, 292
Whiteley, J. H., *Wesley's England* 8
Whitford, John 219
Wilberforce, William 254
Wilkinson, John 81–2, 128–9
Williams, Joseph 9–10, 22, 24, 28, 58, 74–7, 79–80, 84, 97, 99–101, 112–3, 115, 241, 271
Wills, General 3
Winewall 229
Woodhouse, Mrs 170–1
Woodward, Dr Josiah 163
Worsted industry 54–5
Worth, River 273
Wuthering Heights 56
Wright, Susanna 272, 276

Yarm 258, 289
Yeadon 154, 292
Yelling 254
York 33, 125, 263
York Minster 153
Yorkshire Dales 155, 257, 267, 271